A Socioeconomic Profile of South Africa

William Redman Duggan

The Praeger Special Studies program—utilizing the most modern and efficient book production techniques and a selective worldwide distribution network—makes available to the academic, government, and business communities significant, timely research in U.S. and international economic, social, and political development.

A Socioeconomic Profile of South Africa

PRAEGER SPECIAL STUDIES IN INTERNATIONAL ECONOMICS AND DEVELOPMENT

Praeger Publishers New York Washington London

PRAEGER PUBLISHERS
111 Fourth Avenue, New York, N.Y. 10003, U.S.A.
5, Cromwell Place, London S.W.7, England

Published in the United States of America in 1973
by Praeger Publishers, Inc.

Library of Congress Catalog Card Number: 72-91715

Printed in the United States of America

To all Peoples

of all Races

of Africa

CONTENTS

LIST OF TABLES, MAP, AND FIGURE

LIST OF ABBREVIATIONS

ANC	African National Congress
ASB	Afrikaans-speaking Studenter Bond
CNE	Christian National Education
DRC	Dutch Reformed Church
ESCOM	Electricity Supply Commission
EXIMBANK	Export-Import Bank
FAK	Federation of Afrikaans Cultural Organizations
FAO	Food and Agriculture Organization
FOFATSA	Federation of Free African Trade Unions of South Africa
HNP	Herstigte National Party
IDC	Industrial Development Corporation
ILO	International Labour Organization
ISCOR	Iron and Steel Industrial Corporation
NGK	Nederduits Gereformeerde Kerk (DRC)
NUSAS	National Union of South African Students
OAU	Organization of African Unity
PAC	Pan-Africanist Congress
RSA	Radio South Africa
SABC	South African Broadcasting Corporation
SABRA	South African Bureau of Racial Affairs
SACOC	South African Council of Churches

SACTU	South African Congress of Trade Unions
SAR&H	South African Railways and Harbors
SASO	South African Student Organization
SASOL	South African Coal, Oil and Gas Corporation
SWANU	South-West Africa National Union
SWANUF	South-West Africa National United Front
SWAPO	South-West Africa Peoples' Organization
TNIP	Transkei National Independence Party
TUCSA	Trade Union Council of South Africa
UCM	University Christian Movement
UN	United Nations
UNESCO	UN Educational, Scientific and Cultural Organization
WCC	World Council of Churches
WHO	World Health Organization

LIST OF AFRIKANER TERMS

Afrikaners	South African whites of Afrikaans language convention and of Afrikaans cultural background
Baaskap	Boss rule, White supremacy
Bantu	Term applied to all Black tribes of South and South-West Africa
Bantustans	Black African (embryo) nations of the Republic, areas set aside solely for tribal development
Boer	An Afrikaner farmer or the Afrikaner people
Coloured	Those of mixed White and non-White stock
English	Those of British background or birth and of English-language convention—the term also embraces many continental Europeans, as well as resident North American Whites
Highveld	High grassland
Laager	Circle of covered wagons guarding the pioneers from external attack
Plattelander	Plateau dweller
Verkrampte	Literally, cramped or shriveled—ultraconservative Nationalist Afrikaners
Verligte	Literally, enlightened—relatively more moderate Nationalist Afrikaners
Volk	People

INTRODUCTION: THE PROBLEM THAT IS SOUTH AFRICA

The great statesman and phrase maker, Winston Churchill, in a memorable 1939 broadcast, characterized Russia as "a riddle, wrapped in a mystery, within an enigma."

In many ways the Republic of South Africa, too, can bear that characterization. For, with its juxtaposition of extraordinary White wealth and impoverished non-White labor, its historic recognition of legal tradition and its abrogation of human rights, its determination to be at once internationalist and isolationist—to be on the world scene but not of the world scene, to be economically integrated but politically, socially, and racially segregated—South Africa becomes a national contradiction—and an international riddle.

As such, South Africa also becomes an international time bomb, not only in the halls of the UN, but likewise in the corridors of Washington, of Westminster, and elsewhere. She is an international vexation—and a foreign policy problem—for all nations adhering to the rule of law and for all nations with race problems of their own. Partisan and highly emotional tirades have been directed against the South African concept of <u>apartheid</u> ("separate development of the races under White hegemony") from without and within the Republic. Her critics have insisted that something be done by the UN or by Western democracies, acting in concert, to change this racialist hegemony. Programs of external and internal pressures have been suggested toward that end. Most of these international bills of complaint, however, have lacked objective understanding, or full comprehension of the ramifications, of the South African scene.

The present Nationalist regime, as well as its recent predecessors, have been increasingly repressive of the non-White community within the Republic. The Nationalist doctrine of apartheid has been applied to these groups with more and more authoritarian bias—this despite the country's tendency toward economic integration and contradictory political segregation. By custom, by constraint, by legal fiat, and with parliamentary supremacy over all sectors of society, there have been more and more constrictions placed on persons and institutions that voice opposition to the regime. These restrictions have been aimed particularly at the leadership of the press, pulpit, and cultural and educational institutions. White South Africans are arming themselves—by law, by fiat, by expansion of the police and military—to guard against internal upset and external intervention. Thereby, the Nationalist government has extended its control and enhanced its short-term security at the risk of a long-term explosion.

The libertarian objectives and self-determination ideals of other nations run counter to these South African currents. It is for these reasons that so many leaders, especially those in the Afro-Asian bloc, have insisted that some international means be found to alleviate the racial polarization, legal injustices, and the absolute White domination existing within the Republic. New Black African nations to the north and militants in the multinational Organization of African Unity (OAU) demand the isolation of South Africa and help in "liberating" South Africa's non-Whites through efforts of "freedom fighters" from the north. The fundamental concern over South Africa is a fear of the potential for, and grave consequences of, a full-scale Black-White confrontation and explosion in southern Africa. Such a racial conflict would pose extraordinary problems for the United States, both domestically and internationally. It would pose vexing problems for a number of her allies, particularly Britain. It would create new and major fractures within the UN. Such a conflict could become a holocaust for all of sub-Saharan Africa.

South Africa's legal right to continued authority over the "mandate" of South-West Africa (Namibia) after the demise of the League of Nations and South Africa's refusal to place that mandate under UN control have given her international critics additional grounds for complaint. In the last 27 years the UN has passed more than 100 resolutions directed against South Africa, all of these critical of her apartheid policies or of her questionable control over South-West Africa. All of these have been disregarded by the Republic's leaders. There has also been a recurring demand from the international community, newly invigorated by each UN resolution, that South Africa be made the target of UN sanctions and boycotts.

Some external pressures have been successful, resulting in South Africa's expulsion from the Olympic games, from Davis Cup competition, and other sports events. Also effected have been a partial UN arms embargo (1963) and South Africa's expulsion from activities and membership in certain specialized UN agencies. However, efforts to apply broad trade sanctions and financial boycotts have failed. Yet, all such external pressures have only deepened the resolve of South Africa's political leaders and its White citizenry to speed up economic nationalism and self-sufficiency, to arm fully against internal and external threat, to protect the status quo against external challenge. Thus far, no outside pressures have effectively improved the lot of the non-Whites within the Republic and South-West Africa.

The volatility of this "White redoubt" in southern Africa clearly endangers international interests and peace in that area. It also threatens to undermine prospects for peace throughout the African continent. Both short-term and long-term dangers of racial conflict there require a more thorough understanding of the problem. If such a tragedy is to be avoided, it requires, too, the thoughtful consideration of, and use of, effective and timely preventative diplomacy.

It is clear from the complexity of this situation and from its widening international ramifications and continental dangers that the Republic of South Africa requires a watching brief by many countries and by many policy makers, diplomats, businessmen, churchmen, and academics. For these a number of questions must be kept in mind. For example:

Is there any possibility that the present political atmosphere in South Africa is likely to bring about a softening of internal attitudes on the color question? Is that atmosphere likely to engender socio-economic improvements for non-Whites? If not, what other catalytic agents could be employed to initiate such changes?

What factors are present today on the South African scene that could bring about constructive socioeconomic change and racial-political improvement there? Can the present and potential dynamic growth of the Republic, with increasing demands for labor, White and non-White, bring about new and effective solutions to her internal socioeconomic problems? If economic dynamism presents a possible means of solving her racial problems, what then should be the international attitude toward further private, international investment in the Republic? Could these foreign investments provide means of diminishing South Africa's existing racial troubles? In effect, can "enlightened capitalism," international and internal, play a part in finding racial solutions there?

Will the newly created Bantustans (Black African nations of the Republic) be made both politically and economically viable? Will the South African government provide adequate financial and technical backing for these new nations? Will the Republic's natural resources and infrastructure be made available to them? What will be the future of the reinvigorated Black nationalism emanating from the Bantustan program? Will the Bantustans bring about a new and peaceful association of White and Black states in southern Africa? Or will they create new abscesses on the South African body politic?

Are there domestic or international means of moderating the church-state controversy over apartheid presently taking place within the Republic? What is the real place of the rule of law within the Republic, and how much erosion of justice has taken place? Can the running controversy between proponents of apartheid and liberal academic forces be turned to constructive purpose? Can conflict between conservative and liberal cultural forces find sufficient middle ground to bring improvement to the country's social scene?

What is the real significance of South Africa in international terms—political, economic, strategic, and social? Can Western democracies continue their present ambivalent attitude toward South Africa—expressing abhorrence of apartheid, on the one hand, but doing "business as usual" with the Republic, on the other?

Can an effective program of pressures, internal and external, be devised to ameliorate the repressive aspects of life for non-Whites within South Africa? Can this be done without bringing on international confrontation and conflict? What preventative diplomacy can be attempted, by UN and Western nations, to eliminate the abrasiveness and potential international dangers coming out of South Africa? Can the South-West Africa question, with its constant frictions in the UN and elsewhere, be alleviated? In these processes can realistic "dialogue" between South African leaders and leaders of Black nations to the north prove beneficial?

How can the international community prevent or ameliorate the grave risks of racial conflict in South Africa? Is the danger of extending that conflict through southern Africa so great and the resulting infringement upon U.S., U.K., and other Western international interests so critical as to make advisable some projection of these nations into a closer association with the Republic? Thereby, can these nations with special interests in South Africa ameliorate or defuse that situation? Alternatively, is it wiser for the United States, the United Kingdom, and other Western nations to disengage from the Republic, thus isolating her people internationally? Would that international isolation of South Africa only further polarize the internal racial situation and thus result in forsaking 18 million non-Whites? What would be the real effects of sanctions and boycotts, and would these actually help to resolve South Africa's racial tensions? How can the Western nations keep South African resources accessible in event of major regional or world conflict? Can a means be found for releasing South African capabilities—scientific, technical, commercial, educational—for shared development of the African continent? Can timely internal and international diplomatic social action avert creation of an impregnable White redoubt in southern Africa?

At this moment in history South Africa remains a virtually intractable international problem. For years to come she will undoubtedly be an emotionally charged focus to debate, having at home and abroad her "-philes" and her "-phobes," her defenders and her detractors. There are "sanctioneers" who would rule her out of the international scene altogether. There are her proponents who contend that, in apartheid, she alone has the answer to the plaguing problem of racial troubles.

The answer of some, though not all, of the foregoing questions, along with suggestions for improving the racial situation in South Africa, will be found in the following pages. At the least these suggestions may help to clarify South Africa's internal and external position and some of her enigmatic contradictions. Perhaps, some of the answers to this multifaceted problem can only be found in the passage of time. Perhaps, new palliatives and solutions will emanate from a fuller understanding of the character and complexity of the "problem that is South Africa." This is the sole intent, the raison d'être, of this book.

June 1972

A Socioeconomic Profile of South Africa

MAP 1

South Africa: Bantu Reserves

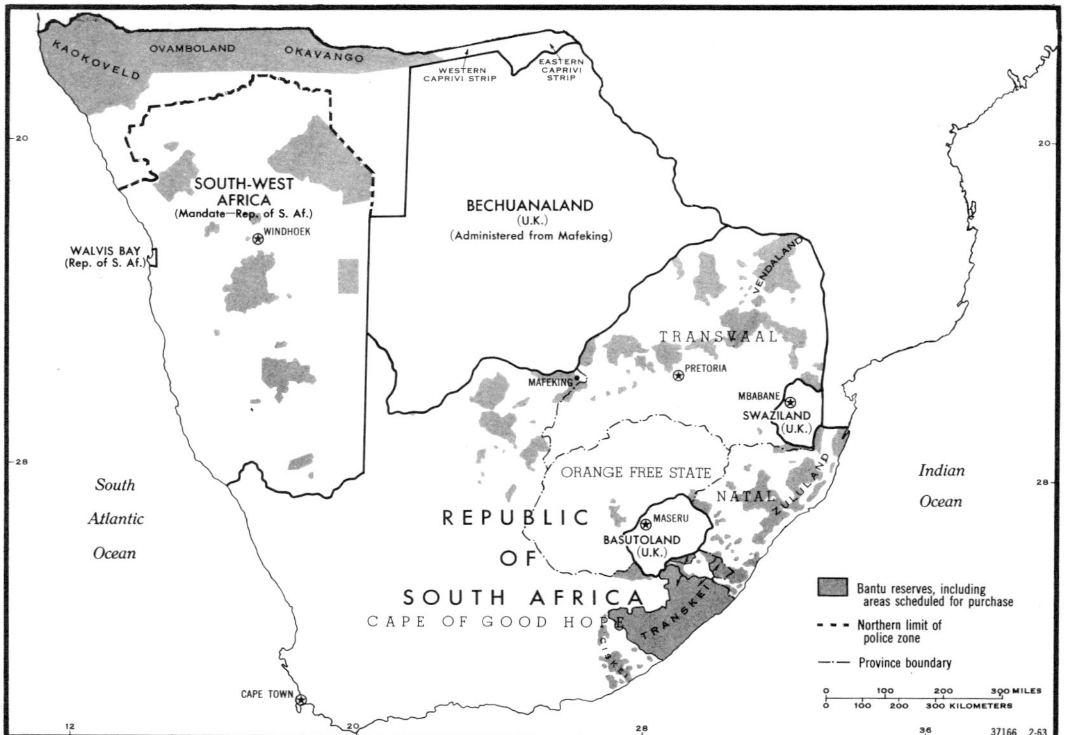

CHAPTER

1

THE COUNTRY'S BACKGROUND

The Republic of South Africa is situated at the southern tip of the African continent. Lying between latitudinal degrees 22 south and 35 south and longitudinal degrees 17 east and 33 east, it has subtropical, temperate, and arid climate zones.

Land area of the Republic is 472,359 square miles, the size of Texas, New Mexico, and Colorado combined. The country has a narrow coastal zone, partially lush and partially arid. From this zone there is a gradual rise through low plateau lands to a large central plateau-land highveld ("high grassland"), ranging from 4,000 to 6,000 feet in altitude. The largest mountain range is the Drakensburg in the southeast of the country, its peaks attaining nearly 11,000 feet.

There are no major navigable rivers in the country and few lakes. Water is scarce and rainfall inadequate. However, frequent periods of drought are sometimes followed by periods of excessive, torrential rains, with resulting heavy soil erosion.

The Republic proper comprises four provinces (similar to American states), which include Cape Province, Natal, Orange Free State, and the Transvaal. As a result of historical cleavages, detailed in later pages, the country has two capitals—Pretoria, the administrative capital, and Capetown, the legislative capital. The country's judicial high court is located in Bloemfontein. There are two official languages, Afrikaans and English.

South Africa also maintains governmental and administrative control over the former League of Nations mandate (and earlier German colony) of South-West Africa. This territory, with a population of 630,000 (all races), covers an area of 318,261 square miles, twice the size of California. This territory lies along the northwest border of the Republic, edging the Atlantic Ocean northward to the Portuguese province of Angola.

South Africa proper is bordered on the north by Botswana, by Rhodesia, by the Portuguese East African province of Mozambique, and by Swaziland. The independent nation of Lesotho is an enclave within the Republic.

In its 1970 census the Republic tallied 21.4 million persons of all races. This included 15 million Blacks, 3.8 million Whites, 2 million Coloureds ("mulattoes"), and 620,000 Asians (primarily East Indians). The annual growth rate for the population as a whole is 3.4 percent, with Whites increasing at 2.2 percent, the Blacks increasing at 3.7 percent, the Coloureds at 3.3 percent, and the Asians at 3.2 percent. In proportionate terms the White population is decreasing, falling from 19.3 percent of the total in 1960 to 17.8 percent in 1970. The present ratio of Whites to non-Whites in South Africa is one to four, contrasting with a ratio of nine Whites to one non-White in the United States. Thus, the problem of finding a satisfactory racial solution and social realignment is far more knotty for South Africa than is that problem in the United States.

Until now the White population has also been divided, culturally and politically. This division resulted from the frictions between Afrikaner and Briton, inspired by the country's settlement history and enhanced by the Boer War. It should be noted, however, that these barriers between Boer (a term denoting "an Afrikaner farmer" or "the Afrikaner people") and Briton are slowly breaking down. Today, the Afrikaner grouping constitutes slightly more than one-half of the total White population and those of British or other European extraction slightly less than one-half. In the face of a quarter-century of Afrikaner control over government, the English-speaking community has become increasingly receptive to Afrikaner doctrine and South African nationalism. This has resulted in part from the country's movement away from the British Commonwealth in recent years. It has resulted as well from broadening Afrikaner participation in business and commerce—their branching out from the traditional vocations of farming and politics. It has stemmed, too, from increasing association on social levels, as well as a new cohesiveness, resulting from increasing international pressures against South Africa. This cohesiveness has inspired a common South African patriotism and determination to protect themselves against an outside enemy, which presumably seeks to sabotage White supremacy and the "South African way of life."

Much of South Africa's history has been influenced by its geography. Remote as the country is, and surrounded on three sides by the Atlantic and Indian oceans, the Republic is more of an island than the southern extremity of a large continent. There are no navigable rivers to serve as channels of colonization. Mountain ranges and the irregular plateau protected against the opening of the upland interiors for nearly 200 years after the establishment of the Dutch and French Huguenot settlements in the region of the Cape of Good Hope.

There came first to southern Africa the Portuguese men of war seeking passage around the Cape. These were followed by Dutch, French, and British ships. The Dutch set up the first permanent settlement in 1652 at Capetown. The representatives of the Dutch East India Company, led by Jan van Riebeeck, established supply depots for water and provisions for their shipping bound to and from the Asian subcontinent. These Dutch, in turn, brought a few slaves to the area and themselves mated with these slaves and the indigenous Bushmen and Hottentot tribesmen whom they found in the area of the Cape. As the White settlements grew, the association with the Bushmen and Hottentots brought on a mulatto grouping known first as "Bastards" and later as "Cape Coloureds."

The remoteness of the area—Capetown is 6,000 miles from England and 5,000 miles from Australia—created the atmosphere for development of a wholly new nationalism—part Dutch, part French, part British, but with predominant Dutch overtones—to become known as the Afrikaners. This group would undoubtedly have been wholly dominant over the entire area known as South Africa had it not been for the discovery of gold and diamonds, with subsequent heavy immigration.

The history of the country is ordinarily deemed by its White historians to have had its real beginnings only from the year 1652. It was in that year that the first permanent White settlement was established at the Cape of Good Hope. Many South African historians appear to have made something of a fetish of the notion that these first Dutch settlers entered only empty spaces when they set foot in southern Africa. They contend that they found there only a few Hottentots and Bushmen. The same South African historians contend that the main bodies of Black African tribesmen only later migrated southward from Central Africa and into those portions of the Republic where they are now settled. These historians contend that the Bantu, or Blacks, have no traditional or legal rights to land already settled by white Dutch forebears.

A recent scholarly work on South Africa by Monica Wilson and Leonard Thompson contests this historical thesis.* That work points out that Portuguese explorers, including Bartholomew Diaz (1488) and Vasco de Gama (1497), came upon settlements of Blacks with their cattle along the country's southeastern shores. These editors seek to refute the Afrikaner historians' thesis that this land was vacant,

---

*Monica Wilson and Leonard Thompson, eds., The Oxford History of South Africa, Vol. 1, South Africa to 1870 (London: Oxford University Press, 1969), Preface, p. 7 ff.

by stating the following: (a) that there is rich archeological evidence of earlier civilizations and economies in precolonial southern Africa; (b) that this archeological evidence has been ignored; (c) that those traditional societies found by the new European settlers were erroneously considered to have been both static and lacking history—presumptions that overlook oral traditions, complex tribal structures, and archeological finds; (d) that the same historians make erroneous generalizations concerning early African societies, e.g., that Bushmen were all hunters and Hottentots all pastoralists; (e) that implicit in academia in South Africa is that it is improper for historians to be concerned with social structure and for anthropologists to be concerned with all races, e.g., historians have concerned themselves with Whites, anthropologists with Blacks.

In sum, Wilson and Thompson argue that statements about "exclusive occupation of defined areas [of southern Africa]" and "of a distaste for mingling" reflect modern Afrikaner preoccupation with race and the present South African social structure rather than historical reality.

Only future historical, anthropological, sociological, and archeological discoveries may finally settle these arguments, pro or con. In any event, in the years that followed the first Cape settlement by the Dutch in 1652, there came into South Africa various other European nationalities as well. There were the French Huguenots (circa 1688), escaping the religious persecutions of Europe. There were British settlers, coming as conquerors and colonizers in the wake of the Napoleonic wars and, afterwards, escaping the economic pressures of the Industrial Revolution in England. Migrants of diverse nationalities came to seek their fortunes in the new found gold and diamond diggings of the Transvaal. As the first of these many groups pressed through Capetown, Port Elizabeth, and Durban, the earlier Dutch settlers were pushed northward. Boer and Briton, in turn, made successful drives against the indigenous Black inhabitants of Cape, Natal, and the Transvaal. Still later the Dutch—now calling themselves Afrikaners—collided in bloody battle with the British settlers and military in the Boer War (1899-1902). Thereafter, with animosity still flaming between the two White groups—Boer and Briton—the four separate geographic and political sectors of South Africa managed to achieve tenuous rapport. Thus, in 1910, the Union of South Africa was founded—bringing together the English-speaking crown colonies of Cape and Natal with the Afrikaner Dutch republics of Orange Free State and the Transvaal.

The principal founders of the Union, Generals Louis Botha and Jan Smuts, believed that it would be possible to reconcile the conflicting Boer and and British personalities, cultures, and political aims all within the British Empire (and later Commonwealth). They made this association with Britain the principal plank of their South African, and, later, United Party, platform. Opposing this view of reconciliation, however, was the Orange Union Party, led by General J. B. M. Hertzog, who was the chief architect of the postindependence Afrikaner philosophy. Although Hertzog had actually joined the first Union Cabinet, nonetheless he represented this nucleus of Afrikaner nationalist thought and the embryo of the present ruling Nationalist Party and philosophy.

During the next three decades (1910-39) there were political groupings and regroupings, coalitions and fragmentations. Throughout the period, however, there remained between the opposing groups the differing view as to the closeness of relations with Britain—the Smuts group for proximity, the Hertzog group for separation.

The beginning of World War II brought on new pressures for withdrawal from the British Commonwealth and formation of a republic. In 1939 the ruling coalition broke up over the war issue. Hertzog and his Nationalist-oriented followers withdrew, these favoring either full neutrality or a benevolent neutralism toward Nazi Germany. Now leading the United Party, Smuts succeeded in taking South Africa into war on the side of the Western allies, though by a close parliamentary vote.

During World War I and again at the beginning of World War II, many South Africans held strong neutralist or pro-German sympathies. Many of the Republic's present leaders were actually interned as pro-Nazi sympathizers during World War II. Those interned included South Africa's present prime minister, John Vorster, and his brother, Jacobus Vorster, present moderator of the Dutch Reformed Church (DRC).

In 1943 Smuts won a sweeping electoral victory. The postwar election of 1948, however, told a different story. The Nationalists, then under D. F. Malan, in association with the so-called Afrikaner Party, won a parliamentary majority. Malan, with the Nationalist-Afrikaner coalition, formed the new government, which was to remain in power for the following quarter-century. The United Party then (as now) became the main opposition. The 1948 election had been fought on the issues of the unclear racial policies of Smuts, on economic issues, and on the renewed desire to break with Britain. (Even in 1972 the first two of these matters remain paramount political issues, the third having been resolved in 1961.)

In 1948 the present Nationalist Party assumed power. There followed the successive premierships of D. F. Malan, J. G. Strydom, H. F. Verwoerd, and B. J. Vorster. The present prime minister, John Vorster, has been in office since 1966. During these regimes of the past 25 years, the major principles of baaskap ("boss rule") and of apartheid have been invoked and activated.

The Union remained a member of the British Empire (and later Commonwealth) until 1961. At that time, under considerable international pressure, coming mainly from the Afro-Asian bloc of newly independent nations, South Africa (to the delight of the Afrikaners) withdrew from the Commonwealth and became a sovereign Republic. The sovereignty of the British ruler was then replaced by a state president of the new Republic (a largely protocol role). The state president is elected to a seven-year term by a joint session of the bicameral Parliament. At the time the Republic was created in May 1961, a new constitution was promulgated. This constitution did not make many innovations or legal breaks with the original Westminster parliamentary-model form of Union.

Under the Republic form of government, as with the Union, real authority remains in the hands of the prime minister, who is the leader of the majority parliamentary party. Under his direction a Cabinet (appointed from the membership of the majority party in the lower House of Assembly) serves as his executive body, directing the work of the legislature and bureaucracy. The bicameral Parliament is composed of a wholly elective lower House of Assembly and a selected upper house, the Senate. The legislative body is supreme. New elections must be held within five years, unless the government falls or earlier elections are ordered by the ruling party. The Senate has 54 members, including two from South-West Africa. Eleven senators are appointed by the president, and 43 Senate seats are filled by an electoral college, consisting of members of the House of Assembly and provincial council members of each province and of South-West Africa. The House of Assembly consists of 166 elected members, 160 coming from the four provinces and six coming from South-West Africa. Though there is a quasi-independent judiciary, there is no supreme judicial authority holding the interpretive constitutional power of the U.S. Supreme Court or the juridical veto of the British Privy Council.

Each of the four provinces has a unicameral legislature elected on the same principles as the House of Assembly. Each provincial government is directed by an administrator, who is appointed by the state president for a five year term. Powers of the provinces are circumscribed and controlled by the central government. All provincial legislation requires central government approval before becoming law. Each provincial government is concerned mainly with hospitals, roads, the direction of municipal councils, and education (other than that for the Blacks).

CHAPTER

2

THE RACIAL PROFILE

For a better understanding of South Africa as a nation, it is essential to comprehend her complex racial structure and her race relations. Problems of race are pervasive throughout South African life, and this pervasiveness means that the question of racial association or conflict is the dominant social theme. These social-group relations have been the product of a number of historical, cultural, and demographic factors that have deep roots. There is an odd amalgam of fear and hate, of trust and distrust, of admiration and envy, of de facto integration and de jure segregation. These combine to produce a potentially volatile national scene.

The previous chapter details the latest (1970) census figures for the Republic. The census reports a total of 3.8 million Whites as contrasted with 17.6 million non-Whites. The salient controlling feature of the South African racial scene is the numerical preponderance of Blacks over Whites in the ratio of more than four to one. The existence of numbers of Coloureds and Asians in the country (these considered as non-Whites) enlarge the racial complexity and racial frictions.

This study now requires definitions for terms for racial designations. In South Africa "Whites" are known as "Europeans." These include descendants of immigrants from all European countries, particularly the United Kingdom and the Netherlands. The word "Afrikaner" generally denotes those South African Whites of Afrikaans cultural background and of Afrikaans-language convention. (On occasion the present ruling National Party seeks to equate the word "Afrikaner" with National Party membership.) The word "English" generally denotes those of British background or birth and of English-language convention. It is a broader term than "British" alone, as it embraces many others of European continental birth or background, as well as resident North American Whites—American or Canadian.

The term "non-Whites" includes "Coloureds," "Asians," and "Blacks." The word "Coloured" means those of mixed White and non-White blood deriving, in the main, from the union of the early White Cape settlers with Hottentots and Bushmen resident there, as well as with a few Malays and imported West African slaves. The word "Asians" means descendants of indentured workers brought from the Asian continent, particularly Indians (Hindu and Muslim), Pakistani, and Ceylonese. This latter racial group includes a few thousand immigrant Chinese and their descendants.

In South Africa, until recently, "Blacks" were characterized almost abusively either as "Natives" or as "Kaffirs." The latter word originated from Kaffraria, the geographic designation given the tribal area of the northeastern Cape Province by early White settlers. Today, in South Africa Blacks are officially called "Bantu." First usage of the word "Bantu" was philological, denoting a broad grouping of similar languages and dialects used by the dark-skinned, mainly Negroid people of a large section of central and southern Africa. The word "African" is not widely used in the Republic as it is confusing, embracing all residents of the African continent, without distinction as to race. Black Africans in the Republic now tend to favor the descriptive term "Black," rather than the official term "Bantu."

As with other areas of Africa and the developing world, the flow of Blacks into urban areas (legal and illegal) has been immense in recent years. It has been estimated that in the decade 1951-60 and again in the decade 1961-70, the increase of Black populations in urban areas of the Republic was double that of the White growth. It has been estimated that, in each of these decades, the White population of municipalities grew by 25 percent; the Black growth for the same periods was 48 percent to 50 percent. Even official census figures of Black populations in these areas are considered erratically low, however, because illegal residents of Black townships, servants' quarters, and workers' hostels would fail to register for any census count. Thus, it is that about two-thirds of the Republic's Blacks live in White-owned areas of South Africa, either in municipalities or on farms. The remaining one-third live in the tribal reserves or in proposed or present Bantustans. These latter comprise only 13 percent of the total land area of the country, though eventually they are expected to provide a livelihood for 75 percent of the entire population.

As noted elsewhere the Coloureds are mainly concentrated in the urban areas of the Cape and the Asians in the metropolitan areas of Durban, Pietermaritzburg, and Johannesburg. Neither the Coloureds nor the Asians have yet been given government-designated separate "homelands."

Although 85 percent of the Whites are urban dwellers, they are actually outnumbered by non-Whites in every major city and town. Furthermore, in White farming areas, Whites are outnumbered by Blacks six to one. The government, with its combination of Bantustans and urban townships, is trying to corral the Blacks into specific and segregated areas, many of these remote from White settlements. This action, presumably for security and "development" purposes, creates great transport, housing, and labor problems for both Black workers and for their White employers.

Despite heavier infant mortality, the birth rates of all non-White groupings consistently run higher than do those of the Whites. As a result demographers estimate the disparity between Whites and non-Whites is expected to grow. It is now anticipated that the ratio of Whites to non-Whites will reach one to seven by the year 2000. At that time projections forecast 22.5 million Blacks, 4.5 million Whites, 4.5 million Coloureds, and over 1.2 million Asians. The number of Coloureds in the Cape Province already exceeds the number of Whites there. In Natal, too, the Asians now exceed the White population. It is important to point out that more than 50 percent of all non-Whites in South Africa are under the age of 25, whereas less than 40 percent of Whites are reported to be in that age category. Thus, these long-range projections of population groupings may underestimate the eventual ratio between Blacks and Whites and between non-Whites and Whites.

The difficult race relations picture in South Africa is made even more complex by a variety of cultures and of development within the various groups. The Whites are the aristocrats and landowners, enjoying political and social privilege, with wide economic affluence. Yet they, too, are divided by the polarization of those of predominantly British and of Afrikaner background. Some of both groups, in the cities, are exceedingly prosperous, but many Afrikaners on farms and in laboring sections of the municipalities are hard pressed.

The Blacks are, in general, manual laborers and agriculturalists, subject to an infinite series of racial, economic, and social restrictions. However, among these, especially in the municipal townships and in the Bantustan capitals, there is now developing a highly educated, sophisticated, sometimes prosperous Black elite. These are the potential economic and political czars of the Black "nations."

The Asians and Coloureds, by contrast, comprise a large intermediate class of shopkeepers, hotel workers, factory workers, and artisans, who together constitute a distinct middle class. There are also many professional men and women—lawyers, doctors, and teachers. Even here, however, there are evidences of economic disparity, as small numbers in each of these groupings are decidedly prosperous, while a high proportion are below minimum subsistence levels. Members of the Asian and Coloured communities enjoy some social and economic advantages over the Blacks. However, they suffer many social indignities and political-legal disabilities in comparison to the Whites.

THE WHITES

The "European" attitude of fear, distrust, and implacable determination to preserve the status quo of "White supremacy" represents the most important single element of South Africa's racial scene. Though the two sectors of the White community—Afrikaner (numbering 2 million) and British (numbering 1.8 million)—differ somewhat in their approach to the problem of race relations within the Republic, there is no fundamental difference in attitude among the majority of both groups. On this policy Afrikaans- and English-speakers differ only in approach. Those of British extraction are more inclined to be less dictatorial than the Afrikaners in application of race laws. For both groups, however, the fundamental policy of continuing White dominance remains the same.

On matters other than race there has been considerable distinctiveness and rivalry between Afrikaner and British segments of the community. Given the long (25 years) primacy of the National (Afrikaner) Party and the movement of Afrikaner from their traditional fields of farming and politics into commerce and finance, many economic and cultural differences between the two groups are now becoming blurred. The schism between these groups is, of course, historic and stems from the animosities antedating and following the Boer War. The resolution of that conflict, which only tenuously amalgamated the two widely differing cultures, is only now slowly merging into a single "South African personality." Though all Whites in the Republic remain known, anachronistically, as "Europeans," they are becoming true "South Africans." Even so, the religious, social, cultural, and linguistic characteristics of these two groups—Boer and Briton—are today, in some respects, more widely variant than are the differences between some Whites and some non-Whites (including Blacks).

The Calvinist ethos dominates the Afrikaner mentality in a narrow, highly legalistic vein—jealous of tradition, sensitive to criticism by outsiders, cognizant of authority of church and state. The British mentality, diffused somewhat by liberal Judaic influences (there are 170,000 Jews in South Africa), tends toward a more easy Anglo-Catholic mentality, apathetic in politics, determined to preserve first of all its commercial and social position, hopefully without having the status quo "boat rocked."

In certain social situations the merging of the two groups is evident. Dual-medium education is becoming more common for Afrikaans- and English-speakers. Intermarriage is increasingly sanctioned by both societies. Three-fourths of the Whites are bilingual. Both the English and Afrikaans languages are increasingly necessary for everyday use in government and business. New intermixing, accomplished by postwar White immigration—German, Italian, Greek, Scandinavian, French, American, and Canadian—to the Republic has served as an added catalyst in breaking down the barriers between Afrikaner and Briton. So, too, has the intermixture provided by new postwar academic and commercial associations. Urbanization and the growth of population has also provided an impetus for breakdown.

At the time of Union (1910) most Afrikaners were farmers and most British were townsmen. The majority of Afrikaners remain semiskilled artisans, laborers, and farmers. However, they are moving horizontally into the cities and vertically into professions, commerce, and finance and into the civil service and the security forces. Yet, the influence of the rural Afrikaner and his conservative mental attitude still permeates and carries great weight in Afrikaner political circles. This results, in part, from the factor of gerrymandering parliamentary constituencies, giving to those rural Afrikaners an extraordinary political weight. Furthermore, the ultraconservative plattelander ("plateau dweller") of the Transvaal and Orange Free State, by sheer numbers, continues to dominate his more liberal Afrikaner associates of the Cape and Natal. The more conservative Afrikaner seeks to fend off external dilution of his culture through a series of religious, educational, and cultural organizations ranging from cradle to grave. Thereby, they seek to keep their volk ("people") corralled within the laager ("circle of covered wagons guarding the pioneers from external attack") of a chauvinistic society. Thus does Afrikanerdom seek to keep its people culturally unique.

This tight control extends even into higher echelons of government, where the operations of the organization known as the Broederbond ("Brotherhood") are legion. This organization, said to number about 8,000 Afrikaner Protestant males,* reportedly dominates assignment and promotion within principal areas of central and provincial governmental services. It exerts considerable control, as well, in the fields of Afrikaner business. (See Chapter 4.)

Operations of secret societies like the Broederbond have brought into the open, however, a dichotomy of attitudes, political and social, within the Afrikaner community itself. This split—which

*Sunday Tribune (Durban), August 30, 1970.

has labeled the more conservative antagonists as Verkrampte ("cramped" or "shriveled") and the relatively more moderate side, the Verligte ("enlightened"), has created major policy problems for Prime Minister Vorster and his senior political aids. There appears to be no fundamental difference between these groups as to maintenance of apartheid and White supremacy—both support it. However, there is a difference as to the rationalization of that policy, as to the approach and application thereof. The conservative Verkrampte, for example, wish to have little to do with the Bantustan concept, believing that too much has already been done for the Blacks. The Verkrampte, too, would prefer to remain isolated from the world—to withdraw from the UN and to build South African self-sufficiency in isolation. The Verligte, on the other hand, seek more relaxed attitudes with South Africans of British extraction—they push for effective implementation of the Bantustans, and support the concept of "dialogue" (diplomatic exchanges, discussions, and trade with other nations of Africa).

Efforts to keep these divergent views in check and their respective proponents within the National Party have proved highly embarrassing for Prime Minister Vorster. In fact, just prior to the 1970 general election, the prime minister was forced to read out of the Party a small clique of Verkramptes (led by a Cabinet minister, Albert Hertzog) to preserve unity among the majority. In any event these divergences of view among Afrikaners have forced the present Nationalist government toward more conservative rather than toward more liberalizing policies and action.

It has previously been stated that, except for a few White intellectuals and political liberals, South African Whites of British background are also essentially conservative on the subject of race. Only among the youth (both British and Afrikaner) has there been in evidence any real trend toward a more liberal bent on that issue. In view of the British tradition, ranging from the Magna Carta to the modern rule of law, that predominately conservative attitude is often difficult for outsiders to understand. There is too often an automatic assumption that South African Whites of British or European extraction (other than Dutch) are liberal in viewpoint on race issues. This is not necessarily true in South Africa. Whites resident there—British, European continentals, and North Americans—may often be as conservative in viewpoint on race issues as any Nationalist Afrikaner. Those of British extraction, particularly within the opposition United Party, have long hidden their support of White supremacy by euphemistic discussion of "trusteeship" or "conferation." The Nationalists have been more blunt with their society of baaskap, apartheid, and Bantustan.

Peripheral differences remain, however, between Afrikaans- and English-speaking as to certain facets of this all-pervading color problem. There has long been a drive, for example, by those politicians of British background (especially among leaders of the opposition United Party) to amalgamate into the White community the Coloured group. This has been inspired in part by fears that the non-Whites, with higher birth rates, will continue to outbreed the Whites. There is also, among British-extraction South Africans, a more relaxed attitude with respect to labor laws and "job reservations." British South Africans, heavily interested in commerce and industry, are the first to suffer labor shortages as a result of these laws and would therefore like to be rid of them. By contrast, the Afrikaner politician wishes to maintain these laws and these separations to insure "purity" of the White race, as well as White domination over the economy and labor markets.

THE COLOUREDS

The two million Coloureds of South Africa comprise an admixture of mulattoes, other Afro-European strains, and Malay. Though legally and socially separate, the Coloureds are, in fact, a historical appendage of the White community. They speak the same languages, Afrikaans and English, with 90 percent of them favoring Afrikaans. They belong to the same religious sects; one-third of them are members of the DRC. With many of them highly educated as professionals and well-trained as artisans, the group comprises a kind of lower middle-class bourgeoisie. On professional and academic levels, on farms, in commerce and industry, they have daily association with Whites—but never as equals. Given these facts of daily life, however, the range of legislation and social consciousness constricting them has made the Coloureds dispirited and anchorless. Coloureds, unlike Blacks, have no "homeland." They are grouped into blighted communities on the edges of major cities of the Cape and Natal. Until recent years they had token forms of parliamentary representation. They now have no real political voice, though there has been an effort to establish a certain communal representation, approved by the government, called the Coloured Persons' Representative Council. (See Chapter 4.)

Though there are certain local factions and recognized leaders, none of these yet appears to have real national stature. However, some of the Coloured "nationalists" have developed a distinct anti-apartheid, antigovernment attitude. Of immediate interest is the tendency of certain of these Coloured leaders to associate with recognized and nationally known South African Black leaders. It remains to be seen, however, whether the Coloured community, shattered in spirit by broken or unfulfilled promises of White politicians, may ever be able to resuscitate itself to become cohesive and politically potent. As the well-known South African author Sarah Gertrude Millin once characterized them, the Coloureds are "God's stepchildren."

THE ASIANS

This group, mainly Indian in origin, numbers about 620,000. (The Asian community usually includes a socially separate but legally similar grouping of Chinese, numbering above 6,000. By contrast the few resident Japanese, mainly businessmen, are accorded the legal position of "honorary Whites.") While politically and socially perhaps the weakest of the racial divisions, the Asian community has a greater cohesion and probably greater economic influence than do the Coloureds. About two-thirds of the Indians are Hindu and the remaining one-third Muslim. These two groups are fragmented by language, caste consciousness, and culture, as it contains Tamil, Telegu, and Dravidian sects, among others. Gujarati, Hindi, and Tamil are the most common languages, with English as the lingua franca. Their forebears came to South African shores during the last decades of the nineteenth century to work as indentured laborers in the sugarcane fields of Natal. It should be recalled that Mahatma Gandhi was one of these immigrants, living in South Africa from 1893 to 1914, working as a lawyer and developing his concepts of satyagraha ("soul force"), or passive resistance, later so successful in helping India attain nationhood.

Family ties and social consciousness remain strong within the Asian community. The group is resolutely determined to improve its own situation through economic and educational channels without awaiting action of politicians. While the great majority of Asians lives in Natal and supplies agricultural labor, catering trades, and semiskilled artisans, there is a growing group of Asian professionals who have become a cultural and economic elite.

The complexities of repressive racist legislation notably the Group Areas Act, which prescribes areas in which Asians (and all the races) can live, work, and be educated, has proved a major uncertainty for the Asian community, as it has been ever more restrictive and destabilizing. As a result underemployment, undernourishment, and underprivilege in housing, amenities, and education are commonplace among the Asians. These economic and social disabilities have kept Asian political pressures at a minimum. Ineffective leadership in recent years has also contributed to Asian difficulties. The resolute and astute leadership of the community in the 1940's and 1950's was decimated or broken by governmental action (banning, exile, or imprisonment). Recent Asian "leadership" coming out the government-sanctioned and government-appointed South African Indian Council (see Chapter 4) has proved, thus far, ineffective, powerless, and unrepresentative of the main Asian community. As a result the Asians have found solace in religion, the family, and communal strength. Instead of seeking political power unsuccessfully against apartheid barriers, they have aimed at acquisition of education and money. Thus, they are similar in many respects to the Coloureds or to the "wandering Jews" of Europe.

THE BLACKS

This group, numbering 15 million, represents 70 percent of the total populace of the Republic. One-third of their numbers remain rooted in a traditional, pastoral-agricultural life of the "tribal reserves." Most of these reserves will eventually become Bantustans. (See Chapter 5.) The remaining two-thirds of the country's Blacks are partially or wholly detribalized and urbanized, living and working in mine compounds, industrial hostels, or in segregated townships clustered around metropolitan centers. These urbanized Black Africans are considered by the government to be only temporary residents in the metropolitan areas in which they work and in which many of them were actually born. By government fiat they are considered only as citizens of the various Bantustans of their forebears. Thus, some Blacks are permitted to live and work temporarily in White South Africa only under sufferance.

Work rules and government regulations usually dictate that Black laborers must be separate from their families, except in those circumstances where township housing is available to long-term employees. Contract labor terms, usually 18 months, and stringent pass requirements for workers and family visitors further complicate freedom of movement for Blacks. (see Chapters 3 and 7.) This creates the anomaly that, though an integral part of the South African economy, two-thirds of the Blacks are politically and socially segregated. The remaining one-third is totally segregated from White society, as well as from their own urban Blacks, many of these members of their own immediate families.

The main body of Black workers is occupied in mining, manufacturing, commerce, and transport. A fair percentage of Blacks are engaged in the various services categories, including domestic work. Some 700,000 of the Black workers are engaged in agriculture on White-owned farms. Many Blacks remaining in the "reserves," especially the women and children, are engaged in subsistence agriculture. A few Blacks hold clerical and teaching posts, and there are a few other professionals—lawyers, doctors, and clerics.

Virtually all South African Blacks are members of the so-called Bantu (meaning "the people") grouping of Africans, these possessing common linguistic backgrounds. The word "Bantu" itself is confusing in its generalization, being now applied equally to all the diverse Black tribes of South and South-West Africa. Within the Republic there are nine major tribal groupings; these include the Xhosa (Transkeians and Ciskeians), the Zulu, the Lebowa, the Tswana, the Machangana, the Venda, the Basotha Ba Borwa, the Swazi, and the north and south Ndebele. Within these nine tribal groupings there are hundreds of lesser tribes. Customs and hereditary situations make them as different from one another as the Finns are from the Greeks or as the Irish are from the Germans. Features, too, differ. A Black African's coloration and physical characteristics depend in large measure on how much Negroid, Hamitic, Nilotic, or other bloods are within him.

Among the Blacks there are four main linguistic groups. The largest of these, the Nguni, includes Zulu, Xhosa, Pondo, and Swazi tribes. All these tribes are located along the southeastern shores and coastal hinterland of the Republic. This group totals about 8 million in number. The second largest linguistic group are the Sotho and the Tswana, living in the center and western sectors of the Transvaal. These number about 4 million. Two smaller groups, about 700,000 Tsonga and 3 million Venda, live mainly in the northern Transvaal. Although all languages of these groups, being Bantu in derivation and structure, have similarities, they are not mutually comprehensible. With each individual linguistic group, too, are dozens of lesser dialects, usually comprehensible within the tribal grouping.

Thus is the Black African community fractured by urban and rural separation, by tribal grouping, by education and employment, and by cultural gradation and social division. To varying degrees tribalism was actually decaying within South Africa over the past half-century. This was the noticeable result of religious, educational, linguistic, and economic changes. This was the result, too, of the mass urbanization. As the combined assaults of economic integration, migratory labor, mission influences, education, and Black African nationalism converged, the Black Africans were moving away from the chief-ruled tribal structure and into a modern Black African social structure. By its apartheid philosophy, represented in the realities of its Bantustan program, the Republic's White-ruled Nationalist government has deliberately sought to reverse this detribalizing—and unifying—process.

Effective in the destruction of tribalism have been the intrusions of other languages, especially English and Afrikaans. Also diluting and reshaping the traditionally animist tribal ways were the influences of the many Christian sects. Within the Christian sector there are fractures involving major recognized Church groupings (Anglican, Catholic, Methodist, Congregational, Lutheran, and so forth) and that recent phenomenon—the "independent" African churches. (See Chapter 8.)

Basing its decision on the above-named nine major tribal groupings, the South African government has predicated its determination of Bantustans, areas set aside solely for tribal development, into autonomous (and presumably eventually independent) nations. At present, however, these areas are in varying early stages of internal autonomy and can be considered only as "colonies," or "embryo nations."

No profile of the Blacks would be complete without a brief description of the "townships." These are ghetto-like Black suburbs of the White cities. The largest of these is Soweto (South-West Township), near Johannesburg, reputed to contain nearly 1 million residents, legal and illegal. The townships contain male and female workers' hostels and thousands of partially subsidized, individual, boxlike houses. Residency therein is granted "tenants" (and their family members) who have long-time employment records in adjacent White areas. Some tenants are permitted to keep "lodgers," such as contract-labor workers and their families. (Blacks can own realty in homeland villages but only have rights of tenancy or lodging in the townships.) There are few amenities in township housing. Most lack inside plumbing and electricity. Illegal "lodgers" are common; crime is rampant; and transport, health, and recreation facilities are inadequate. Police control of entry into townships is strict, and White visitors require permits. The townships are run by municipal authorities under direction of Bantu administration officials. Some townships have elected Black urban councils, but these have little real authority. Demands for housing and hostel space outrun current availabilities. Further expansion of present townships is actively discouraged by the government on the thesis that Blacks should maintain their permanent residence and families only in the homelands.

CHAPTER

3

PHILOSOPHY AND PRACTICE OF APARTHEID

The philosophical basis of apartheid is, in essence, the concept that each racial subgroup is a nation in itself. According to this philosophy the customs, the values, and the daily life of each of the races and tribes resident within South Africa and South-West Africa must be preserved from adulteration by extraneous alien influences. Each racial subgroup is to maintain an individual identity. To lessen chances of adulteration and dilution, each racial subgroup should live and work and develop as much apart from one another as political, social, and economic circumstances permit.

Furthermore, under the concept and theology of apartheid, Western White civilization—and particularly that of the Afrikaner—is considered to be at once the most advanced, inspired, and divinely ordained of all racial groupings. Consequently, the White man—and, again, particularly the Afrikaner—is considered to be the predestined trustee, the guide and ruler, of the less advanced. Thus it is that the Afrikaner culture is decreed to be at the core and the epitome of the South African way of life.

The Afrikaner community is considered supreme, with God-given rights of leadership. They are, in effect, "the chosen people," safeguarding White supremacy and protecting the Afrikaner position of leadership. To that end all political, parliamentary, and legal activity, educational, cultural, and religious actions—even business activities—are aimed at buttressing the Afrikaner position—protecting racial purity—insuring White supremacy. Under no circumstances are Whites to become subject to judgment or authority of non-Whites. In the United States the constitutional concept of integration is presumed to be supported by all arms of the federal government. The South African government insists on segregation.

From the inevitable extension of this thesis comes the additional thesis that only Whites can sit in Parliament, that only Whites can sit on juries, that all skilled and managerial jobs must be reserved to Whites. Each racial grouping is to have its own universities, its own professional levels, its own sports and social amenities (ranging from places of worship to taxis and ambulances). Furthermore, each group is to have its own residential, business, educational, and sports locations, these decreed by law.

Taking this, too, to its final extension, the thesis of apartheid decrees that Blacks are only in urban areas as "temporary workers" —migrants licensed to satisfy the transitory needs of the White "rulers." Even if Blacks are lifelong residents of those areas and several generations removed from their homelands, their only legal right of residence is in those homelands. Those homelands are to be the focus of Black attention—the locus of their families, loyalties, and citizenship. For the Blacks then, this thesis constitutes the foundation-stone of the various tribal Bantustans. For the Coloureds and Asians-still in the throes of being restricted and regrouped—this constitutes the basis of a tenuous communal life on the fringes of the largest cities and White society. These groups, too, remain subject to White domination.

Given this concept of apartheid, for reasons of convenience to the Whites, many Blacks are permitted to remain within White communities, on a transient basis, to satisfy economic and industrial needs. However, it is deemed unwise by the Nationalists to give the Blacks the vote within White South Africa, since the Blacks would, at once, be in the majority. Furthermore, Blacks who are temporary "guests" in White South Africa, away from their ancestral, tribal homes, are not to be accorded a vote in White areas or the national parliaments. Their vote must be exercised only in their tribal legislative elections and within a carefully designated scope of authority and right. Thus, Zulus, whether resident in Johannesburg or in Zululand, are to vote in elections held only in the reserves from which they derive, even though they may be living and working outside that reserve.

By contrast, however, the Afrikaners are forced to recognize both Coloureds and Asians as permanent residents. Thus far, however, they will not accept these groups as citizens or full-scale nationals of the country with voting rights equal to Whites. While there has been particular pressure to give that full franchise to the Coloured, no such "dilution" of the White supremacy concept has yet occurred. Recent moves to set up communal councils for these two groups mark only a token step toward real communal franchise. Both Prime Minister Vorster and former Prime Minister Verwoerd specifically rejected the idea of representation of either Coloureds or Asians in the South African Parliament.

Carrying these themes to their logical conclusions would infer that the present leaders of South Africa envisage full partition of their country. This presumption requires a close, hard look—including an appreciation of South Africa's present highly integrated and effective economy. (See Chapters 5-7 on Bantustans, on the economy, and on labor.) That look must also be directed at the actualities of present-day South African government and daily life.

Since coming into power 25 years ago the ruling National Party, mainly composed of Afrikaners, has carried on an increasingly restrictive policy, systematically implementing a broad program of legislation and decrees designed to segregate all non-Whites living and working in White South Africa. This program is above and beyond the effort to drive back into the tribal reserves under the Bantustan program the majority of Blacks residing within the Republic. The aim of these drives is to fulfill Nationalist political and cultural doctrine by creating a closed and compartmented society to insure continued White domination. The Nationalist aim is to make sure that each racial group would attain to its own home areas and have its own prescribed areas of work, residence, society, and cultural values. This makes the operation of apartheid both vertical and horizontal—the Whites at the top of the national pyramid, the Coloureds and Asians in between, and the Blacks at the bottom—geographically, politically, economically, and culturally.

The policy and practice of apartheid require that everyone in the Republic be labeled according to his racial group. Until the Nationalists came into power in 1948, this racial classification, with a few technical exceptions, had been mainly the result of custom. Racial classification has now been built into law, relating to residence, work, education, culture, and all major amenities. To achieve the absolute in this racial classification, a population register has been created, and, under this register, racial identity cards have been issued to all inhabitants of the Republic. It is now planned to enhance the practice of putting everyone into his racial niche in South African life by use of a "book of life," or comprehensive passport, embodying all vital statistics of each individual, including birth certificate, marriage or divorce actions, work history, driver's license, and immunizations certificate, and so forth. It is presumed that this book of life will be fully operative by 1973.

The arbitrary classification of persons has caused considerable misery, since, on occasion, government officials concerned with race classification have actually split families—labeling one member White, another Coloured, and so forth. Such racial classification henceforth fully determines a person's political and social position—his associations, his work and education possibilities and prospects, his residence, and his major life contacts. On occasion, too, the classification of races has proved ironic. For political and economic purposes, resident Japanese businessmen have been given the title "honorary Whites." The Chinese community, for some purposes, has been construed as Asian, for some purposes, as Coloured or White. Visiting foreign Black African dignitaries, including American Negroes, on occasion, have been considered as "distinguished foreign visitors" who are racially unclassified. Thus, they have been permitted access to some White amenities, including specified hotels and restaurants.

Though not legally prohibited until recent years, the intermarriage or sexual association of Whites and non-Whites has been frowned upon by South African society for decades. More recently, with new legal leverage and local police emphasis, there has been an unusual (and thus far unsuccessful) effort to stamp out all sexual associations across the color bar. Intermarriage between White and non-White is now illegal. If intermarriage occurs between members of differing non-White race groupings (as, for example, marriage of a Coloured to an Asian or a Black), then the racial classifications are changed to equalize the partners at the lower level of the racial pyramid.

Earlier legislation had prohibited both mixed marriages and sexual relations between Whites and Blacks. In 1950 the Immorality Amendment Act was extended to prohibition of sexual associations between Whites and all non-Whites. Several hundred persons of all races, but predominantly White males cohabiting with Black and Coloured females, are now convicted each year of crimes involving miscegenation or other immoral association between the races. Attesting to the social pressures involved, six White men committed suicide in a three-month period alone (December 1970 to March 1971) when so charged. The recently enacted Prohibition of Mixed Marriage (Amendment) Act has further complicated the racial-marital situation. It provides that any White male person who is a South African citizen or domiciled in the Republic who enters into a racially mixed marriage outside the Republic cannot have that marriage recognized within South Africa. Such a marriage is deemed to be void. Partners to such a marriage are to be prosecuted if they return to the Republic. This legislation is prejudicial to the wife and children in such a partnership, as the South African husband could return to the Republic and avoid all responsibilities of such a marriage.

Blacks and Asians are extremely restricted as to both housing and movement, the Coloureds less so. Asians are not allowed to travel or move from one Province to another except under temporary permit and for good reason. The Blacks are allowed outside their reserves only for the purpose of seeking work within White South Africa during a 72-hour period. Exceeding that time, unless they obtain approved employment, they are subject to fine or jail. Legislation to insure that only the number of Blacks actually needed in urban areas be permitted there annually becomes more strict in enactment and implementation. This legislative control is consolidated under a so-called Bantu Laws Amendment Bill, which is both harsh and extensive. More than 1,800 Blacks were prosecuted daily for "offenses" under various pass laws during fiscal year 1970/71 alone. The minister of justice reported in the House of Assembly in March 1971 that 42 percent of all prisoners serving sentences of up to four months have been imprisoned for violation of "influx control" laws.[1] More than 33,000 Blacks were returned to their "homelands" from urban areas during 1970.[2] Special efforts have been directed to insure that all control of Blacks in metropolitan areas be the responsibility of the central government, which, to date, has been considerably more stringent in its treatment of Blacks than have municipal authorities.

The Group Areas Act of 1950 established a zoning program for all areas of White South Africa. This legislation demarcated areas designed for each racial group and subgroup for work and residence. Massive relocation and dislocation of housing and businesses occurred under this act. A few central areas of cities that have been too difficult to sort out among non-White groups remain only temporarily available to all three—Coloureds, Asians, and Blacks. These areas, however, are under continuing governmental scrutiny and will eventually involve relocation. Gradually, however, such areas are becoming fewer, and single racial groupings within prescribed areas are the norm rather than the exception. Sorting out is accomplished by moving members of one group from the area, then proscribing members of that group from buying, inheriting, or locating within the area. There is considerable enforced movement of urban groups, the Whites being the least affected by these new demarcations, the Coloureds and Asians probably most affected. When urban Blacks are moved to townships, they are given only tenancy or lodging rights in the houses they occupy. They are only occasionally allowed freehold title to property in the homelands. Blacks are not permitted permanent residence in White, Asian, or Coloured areas. Asians and Coloureds are permitted title thereto only in highly restricted localities. As to residence on farms White farmers are permitted only a specified number of Black workers on that land. Squatters on farmlands in excess of those essential laborers are forcibly removed to their hereditary tribal reserves.

All non-Whites are restricted as to the nature of work they may take up, as to the level of work to which they may attain, and as to salary they may receive. Many restrictions are statutory. Others result from apprenticeship practices or custom. Furthermore, conditions of work and rights as to collective bargaining are severely restricted for all non-Whites, but especially for Blacks. Supervisory, technical, and managerial jobs are done by Whites. Some service and intermediate industrial foreman jobs are permitted to Coloureds and Asians. Unskilled jobs are done by Blacks. (Black labor unions are not officially recognized. See Chapter 7 on labor.) Strikes by Blacks are illegal, and penalties for work stoppages are severe, usually involving return of striking Black workers to their tribal reserves at once. Under archaic laws it remains a criminal office for a Black to quit his job unilaterally or to fail to carry out his terms of contract. This sector of law has been further strengthened by the determination that Black domestic and commercial-industrial workers must serve one employer for at least ten years before then becoming eligible for rights of tenancy in a nearby township. Until then, he is usually prohibited from having his family with him. Meanwhile, even though married, he must live in bachelor workers' hostels run by government or municipality, in quarters supplied by his employer, or illegally or legally with friends or relatives already resident in established townships.

With few exceptions, such as streets and stores, public amenities are rigidly segregated. Apartheid legislation with respect to these amenities, including churches, universities, hospitals, and transport (trains, buses, taxis, and ambulances) has become increasingly restrictive toward all non-Whites, but especially Blacks. The segregation also applies to hotels, theatres, restaurants, park benches, beaches, entrances to public buildings, and sports events. Posted signs direct traffic on most amenities—inviting Whites, excluding non-Whites, and vice versa.

In the field of health the separation of races is clear-cut in the public area but somewhat more hazy in the private area. In general, the Whites are served by "Whites only" hospitals, staffed by Whites. White doctors, however, constitute an important element of the operation of government hospitals for the non-Whites, these serving only non-Whites. Church-supported mission hospitals have been an important element of the social scene throughout the African continent in the past century. In South Africa these are steadily being taken over, or subsidized and controlled, by provincial governments.

In 1948 there were hospital beds for 20,000 Whites and 30,000 non-Whites. In 1967 there were 40,000 for Whites and 94,000 for non-Whites. The general health and longevity situation of non-Whites, however, is still unsatisfactory when compared to Whites. Vital statistics[3] tell an interesting story. The latest available figures on the life expectancy of various members of the racial groups were as follows: (a) White men, 64.7, and White women, 71.6; (b) Coloured men, 49.6, and Coloured women, 54.2; and (c) Asian men, 57.7, and Asian women, 59.5. There are no figures for Blacks available, as registration of births and deaths for these are incomplete. In 1970 the infant mortality rates (number of infants per 1,000 live births who die in their first year) were as follows: (a) Whites, 21.2; (b) Coloureds, 132.0; (c) Asians, 36.5; and (d) Blacks, 101.2. Occurrence of tuberculosis, reported for 1970, was as follows: (a) Whites, 824; (b) Coloureds, 6,608; (c) Asians, 957; and (d) Blacks, 55,398. Malnutrition is rife in Black African areas but there are no reliable statistics. Kwashiorkor is no longer a notifiable disease for statistical purposes, but drought and ignorance of nutritional needs make this disease an ongoing tribulation among non-Whites.

An integral part of the apartheid policy has been in the underlying thesis that legislation—and civil administration—is designed to put down all concerted resistence to it—whether White or non-White. From 1950, when the severe Suppression of Communism Act was passed, the Nationalist government has gradually hardened its legislative capabilities on this score—derived from the philosophy that it equates opposition with Communism. Thus, the civil liberties of all races, as well as all opposition, have been gradually circumscribed and, in some areas, proscribed. Freedom of speech, freedom of assembly, formation of opposition political parties, freedom of press, freedom of work and of movement, even freedom of religious activity have been impaired or precluded.

There are various exceptional statutory and administrative restrictions on the South African judiciary that effectively bind the "arms" or norms of traditional Western democratic justice. For example, the law courts are forbidden to judge the validity of any act of Parliament, except language acts. Courts may not issue orders for detainees to be released. The attorney general can order a judge to refuse bail. Retrospective legislation is on the books. Prosecution witnesses can be jailed and defense witnesses ordered not to testify. Court verdicts that have gone against the government usually are followed by statutory amendment to close the "loopholes." Thus, there is in force in South Africa a definite control of judiciary by the executive and the legislative arms.

All standard privileges of free assembly and society have gradually been diminished or erased for non-Whites under the Nationalist regime. It has been difficult for liberal voices to be raised in opposition, but doubly so for Blacks. While there is still some liberal and independent political thought voiced in the English-language press and in a few Afrikaner journals, even these groups are hard pressed. All liberal White opposition in national, provincial, and municipal parliamentary bodies has become weaker. The continuing presumed independence of the judiciary is also hampered and straitjacketed by the necessity of applying unjust laws under an authoritarian parliamentary regime that is all-powerful. The 1950 Suppression of Communism Act and subsequent similar laws (particularly the

Terrorism Act of 1967) have constantly set the tone that liberal opposition to the Nationalist regime is as bad as or worse than Communism, since such liberal thought and action is presumed to promote internal disorder and change. As a result many leaders of liberal movements, members of all races, have been exiled, banned, or detained without the right of habeas corpus. Such arbitrary action has enabled the government to move against any opposition without giving defendants and detainees adequate recourse to the courts. House arrest and lengthy detention without trial are common. The accused are considered guilty until and unless they can prove their innocence. Arrests of political suspects can be made without warrant, and detainees may be held for 180 days without trial. They may also be re-arrested and redetained for another 180 days after serving out the original detention. Definition of "sabotage" or "treason" is extensive. The government's police powers enforce and reinforce apartheid. In most Western nations it would ordinarily be presumed that such powers would be applied only during a state of emergency. In South Africa that state of emergency is ongoing and an undeclared norm.

The South African Institute of Race Relations issued a formal statement in January 1968 decrying the legal situation in the Republic. It opposed banning without recourse to the courts. It agreed with right of government to take such steps as are necessary to safeguard the state from Communist or other subversion and accepted that the government must be alert. However, the institute contended that the present powers of the government exceed those required to meet the present dangers and the government has interfered with established rights of individuals that should prevail in a society which claims to respect standards of Western civilization. In bypassing ordinary judicial process, the institute stated that the government was not only undermining a basic bulwark of its Western democratic society, but was, at the same time, strengthening in the world at large an undesirable image of South Africa. The institute called on the government to restore the courts of South Africa to their rightful place and allow them, on basis of evidence presented, to convict or discharge those now arbitrarily banned or detained.

Because of the broad definition of "Communism" and "liberalism," freedom of speech, of press, and of assembly has been ever more severely curtailed since 1948. So, too, have the governmental actions over press, including books and newspapers, films, and radio. (There is no television as yet in South Africa, presumably because of governmental fears that public exposure and reaction to foreign events would prove difficult to control.)

The South African government may now censor, ban, or prohibit any book, film, press article, or other publication that it considers inimical to itself, or which it believes may engender hostility between

White and non-White, or which furthers concepts or ideas of Communism. Backers of periodicals are required to deposit up to rand 20,000 (approximately U.S. $27,000) as insurance against possible banning of the publication in the future. Publication of statements by, or quotations from, banned persons are also prohibited. (See Chapter 8.)

A recently published book by Anthony Mathews, Dean, Faculty of Law, University of Natal, makes a clinical analysis of South Africa's legal scene.[4] The book shows how security laws have become an integral element of the apartheid system. It states that the government regards opposition to its policies and outright subversion as virtually indistinguishable. It contends that security laws are making it possible that all opponents of the system can be declared persona non grata and can disappear into detention without trial. He calls for taming governmental authority, subjecting it to the rule of law.

Mathews makes six premises: (a) a government committed to pursuit of group power might initially avoid repressive measures, but rising demand will force it to make concessions or to repress its opponents; (b) discontent of excluded groups will take forms of protest and pressure that the system permits; (c) a government committed to make no compromise will then denounce use of available channels of dissent, closing them off by legislation; (d) the opposition will operate outside the system, using nonviolent methods to secure recognition; (e) these, in turn, will be countered by security laws, forcing opposition into allegedly subversive action; (f) security legislation will abolish remaining vestiges of liberty, placing the government in a position of total power.

Mathews says these foregoing steps have been exemplified by recent South African history. He believes that accommodation will begin only when pressures are irreversible. He apparently believes that if violence can be avoided in the Republic, rule of law may yet prevail. This requires liberalization leading to political equality of all races in a national parliament and a federal system. He believes this could be based on essential elements of a constitutional democracy already present in the Republic—a self-sustaining, modern economy with resources for creating a stable middle class; representative institutions; an advanced system of public administration; and a liberal tradition of law. As a prelude to a federal framework, Mathews recommends liberalization and elimination of apartheid laws, including job reservations; expansion of education; removal of barriers to land ownership by non-Whites; permanent residence rights for all workers; and progressive introduction of non-Whites into regional and, eventually, national politics. He contends that separate development cannot produce the "separateness" that the White leaders desire.

No consideration of the philosophy and practice of apartheid would be complete without some discussion of two arch proponents of Afrikanerdom and the system of separate development. Though earlier Afrikaner leaders—Hertzog, Malan, and Strijdom—had great influence in establishing the dogma of Afrikaner nationalism, the two most recent prime ministers of the Republic have had immense influence. Hendrik Verwoerd was chief architect of the philosophy of apartheid and the Bantustan concept. B. J. Vorster has been the principal activator of those ideas.

Verwoerd, prime minister of South Africa from 1958 till 1966, was born in Holland in 1901. He lived in South Africa as a child but was educated at German universities. He later taught psychology and sociology at the University of Stellenbosch. From 1937 to 1948 he was editor of the Johannesburg Afrikaans-medium daily, Die Transvaler. This newspaper was an important mouthpiece of the National Party and, as such, gave Verwoerd national stature. During World War II his editorial activities proved him to be anti-British, anti-Semitic, and pro-Nazi. He was nominated to a senatorial seat in 1948 and led the National Party policy group in the Senate for the next several years. In 1950 he was appointed minister of native (now Bantu) affairs. In that position he created much of the legislation that now governs Black life in the Republic.

Verwoerd first set forth his philosophy of apartheid in a parliamentary speech, as a policy of growing from one's own roots, through one's own institutions, and by one's own powers. . . . He later interpreted apartheid as an actual, territorial separation of "European" and "Bantu" by insisting on creation of territorial homelands for the Blacks. In effect he sought to retribalize the Blacks. He was to carry his ideas further through his selection as prime minister in 1958 after Prime Minister Strijdom's death.

In Verwoerd's early speeches as prime minister he again emphasized his rigid political theories. Almost at once he rejected a more liberal policy toward Coloureds, and he forced revocation of parliamentary representation (by Whites) of Black African interests. It was he who led South Africa in 1961 out of the Commonwealth and into Republic status. In January 1962 he announced the first steps to be taken in creating the Bantustan "homelands," beginning with the Transkei. Throughout his rule as prime minister he was firm in his control of his party. In his exposition of his philosophies he was intense and self-righteous, considering that he had an almost Divine mission to protect Afrikanerdom and White rule.

Prime Minister Verwoerd was assassinated in 1966 in the House of Assembly in Capetown. Soon, thereafter, the well-known author Alan Paton, in a newspaper study of Verwoerd,[5] claimed that the prime minister had more solid White backing at his death than he had upon assumption of his premiership. This, said Paton, was because "many who thought him dangerous now looked upon him as a bulwark against danger." While Paton condemned Verwoerd as a racialist in his earlier public years, Paton believed that he became somewhat more "benign" on issues of race in his later years. His greatest feat, said Paton, was in the way he took his predecessors' concept of baasskap and replaced it with the concept of separate development. Thus, he won to his side the intellectuals and churchmen and resuscitated some progressive ideas in Afrikanerdom. Paton considered Verwoerd to be a man of considerable political stature and administrative skill. Said Paton, "he could have been great under different stars" (in a less-narrow society).

The Republic's present prime minister, B. J. Vorster, first appeared on national and international scenes when he was appointed Verwoerd's minister of justice in 1961. He was born in South Africa in 1915 and graduated from the University of Stellenbosch. After studying law he practiced in the Cape and the Transvaal. He was interned by the Smuts government during World War II for his alleged pro-Nazi sympathies. He was elected to Parliament in 1953 as a Nationalist member from the Transvaal. In 1958 he was appointed deputy minister of arts and sciences in Verwoerd's Cabinet. Appointed minister of justice in 1961 he thereafter specialized in improving the conditions and capabilities of South African police and internal security. He became prime minister in 1966, following Verwoerd's assassination. Prime Minister Vorster is not a gregarious and hearty type of extrovert politician. He is far more serious-minded. He is extremely effective as a platform speaker and in parliamentary debate.

Responding to a query as to whether Whites in South Africa claim a special position for themselves,[6] Vorster said

> the Whites do not claim for themselves a special position which they are not prepared to accord to the various Bantu people within our borders. Just as they are prepared to recognize the special position of these groups in the areas where they have been traditionally and historically settled, the Whites claim the same rights in the areas traditionally and historically inhabited and developed by them. . . . Why are you experiencing peace and quiet in this country? It is because the mass of the Black population knows, understands and accepts that separate development doesn't work only to the advantage of the White people, but that it also works to the advantage of the Black people. . . .

Prime Minister Vorster was questioned further by U.S. News and World Report as to what would be South Africa's reactions if the UN tried to end the mandate over South-West Africa. Vorster was definite. He restated his foreign minister's policy exposition in New York that "South Africa would resist with all the power at its disposal any attempts which endanger the safety of our country or of the peoples committed to our care. . . ."

Asked about his relations with Rhodesia and the Portuguese territories (Angola and Mozambique), Vorster replied:

> It stands to reason that all states in Southern Africa will and must work as closely together as possible, because it is in the interest of each and everyone of us to do so . . . the new [Black] states, the former Protectorates, hold no danger for us. We want to work with them as independent Black states, to their advantage and to our advantage. There is no reason whatever why the closest of ties should not exist between them and us as . . . between good neighbors . . . cooperation between all States of Southern Africa will continue to grow . . . we want the best possible relations between all countries, White and Black, in Southern Africa. . . .

Responding to a query on "partition" of the Republic, Vorster replied that" the country is, in fact, partitioned as between Blacks and Whites . . . [that] done back in 1936. . . . Questioned on eventual federation of White and Black territories, Vorster said:

> You can't at this stage say what the ultimate outcome [of Bantustans] will be whether you will have a federation or conferation . . . our policy is one of leading the various Black nations . . . to self-government. . . . Having become independent politically, they will realize at that time, and we will realize, that economically we are inter-dependent, and whatever relations can or will flow from that will have to be decided in the future . . . [independence for the Bantustans] is the policy of the National Party. . . . We know that segregation is practical and can work. . . .

Delivering his first speech as chancellor of his alma mater, the University of Stellenbosch, in February 1971,[7] the prime minister said that apartheid could not be practiced without applying an "element of force." However, he believed that it was totally wrong to neglect a man's identity. He added that the most pressing question in South

Africa today was the peaceful coexistence of the various races in the future. "One thing is absolutely necessary: you cannot allow unrest or violence." He would not accept the argument that the White group should incorporate the best of the other groups. This had only caused trouble in the past. He added that the Coloured people were not an accessory to the Whites. "You will discover there are rules and codes in any ordered society. . . . Without fences there can be no freedom. The worst slave is he who escaped authority. . . ."

The prime minister's views on the policy of segregation as opposed to integration—of multinationalism as opposed to multiracialism—are perhaps better explained in yet another platform. Speaking before a recent National Party rally, he said, inter alia, that he did not consider himself to be better than a man of another color, but that "God in His wisdom had made people different" and that gave him (the prime minister) the right to maintain that difference. He added that, to avoid racial friction in the Republic, the Mixed Marriage Act, the Immorality Act, the Separate Universities Act, the Group Areas Act, and similar legislation would remain on the statute books in order to help maintain that difference. He also said that the time had arrived in South Africa where promises already made to the non-White population had to be carried out. South Africa had but two clear alternatives—multiracialism or multinationalism. The prime minister emphasized that only the National Party concept of multinationalism could safeguard the future of the White "nation" in the Republic, as well as those interests of the non-White "nations." Multiracialism in South Africa "would lead to the greatest chaos."

CHAPTER

4

THE POLITICAL SCENE

THE NATIONAL PARTY

The Afrikaner National Party has been in power in South Africa since 1948. Successive Nationalist regimes in power since that time have aimed at centralizing government, strengthening the Afrikaner politico-cultural traditions, and pushing the Black African majority back into their "homelands." With its political clout mainly centered in the rural areas of the Transvaal, Free State, and eastern Cape, the Nationalists have helped to keep themselves in power by gerrymandering tactics that favor their rural constituencies. At the same time, until recently, they have maintained a highly disciplined party organization, keeping an iron hand over civil service and workers in government-operated corporations, such as the extensive South African Railways and Harbours (SAR&H). The Nationalists have also succeeded in retaining their grip over such a long period by playing on patriotic urges to defend the status quo against encroachments of "liberalism," Communism, and swartgevaar ("Black peril"). Cohesion of the Afrikaner populace in cultural, religious, and educational groupings, together with a slight increase in the ratio of Afrikaner to Briton, has also aided the Nationalists in retention of political superiority. So, too, has the surprising political apathy of the more business-minded British sector of the society. Leadership is exerted from the top through Cabinet and party caucus to "grass roots" provincial and local organizations. Parallel vertical control is maintained through all the machinery of Afrikaner life—political, cultural, religious, and business. A typical Afrikaner is as deeply engrossed in his politics as are the Jews or the Irish.

Throughout its present long reign the National Party has maintained solid parliamentary majority. As well, it has gained control over three of the four Provincial assemblies, lacking only the British-oriented United Party control of Natal. The Nationalists also maintain control over the South-West African Assembly. Until 1970 there was a steady increase in popular support of the Nationalists. In that election year, however, the main opposition United Party made inroads against the Nationalists in urban areas. Their successes resulted in a gain of eight parliamentary seats by the United Party, leaving the Nationalists with a parliamentary total of 118 seats. By 1972 the United Party held a total of 47 of 166 seats in the House of Assembly, with the splinter group, the Progressive Party (formerly United Party) holding only one seat. Thus, the Nationalists continue to hold a safe two-thirds majority.

The gains made by the United Party in recent years may be attributed to a combination of political and economic difficulties. These include inflation, labor shortages, corruption in government (including allegations against certain cabinet ministers), and the increasing international pressures against South Africa, especially in the realm of sports.

In recent years a cleavage has occurred on the right wing of the National Party that, though weak, has threatened the solidarity and discipline of the party. This right-wing defection has resulted in creation and wide usage of two defining terms—Verkrampte for the ultraconservatives and Verligte for the less-conservative regular Nationalists. Undercurrents of that cleavage appear to remain within the party as well, though some of the dissidents were read out of the party prior to the 1970 election. At that time the dissidents, led by Albert Hertzog, a former cabinet minister, formed the Herstigte National Party (HNP), which unsuccessfully challenged regular Nationalist and other parliamentary candidates in a few heavily conservative constituencies. The HNP won no seats. The HNP has continued to maintain its form as a political party, with candidacies in recent by-elections and with radical right publications. This effort, however, has been one of nettlesomeness to Nationalist leaders rather than of major danger. More important, however, is the immeasurable group of right-wingers, said to tacitly favor the verkrampte line, who remain within regular Nationalist ranks. These are reputed to be more numerous than supposed and may include one or two present cabinet ministers. The difficulty has occurred over party differences on the issues of international associations (including sports events); on the Bantustan concept, of which ultraconservative right-wingers disapprove; and on the issue of "liberalism" and how to handle it as a threat to Afrikaner culture.

The well-known South African author Leo Marquard, in an address to the Institute of Race Relations in 1968,[1] characterized these two antagonistic groupings. He said Verkramptes were "those who maintain that South Africa grew strong through its vigilance and . . . should not bow the knee to foreign and false gods of Liberalism in disguise . . . the Afrikaner should glory in his isolation. . . ." Marquard sees the Verligte as "those who think that Afrikaner nationalism not only can afford to relax its exclusiveness as a White group . . . but will be compelled to do so as a White group on a Black Continent. . . ." Marquard believes that many of the Verkrampte are young people, artisans, students, and professionals who have long been exposed to the Christian (Afrikaner) National theories of education. To balance these, on the Verligte side, is yet another increasingly vocal, youthful group, centered mainly in the Afrikaans-medium universities of Stellenbosch and Potchefstroom. He and other observers tend to believe, however, that the two Afrikaner dissident groups, Verkrampte and Verligte, are not fundamentally divided on the issue of race and White domination, but rather on the application.

The "moderate" Afrikaner intellectuals believe that the government is not going far enough and fast enough in liberalizing its apartheid laws. They believe it essential to keep ahead of both economic needs and political pitfalls. For example, the "moderate" Afrikaner intellectuals (like most members of the opposition United and Progressive Parties) decry the idea of "partition" of the Republic a la Bantustans. They do not believe that this will alleviate the situation of race tensions. They argue that these concepts are anachronistic since de facto economic integration proceeds apace and the Blacks become more urbanized.

Thus far, the Nationalist government under Prime Minister Vorster has effectively squelched any major unrest, right-wing or left-wing, within the Nationalist ranks. That squelching, however, has required many compromises and has resulted in considerable ambivalence, passivity, and contradictory statements on the part of both prime minister and cabinet.

Within Nationalist ranks, above and beyond the race question, there remains a xenophobic nationalism and antipathy toward things British. This has resulted from the long history of conflict between Boer and Briton in Southern Africa, culminating in the Boer War. The feeling has been given further fuel and flame by the activities of the two world wars and by the determined battle of the Afrikaner to create a Republic. These historic antipathies, real and imagined, have fostered Afrikaner nationalism, which, in turn, has begun to mould itself into a new South African patriotism. The strength of the National Party stems, in part, from its historic sectionalism (Transvaal, Free State, and Cape rural). The strength stems, too, from its control over its membership and from the institutions that bolster that authority. The party is held together tightly by this network of institutions and by the historical-cultural mythology that this group of institutions constantly evokes.

Chief among these politico-cultural groupings is the highly influential secret society, the Broederbond. This group of Afrikaner leaders is of central importance, not only in guiding the party but in operating the main divisions of government, the church, the media (especially radio and Afrikaner newspapers), and even in some fields of business where Afrikaner investment is heavy.

The Broederbond, operating in secrecy, enforces conformity and, in modern terms, racial extremism. It appears to have had a growth in power in recent years, mainly because of the extension of Afrikaner influence into new fields of activity. Its key influence remains its capability of insuring promotion of Afrikaners of the "right" political hue, thus stifling dissent and insuring political conformity. The Broederbond was long headed by P. J. Meyer, chairman of the South African Broadcasting Corporation. (That entity holds a total monopoly over radio and embryo television establishments in the Republic.) The Broederbond is now headed by Andries Treunicht, leader of the right-wing Nationalists in the present South African Parliament. Every prime minister since 1948 has been a member of the Broederbond, as have a majority of Cabinet ministers and three-quarters of all the Nationalist members of Parliament.[2] Leaders of the DRC, many principals of the Afrikaans-medium universities, and hundreds of upper-echelon bureaucrats, academics, and newspaper editors are members.

Opposition to the Broederbond is hampered by its very secrecy and by its very successes. Its current emphasis on loyalty to South African White Afrikaner society and opposition to Communism, to Black Nationalism, and to danger of foreign subversion strengthens its hand.

The DRC is the second most important nationwide Afrikaner institution. It has always held a major role in shaping Afrikaans cultural, linguistic, and ethical influences. The church remains a major foundation-stone of the National Party philosophy and of the country's education. Over 50 percent of the White population is of the Dutch Reformed faith. In smaller urban and rural communities, this membership is predominant. A heavy proportion of the Coloured community is also numbered among DRC membership. Many thousands of Black Africans are adherents of that faith as well. A high proportion of the Dutch Reformed ministers are members of the Broederbond. Many of the pastors, too, are heavily involved in local educational activity and in the directorates of business. Although there have been few dissidents among liberal-minded DRC clergymen, these acts of opposition have usually resulted in excommunication or Coventry for those dissident clerical rebels.

The religious tenets of the DRC stress respect for authority, the ethnic concept of the Afrikaners as a chosen people, the Biblical "justification" of apartheid, and the religious justification of preserving and strengthening Afrikanerdom. All these ideas stem from a tight-lipped and stern seventeenth-century Calvinism propagated by the Dutch Reformed predikant and pulpit. In opposing the intrusions of the more liberal foreign church influences (Anglican, Catholic, Methodist, Congregationalist, and so forth) the DRC remains a bastion of the National Party structure.

Apart from the Broederbond and the DRC perhaps the most effective arm of Afrikaner politico-cultural influences is that sector of the church-educational activity known as the Christian National Education (CNE) group. This body seeks to define Calvinist Afrikaner doctrine in educational terms through control of curriculum, syllabus content, and extraordinary control of teachers. This body even goes so far as to enhance the authority of the state by decrying unions as exploiters of labor. A 1951 doctrinal output said, for example, that the state should protect the workers from the employers rather than leaving them to unions, "as in the liberal, democratic state." Thus it is that, in the Afrikaans-medium school and college, the student concurrently receives indoctrination in both Calvinism and in Afrikaner nationalism. It has been this body, too, which has protected the medium of the mother-tongue, Afrikaans, against intrusion of outside languages. Even the creation of some dual-medium schools and universities has not impeded the flowering of Afrikaans. That language is probably in a stronger position in South Africa today than it has been since the country's establishment as a nation in 1910.

Yet another organization, the Federation of Afrikaans Cultural Organizations (FAK), has historically supported all the foregoing bodies in backing Afrikanerdom and the National party. Its work has been to unify cultural, educational, and even business interests in support of Afrikanerdom. Established in 1929 the FAK was reputed, subsequently, to have expanded through a wide range of activities and cultural organizations, numbering more than 300 bodies. These included not only educational, church, and business councils, but charitable organizations and student and youth groups as well. It was particularly effective in building up Afrikaans artistic and literary effort. It created Afrikaner associations parallel to the international Boy Scout, Girl Scout, and Red Cross operations. All of these activities, of course, not only created new cleavages between Afrikaans- and English-speaking groups of the White community but intensified pride in the nationalism of the Afrikaner. Its main component is the Institute of Christian National Education, which insures that churches, schools, youth groups, and the like follow the principles of the party line. Though integrated with Broederbond and DRC leadership at the national level, FAK bodies work mainly on local and provincial levels.

THE UNITED PARTY

At this writing the main opposition party is the United Party, led by Sir de Villiers Graaff. This party now holds 47 seats in the national Parliament, as well as controlling the Natal Provincial Assembly. Its following is large in the urban centers, and its membership also has good representation in the larger municipal governments. The party is historically British-oriented, though a few dissident Afrikaners have joined its ranks. The United Party can be considered a kind of catchall of opposition forces, ranging from liberal academics and newspapermen to highly conservative businessmen and gentleman farmers.

As external pressures have mounted against South Africa on world fronts, including the UN, the tendency of the United Party has been to become increasingly conservative, especially on color issues. The single common denominator within the United Party is opposition to the Afrikaner domination of the country. On economic, defense, and other major issues, however, the United Party does not differ greatly from the Nationalists. In one other area of government—namely, the protection of civil rights and independence of the courts—the United Party comes into direct conflict with the Nationalists. Most United Party leaders are outspoken in their condemnation of authoritarian supralegal tactics of the Nationalists and in what they see as massive violations of individual civil liberties, including abandonment of the right of habeas corpus. Many United Party leaders, too, are outspoken in their belief that the Nationalist leaders, even the prime minister, are too much under the influence of the secret Broederbond. Indicative of this attitude was a recent speech made by the United Party parliamentarian and "shadow defense minister" from Natal, Vause Raw, accusing Prime Minister Vorster of "murdering international sport" for South Africans under direct pressure from the Broederbond.

The United Party is neither so well organized nor disciplined as the National Party. Part of this lack of cohesiveness stems from an aging and sometimes listless leadership of a party that has been out of power for 25 years. Part of the lack of cohesion comes from the fact that many presumed supporters of English and other European backgrounds are much less interested in politics than in business and sports. The tendency of the United Party to "go along" with the Nationalists on race issues also brings out accusations by its own liberal wing, including intellectuals and youth, that the United Party is actually a "status quo" party and not an opposition party in the fullest sense. It still gives full emphasis to the concept of continued White leadership, but does not brook any idea of independent Bantustans.

It presumes the Nationalist policy to be a policy of partition and fragmentation of the Republic.

Most United Party members believe that apartheid is eventually doomed to failure—that the Bantustan concept is unworkable. They particularly condemn the operations of "job reservations," believing that economic growth may somehow eventually alleviate the race problem. They generally support improved housing and amenities for all non-Whites, as well as elimination of pass laws. They generally sponsor the right of ownership of land in the Republic for all non-Whites. United Party leaders seem exceedingly cautious and somewhat fuzzy on the issue of race—as to just what policy should replace that of apartheid. They champion a highly complex theory of an eventual multiracial "confederation," with partial non-White representation in a central parliament. This they believe can defuse and prevent racial frictions. Even so, today, most United Party constituents seem to continue to support the general concept of White supremacy in a diluted form. They believe, however, that Coloureds should attain to a separate common roll. They contend that this acceptance of Coloureds is obligatory in recognition of the latter's "White heritage." It would also bolster population numbers on the "White" side.

The United Party advocates universal franchise for Whites, plus universal franchise for Coloureds on a separate role, with Coloureds representing Coloureds in the Parliament. They recommend similar enfranchisement for Asians, but with Whites representing the Asians in Parliament. They envisage eight White representatives of Black interests in Parliament, along with a select committee to maintain contact with Black African opionion, both in urban complexes and in Bantustans. They see a form of subordinate self-government for each racial group, with a loose confederation or federal parliament based on the foregoing separate electoral rolls.

The United Party leader, Sir de Villiers Graaff, has stated that his party differs from the Nationalists in four basic ways: (1) The United Party wants one authority over the whole of South Africa; the Nationalists want to break up South Africa into eight separate Black States and one White state; (2) the United Party wants the Bantu reserves developed and administered by the Bantu themselves, these to remain part of the Republic on a federal basis; the Nationalists want eight separate Black states, each with its own independent parliament; (3) the United Party wants communal councils for non-Whites for those not otherwise represented (such as urban Bantu, Coloureds, and Asians), these included in the federation; the Nationalists want Asian and Coloured councils that will move toward separate parliamentary status; (4) the United Party wants non-White groups (communal and tribal) to have a voice in the central Parliament; the Nationalists want no representation for non-Whites in the central Parliament, even though these groups had it years ago.

It should be added that leaders of the United Party have recently come under criticism from their own followers. These critics are seeking a reassessment of the established United Party policy on non-White representation in a future Republic parliament. They contend that Coloureds must be represented in all three tiers of government. The critics also ask a reassessment of the party's refusal to accept Bantustans as political realities. Party leaders have countered these critics by insisting that party differences on racial theories should be down-played and attention of the Republic electorate should be directed to condemnation of Nationalist government failures on socio-economic issues, bureaucratic growth, and totalitarianism.

The real potential of the United Party can best be judged at the next general elections, due in 1974 or 1975. In that contest for the voters the ramifications and burdens of the Nationalists' Bantustan program will have become more clear, and the economic strength of South Africa, overburdened by inflation and monetary fiscal policies, will have been truly measured. Given more dynamic leadership and the backing of the ordinary voter, beset by economic problems, the United Party could well return to power within the next decade.

THE PROGRESSIVE PARTY

The Progressives originated in 1959 as a result of the breakaway of 12 members of the then United Party House of Assembly membership. These dissidents, young idealists and intellectuals, were dissatisfied with United Party leadership and policies. Their major opposition lay in their belief that the United Party leadership held views too close to the Nationalists on matters of race.

The 1961 elections saw the defeat of all but one of the breakaway group. Their lone representative in Parliament at present writing is the well-known and courageous Helen Susman, of Johannesburg. The party today is urban-centered, containing a number of students, academics, professional men, and business leaders. The party has been financed primarily by "enlightened capitalists," such as Harry Oppenheimer, chairman of Anglo-American Corporation.

The Progressives advocate a common electoral roll for members of all races. They do not advocate "one man, one vote" but rather a qualified franchise for all electors, based on educational, income, and property standards. They also believe in a bill of rights, seeking entrenchment of constitutional rights and civil liberties, regardless of race. Because of its insistence on a broad qualified franchise to include non-White voters, it appears to have no real prospects of becoming a serious rival, either to the Nationalists or the United Party. Perhaps its greatest effectiveness would be to realign itself with the United Party to bring about more progressive and lucid policies on race and economic questions. It is evident that the United Party would prove to be a much more effective opposition force if its leaders could succeed in reversing the Progressive breakaway. However, at this time there appears to be no prospect for the reunion of the Progressives with the United Party.

THE LIBERAL PARTY

It should be noted that the small but militant multiracial Liberal Party, which championed the concept of integration of races, political and economic, was disbanded in 1968 under government pressure. This party had been led by Alan Paton, the famous author of Cry The Beloved Country and a notable biography of J. H. Hofmeyr. Other party leaders included Edgar Brookes and the former president of the University of Natal, Ernest Malherbe. The party was notable for its courageous utterances against apartheid and condemnation of the government's violations of the rule of law. It was also notable for the fact that its membership and rallies were composed of all racial coloration. Most of the White liberals have now associated themselves quietly with either the moderate wing of the United Party or the Progressive Party.

NON-WHITE POLITICS

The non-White political scene requires individual discussion of the vastly differing Black, Coloured, and Asian situations. As has been seen in so many other sectors of South African endeavor, non-White politics are contradictory and sometimes mystifying to the outsider. Here, too, countervailing pulls are present. At times, for example, each of the non-White communities has demonstrated spontaneous and effective leadership. At other times, always cognizant of the effectiveness of the government's security apparatus, non-White leadership has been ineffectual and grass roots political response weak—even on community issues of considerable importance. Illustrative of the divergent tendencies have been the Asian reactions to the group areas removals and the Black African reaction to "Black spot" removals, such as the much publicized and inhumane Limehill. Yet, on other occasions, results have been surprisingly impressive. The Capetown non-White march of 30,000 in protest to Sharpeville was exemplary of political activism. Here, the long-range extraordinary patience of the non-Whites is shown in contrast to short-range, sometimes surprising demands for satisfaction of their immediate needs.

It will be recalled that, in years past, both Coloured and Asian voters had some representation in the national Parliament, either token or real. Successive White supremacy governments, however, eliminated all such central government representation and privileges of national franchise. As noted previously, the doctrine of apartheid holds that Coloured and Asian communities are neither politically nor culturally on a level with the Whites. Recently, however, both groups have been permitted some localized communal representation, largely advisory, through the Coloured Persons' Representative Council (partially elected and partially nominated) and the South African Indian Council (wholly nominated). It is assumed that some additional powers of regional self-government will be extended to these groups but the progress is slow.

The Coloureds

The Coloureds have had a long and troubled history of enfranchisement and disenfranchisement. As far back as 1854 the then colonial British government of the Cape granted first representative and later (1872) responsible government to the Cape Colony. At that time all male citizens who could satisfy a modicum of literacy and property tests were entitled to become voters. Later, too, in the British colony of Natal, there was no color bar. In both colonies, however, only a few Coloureds managed to become enfranchised. In the Boer republics—the Transvaal and Free State—there was, from the beginning, an absolute color bar. When the first discussions on union began in 1908, there was a clash on the issue of enfranchisement and suffrage for non-Whites on the common role. The argument was finally settled by permitting provincial laws to remain in force for the time being. At once, the political situation of the Coloureds began to erode when representation in the National Assembly was reserved solely for Whites. A further infringement of Coloured electoral power occurred in the Separate Representation of Voters Act (1956) when the community was forced to accept four White representatives in Parliament on a separate electoral roll. Even this White representation of Coloureds in Parliament was finally abolished in 1968.

The Coloured Persons' Representative Council was created by the Republic's Parliament in 1964. In 1968 the council was expanded and given new powers. At present it is composed of 40 elected and 20 government-nominated members. The elected members are chosen by universal communal franchise on geographical basis. The first national election for the council occurred in September 1969.[3]

An executive committee of five members directs the activities of the council. The government retains a certain control by the power of appointment of the chairman by the state president and through the capability of nominating one-third of the council membership. It serves as a liaison to the prime minister and to other Cabinet members on matters relating to the various Coloured communities of the country. The state president is given authority to confer new powers on the council if that is deemed advisable by the National government. The so-called laws enacted by the council are presumed to have the power of parliamentary action. In fact, however, no such law could be passed by council without the prior approval of the minister of coloured affairs and other Cabinet members concerned. Thus, the council is mainly an advisory body, with some communal responsibilities. The Coloured executive is empowered to deal with education, social welfare, and certain aspects of local government, insofar as these affect Coloureds. The council is not granted ordinary powers of taxation but presently administers a budget of Rand 50 million yearly under central government supervision. Coloured administrative officials are eventually expected to replace White administrators.

The entire political alignment of the Coloured community is in a state of flux. There have been as many as nine small political parties in the field seeking majority control of the Coloured Persons' Representative Council but none of these has, as yet, attained majority control. In fact, the strongest of these, the Labour Party, adopted a militant, antiapartheid attitude in the September 1969 election campaign, thus running afoul of Pretoria. The other parties, the largest of which was the Federal Party, by contrast, openly or tacitly accepted apartheid as the only political means by which they saw concessions for Coloureds obtainable from Whites. Labour leaders countered that they could fight apartheid from within the council if elected. The Labour Party won 26 of the 40 elective seats at that time. The progovernment Federal Party won 12 seats and the National and Republican Parties, one each. The government, to retain "back-room" control, then chose all nominated members from the progovernment Federal Party. Of these, 13 had actually been defeated candidates in the election. One of these was Tom Swartz, leader of the Federal Party, who, as well, became the government-appointed chairman of the five-man executive committee of the council. Thus, the Labour Party, which had fairly won the election, found itself the election loser and in the position of being the opposition party.

When the council first formally convened, the minister of Coloured affairs (M. Viljoen) reminded its members that anything done by the council must be done "within the framework of apartheid." In this and subsequent meetings only a few motions were introduced. One of these sought "equal pay for equal work" by Coloured and White professionals and was passed unanimously but was not accepted by the South African government. The 1971 meeting was boycotted by members of the Labour Party after defeat of a Labour Party motion that the council be abolished and that members thereof be permitted to take seats in the Republic Parliament. The Federal Party then and since insisted that the Coloured community must go along with the government as best it can in the view that only by such a course can it achieve anything for the Coloureds. However, most of its members appear to be discontent with the Republic's policy of separate development. The Labour Party, on the other hand, is fully pessimistic as to the value of the council, but continues to utilize the council chambers as a mouthpiece through which it can express antiapartheid political views with some legal protection under the roof of the government-packed council.

More than 100 Transvaal and Cape Nationalist academics recently pleaded for integration of the Coloureds with the Whites.[4] In response, however, Prime Minister Vorster condemned the academics as "politically irresponsible" in proposing this integration of the Coloureds. Afrikaner intellectuals and United Party leaders continue to press this point home. The National Party counters by stressing "parallel development" for the Coloured, rather than "separate development." They likewise insist that the Coloureds cannot have their own homelands but must continue to "enjoy" a subordinate urban association with the Whites.

The Asians

The Asian people of the Republic have been undergoing considerable social change in recent years. Within the strictures of apartheid, they have sought to improve themselves both economically and educationally. Politically, they have not progressed as far as either Blacks or Coloureds.

The first Asians, Muslim Malays, had been brought to South Africa as early as 1667.[5] The first great wave of Indian migrants came in the 1860's, when indentured workers were brought from India to work in the sugarcane fields of Natal. In 1896 the Indians were disenfranchised in Natal. Though only a few hundred Indians lost their voting rights as a result, the principle of the color bar was thus becoming entrenched. In 1909, with the formation of the Union, both Asians and Coloureds lost their national franchise on their national common role. (At that time there were reportedly 200 non-White voters in Natal, mainly Indians, and over 22,000 in the Cape, these mainly Coloureds.)[6]

The 1896 act of disenfranchisement in Natal had provided a political opening for an obscure lawyer, who was destined to become world famous. Mohandas Gandhi, who resided in South Africa from

1893 to 1914, had formed the Natal Indian Congress in 1894 to combat the disenfranchisement of the Indians. From that small beginning, Gandhi devised his own nonviolent principles of passive resistance, or "soul force," later to prove so effective in India.

Subsequent Indian political associations were to be created in Natal and the Transvaal, these in protest of pass laws, land restrictions, disenfranchisement, and general segregation practices. While the Gandhian theories were activated by Asian groups many times in the next six decades (sometimes in association with Black nationalists), they were never widely supported by the Indian community nor were they truly effective. Instead, especially in the 1940's and 1950's, they resulted in bannings, detention, and long imprisonment of many of the most ardent of the Asian leaders. By 1961, when the Republic came into being, most of the Asian political organizations had disintegrated. As a result, in recent years, there has been a paucity of effective, widely accepted leadership of the Asian community.

The South African Indian Council was created in 1964, with 21 members nominated by the central government with purely advisory responsibilities. A subsequent (1968 act) created a statutory council of 25 members chosen by the central government. Council members hold office for three years. The minister of Indian affairs selects from the council the chairman of a five-man executive. Members of the council select the other four members. The council has advisory and consultative powers only. It provides a liaison link between the Asian community and the government. The government has promised that an elective body will eventually be set up.

Present membership of the council includes wealthy businessmen, industrialists, merchants, and labor leaders. The chairman of its executive body is A. N. Rajab, a wealthy businessman. Although the council's main function was presumably to give the Asian community some control over its own affairs, as a nominated body it is considered by many Asians as a "stooge" of the government and unrepresentative of real Asian aspirations. Furthermore, its activities have not been publicized, and much of the criticism leveled at the group results from the fact that it seems only to rubber stamp Pretoria's decisions with respect to Asians behind closed doors. Asian critics of the group contend that it cannot represent the best interests of the community until it becomes an elective body.

Frustration of the Asian community over failure of this group to protect community interests has led to resuscitation of a militant Gandhian group, the Natal Indian Congress. Its leaders claim that it is better able to represent the Asian community's best interests. Leaders of the far more conservative South African Indian Council contend that any demonstration of militancy by the Asian community will only harden the attitudes of the Afrikaner Nationalist government against the Asians.

The Blacks

From the onset of the Union, the Blacks were effectively disenfranchised. They were left with only token representation in the national Parliament in the first decades thereafter. Growth of numbers of both educated Blacks and of urbanized Blacks did not, in those early decades, provide a broad-based African nationalism sufficiently strong to press against political dominance of the Whites. The fear of swartgevaar removed from the White community any thought of Black enfranchisement. Eventually, even the Black token representation (by Whites) in the national Parliament was removed.

There were, despite all difficulties, some organizations that sought to bring African nationalism into being. A number of these, either local or provincial in scope, appeared during the two decades prior to formation of the Union. Most of these were formed by the educated elite, graduates of Christian mission schools. The South African Native National Congress (founded in 1912) brought on a more active Black militancy, but it concentrated more on labor union matters than on a national political amalgam.

The African National Congress (ANC)—established in 1923—sought to overcome tribal divisions and to make Black political ideology cohesive. During the next four decades the activities of the ANC concerned itself with passive resistance (often in association with the Asians); petitions to governments and delegations were sent abroad. Passage of the Native Representations and Native Lands acts of 1936 spurred new Black nationalist thought and action. This was based, in part, on growing distrust of vague promises of White politicians that land and votes would eventually be forthcoming.

During and after World War II new social pressures and incoming Nationalist regimes brought on contradictory pulls for the Blacks. Industrialization and urbanization, on the one hand, brought Blacks and Whites closer together in the economic sphere. On the other hand, new racially oriented legal barriers and administrative dicta created new separatist social patterns and polarization of the races throughout the nation.

African nationalist efforts post-1948 can only be measured as spotty. Asians and Coloureds had the obligation of seeking cooperation with the Blacks as, together, they faced many of the same economic changes and political-social burdens. Industrialization and urbanization of the dynamic postwar economy provided a common meeting ground for all three non-White groups. There were many common ventures, educational and economic. There were common political purposes to be found in non-White opposition to baasskap and apartheid. It might be assumed that there was the newly activated Afrikaner political milieu against which all non-Whites had to press. There was the imposition of new, and sometimes tyrannical, White supremacy laws to contest or to suffer. Yet, efforts to bring Blacks and Asians together on a nationwide scale failed. In fact, the bloody Durban race riots of 1949, pitting Blacks against Asians, emphasized the underlying antipathy between the two groups.

The various non-White communities apparently failed to grasp these opportunities to unify after World War II, partly because of inadequate nationwide leadership and partly because of differing cultures and political goals. Even within the four separate provinces of the Union, there was great disparity of resistance, energy, and willingness for struggle. Natal and the eastern Cape seemed invariably to be ahead of the rest. It appeared the move for African nationalism and resistance reached its apogee in the country in October 1952. Thereafter, it was constricted, fragmented, repressed, and eventually broken. The breakage occurred not alone from the effectiveness of the South African security forces, but, as well, through fears of one non-White group toward another and increasing non-White passivity. Infiltration of Communist and pro-Communist elements into the Natal Indian Congress and the ANC provided more grist for governmental action against even legal and constructive non-White efforts to unify politically.

By 1952 the ANC membership was reported to be in excess of 100,000, most of these being in the Cape and Natal. Chief Albert Luthuli (who was awarded the Nobel Peace Price in 1960 for his nonviolent aims) had become president-general of the ANC. He sought to make that organization not only nonviolent but interracial. He led several "defiance campaigns" in the following three years, these directed against pass laws, against Bantu education legislation, and against elimination of freehold property rights for Blacks. In the face of White intransigeance and considerable non-White passivity, these were not nationwide in scope or in success. However, the defiance campaigns were followed by a number of civil disturbances that, in response, brought from the Union government mass arrests and more restrictive legislation.

In 1955 a congress of the people was called by the ANC, the South African Indian Congress, the radical (allegedly pro-Communist) South African Congress of Democrats, the South African Coloured People's Organization, and various non-White trade unions. The congress adopted a "Freedom Charter," which attempted to meld together the ideology of the 1943 Atlantic Charter (of Roosevelt and Churchill) with the ideological aims of South Africa's non-White nationalists and White "integrationists." Claiming that South Africa belonged to its peoples of all races, it sought to remodel South Africa into a democratic state, based on majority rule. It sought thus to achieve citizenship and participation in government for all non-Whites.

The charter set up a bill of rights and appended certain socialistic theories, which included nationalization of minerals and of industrial-financial undertakings. There was immediate reaction against the charter from two sources. The more conservative monoracial wing of the ANC began to coalesce against these and other ideas propounded by Luthuli's ANC leadership. This right-wing Black group of dissidents was just four years later (1959) to form the militant, all-Black Pan-Africanist Congress (PAC), led by Robert Sobukwe. It also attained a membership exceeding 100,000. The South African government reacted in yet another way, developing an extensive "informer" network and making new arrests of non-White leaders. Many of these leaders (including Luthuli and Sobukwe) were charged with "treason" and later imprisoned or banned. (Luthuli was still "restricted" in 1968 at the time of his death, having been under ban and house arrest since 1959.)

Both the ANC and the PAC appealed to the same frustrations among the Blacks—and the same basic ideals of nationalism. They differed, however, in attitudes on relations with Whites and other non-Whites. Both organizations aimed at removal of apartheid restrictions on Blacks and eventual establishment of a nonracial, non-Communist democracy. The ANC was multiracial from the start. The PAC insisted on organizing only the Blacks at the outset. The PAC sought direct mass action immediately; the ANC was more gradual and more interested in nonviolent forms of protest. Both organizations were banned from 1960. (A stay-at-home strike attempted in May 1961 failed largely because the PAC failed to join in.)

The militant African nationalism that swept the rest of the African continent during the 1950's and 1960's spread only a few fires into South Africa. These, as they broke out, were gradually extinguished by government action against leaders and by mass apathy of the non-White majority. While the postwar leaders tried to inspire their followers into massive, nonviolent action—general strikes and passive resistance—none of these caught on nationwide.

Campaigns of violence and sabotage involving Black African groups known as "POQO" and "Spear of the Nation" also proved ineffective. They resulted in only further imprisonment for Black leaders not directly associated with these violent episodes.[7] By the mid-1960's both the ANC and the PAC were either dead or "underground" within South Africa. Many leaders of both groups had escaped into exile and were heard from only occasionally from UN and tropical Africa platforms.

There was surprising conservatism among the Black majority. There was little truly national leadership uniting urban and rural Black Africans of all the provinces. Though there was antipathy to the White man, there was the belief among rank and file Blacks that mass action, violent or nonviolent, would only beget corresponding government reaction. The Black mass apparently concluded that massive protest would only result in new insecurity for all non-Whites, especially for the Blacks.

Associations, clubs, and societies have been an integral part of African life for decades past. These range from church groups, to teachers' associations, to commercial organizations. These have all formed the nuclei for more widespread political association. (Their extent is measured by the recent mushrooming of the African "independent church" movement. Over one million Blacks were reported to be members of the Bantu separatist churches as early as 1936. Membership in these groups today is estimated to be in excess of three million.) This tendency to form associations has provided some cohesion between urban and rural Black cultures. It has also made the Black political awakenings, and institutions emanating therefrom, open targets for government security action.

Furthermore, it is easily seen that the nationalism that binds the Afrikaner into a single politico-cultural community is not present among the Blacks, who are disparate in language, in culture, and in education. The fiery "African nationalism" that brings on truly national political unity has not yet flowered in South Africa. Not even in the halcyon days of Chief Luthuli and his ANC was that unity of purpose and of action achieved. A Black African political unity will not be achieved in South Africa until an amalgam of traditional rural views with urban Black views, combining language, culture, leadership, and aims, is attained. Thus far, the deliberately divisive governmental program of the separate Bantustans has prevented emergence of that national unity for the Blacks.

CHAPTER

5

THE BANTUSTANS

South African Whites fear their own submergence by the Black race. Most Whites are determined to maintain their racial "purity" and their dominance of Whites over non-Whites. Since the Nationalists came to power a quarter-century ago, this fear has intensified, resulting in determination of the Republic's political leaders to find new ways to defend against the "Black peril." Thus, since coming into power, the National Party has been putting into effect an increasingly broad program of laws and fiats aimed at total segregation of Blacks from Whites in both urban and rural areas. This effort has culminated in the concept of apartheid and in the so-called Bantustan program.

The essential aim of apartheid and the Bantustan programs has been to compartmentalize the society of South Africa. Therein, each racial component has its place and each Black African tribal group has its prescribed "homeland." Contained within each racial box would be all major activity—work, society, and culture. Whether justified or unjustified, there appears to be an underlying feeling of safety to be afforded the Whites by this concept. In any event it embodies a barrier to (and reversal of) movement of Blacks into the cities, and by separating the tribes, utilizes the old colonial idea of "divide and rule." It thus "buys time" for the status quo of White supremacy.

The Bantustan concept—an idea for development of eight separate, semiautonomous (and perhaps eventually independent) tribal "nations" of South Africa originated with the government-sponsored Tomlinson Commission Report of 1954. This report proposed a drastic program for the country—redirecting it away from racial integration and toward segregation and separate development. The commission stated that the native reserves were poverty stricken, that one-half the adult males of those reserves were away in the Republic at any one time, and that productivity was declining. It recommended removal of one-half the families from the land, encouragement of full-time farming with freehold title, and industrialization and construction of Black African towns. Emphasis was to be on development of reserves themselves rather than on adjacent White areas. It urged that $300 million be spent within ten years to raise the carrying capacity of the reserves. If this were not done, the commission prophesied that, by the year 2000, there would be a proponderance of 17 million Blacks in the White areas of the country. White private capital was deemed essential for the task to hasten the Bantustan development. The commission thought that Whites and Blacks might be numerically equal in White urban South Africa by the year 2000 if the Bantustan program were effective. The commission admitted that, even if development of the reserves were a spectacular success, Blacks permanently resident in White South Africa would even then outnumber Whites at least two to one. The rural Blacks would be held on the land; the urban Blacks would be retained in their present locations. The net effect would be to curtail the influx of Black upon White and to accompany that restriction with a program of retribalization.

The Tomlinson Commission recommended that 110 existing "native" reserves be consolidated into seven (later eight) tribal nuclei. Consolidation of these areas would enable the Bantu to develop gradually their local and regional governments to a stage similar to existing South African provinces. Such political development, the commission stated, would presage similar political configurations throughout southern Africa, by which certain parts of the continent would be reserved for Europeans and to which Blacks would be allowed entry only as migrant laborers and without political rights.

While accepting the philosophy and much of the argumentation of the Tomlinson report, Prime Minister Verwoerd (then minister of native affairs) rejected some of its major recommendations. He did not accept the need of costly large-scale development and rehabilitation. He contended that only one-quarter of the sum proposed by the commission for the first decade of the enterprise would be necessary. Verwoerd also ruled that Black African ownership of land within the reserves would not be freehold but would continue in tribal or communal ownership. Verwoerd was adamant, also, against the notion of allowing White capital into the reserves, although many of his party followers believed (and continue to believe) that action indispensable to the Bantustans' success. Verwoerd stated that "if the Bantu, when they are in full control, wish to invite White firms, that is their affair." Furthermore, he did not clarify the meaning of the phrase "when they are in full control," thus leaving obscure any target dates for eventual autonomy or independence of those territories.

Thus it was that Verwoerd (as prime minister) created and activated the Bantustan program. He did so by promulgating the Bantu

Self-Government Act of 1959. This act removed from the Union Parliament all remaining representation of Africans by Whites and introduced the concept of nationhood for specific ethnic groups. At the outset the designated "territorial authorities" were to maintain contact with the central government through commissioners-general (or "ambassadors") who were White South Africans appointed to guide and advise the upcoming authorities on applicable government policy.

Based on existing tribal groupings and eventual consolidations, these Bantustans are to include:

The Transkei, numbering two pieces of land area, is to be united with the Ciskei, numbering 17 pieces of land. The amalgamation or union is to be known as the Transkei. These are located in the northeastern Cape Province, bordering on Natal. This grouping represents a total population of 2.2 million located in the reserves, plus an additional 1.8 million migrant Transkeians-Ciskeians working in urban areas of the Republic. Total land areas represent about 5.5 million hectares.

Kwa Zulu is composed of 29 noncontiguous pieces or reserves scattered throughout Natal. These are estimated to contain some 2.1 million Zulus, while an additional 1.9 million Zulus are reported to be working in the urban areas of the Republic. Land area of all Zulu reserves is estimated at 3.2 million hectares.

The Lebowa, located on three noncontiguous pieces of "homelands," are located in the northern Transvaal. Population of this grouping is estimated in excess of 1 million in the reserves, with an additional 900,000 in urban areas. Land area comprises 1.7 million hectares.

The Tswana live on 19 pieces of homeland located north and west of Pretoria. A "mixed" community authority has been created that falls under the Tswana Territorial Authority—there are the Tswana, Ndebele, Pedi, and peoples of Sotho, Venda, and Shangaan origin living there. They number 885,000 persons resident in the homelands, plus an additional 1.1 million in urban parts of the Republic. Their land area embraces 3.3 million hectares.

The Machangana live on four noncontiguous pieces of homeland located in the northeastern Transvaal. They number 268,000 persons resident in tribal areas, plus 344,000 in urban parts of the Republic. Land area embraces 891,000 hectares.

The Venda are located in the northern Transvaal on three noncontiguous pieces of land. They number 251,000 resident in the reserves, plus 106,000 in urban parts of the Republic. Land area comprises 804,000 hectares.

The Basotho Ba Borwa are located on one piece of land and resident in the eastern Transvaal and Orange Free State. They include 144,000 residents in the tribal area, plus 1.3 million in the urban areas of the Republic. Land area embraces 52,000 hectares.

The Swazi are located in the eastern Transvaal, living on three noncontiguous pieces of land. They number 112,000 resident in reserves, plus 386,000 within urban areas of the Republic. Land area comprises 290,000 hectares.

The north and south Ndebele population, estimated at 125,000, have not yet been assigned a tribal homeland. A government liaison officer reported that they would have to live either in the Tswana or Lebowa homelands.

There is, at the present time, little likelihood for real capital in any of the reserves, not only because White capital has been excluded, but also because the reserves are not well-endowed with resources, other than unskilled labor and overused land. Infrastructure is lacking, except close to White areas, and local economies are primarily subsistent—agricultural and pastoral. As means of furthering the economic viability of the various Bantustans, thus making them more attractive to the Blacks as real "homelands," the South African government has undertaken several economic tacks.

The Republic's first tack involved assignment of budgets from central government funds into special separate funds, such as those specifically designed for use of departments now given over to the Transkei (education, roads and works, and so forth). This has been, in part, a paper transfer financially, but a real transfer administratively. For a long time in the future, it will involve the South African government in discussion with territorial authorities as to just what proposition of local Bantustan governmental costs is to continue to be borne by Pretoria or which must be found from territorial local sources.

The second economic tack undertaken by the Republic's government in recent years has been the plan to develop the so-called border industry program. This plan, devised in 1960, has been designed to encourage domestic and foreign entrepreneurs to create new industrial establishments along the borders (but still in White areas) of the various Bantustans. These ventures would have the aim of decentralizing industry away from overindustrialized metropolitan centers. At the same time, they would utilize unskilled and semiskilled Black labor resident within the Bantustans. The government promised tax concessions, as well as support of essential power, water, transport, and housing needs for the new industrial entities. White enterprise and capital would thus come to the Bantustans but would not be located within the Bantustans.

Official South African government information circulars have indicated that some 315 industrial concerns, employing some 87,000 workers (including 68,000 Blacks), had been established in the border areas by the end of 1970. Government help totaling Rand 119 million was given these ventures by the end of 1970. This help included loans, tax concessions, aid on costs of transport, power, water, and housing.

The main concentration of these ventures established and planned has been in some 70 localities in Natal, the Transvaal, and eastern Cape. Illustrative of the concentrated development has been the new town of Hammarsdale, near Pietermaritzburg, in Natal. In the past decade some 13 new industries were established there. Textiles, food processing, and timber processing are among the new ventures. By 1968 some 6,000 Blacks and 400 Whites were employed in the Hammarsdale complex. This and other similar establishments have required parallel development of infrastructure—power, water, housing, and so forth.

It has been estimated that, by the end of 1970, some Rand 430 million had been invested in the border industries from public and private sources. Of this total it has been estimated that the government's Industrial Development Corporation (IDC) contribution, in the form of loans and concession grants, amounted to some Rand 119 million. Industrialists and economists still appear to look upon these ventures with some hesitancy. The industrialists fear removing themselves from centers of population and established markets or railheads. They also fear the lack of infrastructure. Economists express the view that these new ventures are not yet large enough to meet the demands of the upcoming Black African labor force from the reserves (now estimated at 40,000 annually). Industry and some Bantustan authorities were not impressed, as well, by economic impediments—transport, power, housing, and so forth—that the border industry program created. It also created new problems for the potential Black worker, who was often many miles distant from the borders. Some South African industrialists still remain skeptical of the program, believing the government makes the case for "border industries" mainly for political reasons.

Yet a third economic aid for the Bantustan program was the Bantu Investment Corporation, established by the government in 1959. This entity has attempted to encourage establishment of small industries and businesses within the various Bantustans through loan programs made to the Blacks. Its capital and activities are relatively small.

A more recent tactic espoused by the South African government has been to encourage the principle of licensing or long-term leases for South African industries agreeing to establish "agencies" within the "homelands." Like the "border industries," this program is still in the formative phase and cannot yet be fully evaluated. While it is recognized that this is a device to encourage White capital into the reserves on a long-lease basis as a partial protection to Black business and political needs, the White capital is wary of the vagaries of the Bantustan concept, fearing either too much central government direction, on the one hand, or possible eventual Black "nationalization" of White industry, on the other.

Yet another prospective source of capital for the Bantustans may be that of foreign aid and foreign investment. Certain Bantustan leaders have espoused and openly discussed these prospects with capitalists abroad. It is not believed, however, that the South African government would, at this stage, welcome such activity. It remains a possibility, however, if the Bantustans attain real autonomy. This would follow the precedent of Botswana, Lesotho, and Swaziland, which, though heavily dependent on South Africa for economic, political, and geographic reasons, have been able to develop their own outside sources of private investment and of foreign governmental aid.

Again, on the economic side, has been the sensitive question of Bantustan access to, and control over, unexploited natural resources within their own borders. In the minds of the South African government officials, there is no question as to the right of these peoples to agricultural resources, but mineral resources appear to pose a different question and may become even more sensitive in the near future. Discovery of oil, for example, in either Transkei or Kwa Zulu would create real abrasions between Pretoria and Bantustan leaders. Proceeds from the valuable platinum mines of the Transvaal, these mines lying partially in Tswana Bantustan lands, has already provoked controversy. The Tswana are permitted a portion of the profits of these. As their autonomy increases, they are likely to demand more. The question also arises with Kwa Zulu concerning control over the new seaport of Richards Bay, with its attendant industrial activities.

One sees today the Bantustans in varying states of political evolution and movement toward "nationhood." The Bantu Homelands Constitution Act (No. 21) of 1971 reaffirmed the intention of the South African government to lead each individual Bantu "nation" to self-government and ultimate independence. A blanket measure, applicable to all Bantustans and coalescing previous legislation thereon, it also laid out a general pattern for movement toward that goal. These procedures included some details of financing, powers of legislation, recognition of the official African vernaculars within each territory, and so forth. It would be redundant to describe in subsequent paragraphs the progression and present "colonial" status of each of the Bantustans. It is considered more useful, therefore, to discuss in detail the economic and political problems of the Transkei (the most advanced of these embryo nations) and of Kwa Zulu (which faces perhaps the greatest problems of all, owing to its diverse and disparate parts).

A fairly consistant pattern of evolution has been adopted, and thus far followed, by South Africa for all the Bantustans. In each of these territories (as has been the history of the advancing Transkei) a legislative group (first nominated and later partially elected) brings parliamentary procedures into being. At first, the membership of this grouping is based on each territory's traditional conclave of chiefs. From this legislative grouping is selected an executive committee, headed by a chief executive (or incipient prime minister). This executive group, in turn, is presumed to be destined for Cabinet status and ruling party leadership. Various governmental activities (education, roads, agriculture, and so forth) are thereafter transferred by Pretoria to the administrative control of the executive, with the legislature playing a supporting role. However, as with the Transkei, the central government at Pretoria retains control of defense, foreign affairs, internal security, and the real powers of the purse. All these moves are aimed at an eventual, presumably independent, government for the Bantustans through the foregoing decolonizing states. The result would be a modified, Westminister-model government, similar, in many respects, to that of the South African Republic. Target dates for independence of these territories are still only vaguely inferred by South African officials, although Prime Minister Vorster has stated that the Bantustans can have their independence "when they ask for it."

THE TRANSKEI

The Transkei, homeland of the Xhosa and Pondo tribes, has been considered both the prototype and showpiece of the Bantustan doctrine. Located in the northeastern section of the Cape Province, bordering on Natal, it covers 16,500 square miles. (The South African government apparently intends to unite the Transkei with the Ciskei just to the south.) The Transkei is a hilly, rocky area, with altitudes varying from sea level to 6,000 feet. A sparse, beautiful, lichen-like summer grass covers much of its rolling terrain, making the land appear deceptively fertile. Transkei's soil is eroded and poor, despite its short-lived grassy beauty, and the entire region is subject to severe perennial drought. The land is cut by many small streams emptying into the sea through deep valleys and clefts in a rockbound coastline of 280 miles. That coastline contains no seaports. The only real port in the region is excluded from Transkeian control, as it is considered a "White spot." That city, Port St. John, along with several other mainly White communities located physically within the Transkei, remains in Republic hands and, as such, are political bones of contention.

The Transkeians are mainly subsistence farmers, raising livestock (sheep, goats, pigs, and cattle) and some corn, fruit, and tea. Yields of all foodstuffs are low and of poor quality. The territory annually requires imports of more than 150,000 tons of corn, the main staple food.[1] While agricultural experts have attempted, in some measure, to encourage improved farming methods, including terracing, stock dipping, and so forth, the territory's output remains at low levels. Only a massive agricultural effort—probably involving communal farms, soil erosion defenses, and irrigation schemes—may ever make it modestly self-sufficient and viable. There is some effort to develop cash crops, such as flax, pyrethrum, phormium tenax, and tea. There is also some effort to develop forest plantations. There are a few small industrial ventures, but these are largely dependent on development of a real agricultural base. Mining has not yet been developed, but deposits of copper, nickel, and coal are reported to exist. The Xhosa Development Corporation, an offshoot of the Republic's Bantu Investment Corporation, has underwritten a number of local enterprises.

The territorial capital, Umtata, population 20,000, is a segregated city. It contains distinct racial enclaves, including all-White hotels and all-Black hotels. The Black enclave contains the majority of inhabitants, including Black administrators and workers; the White enclave contains those White civil servants staffing major administrative posts, plus the remnants of a long-established White settler society. The city, despite being the first Bantustan capital, is still governed as a White spot. This again shows up the dichotomy of the South African system of apartheid.

The paramount chief of the Xhosas, Kaiser Matanzima, bears the title of chief minister of the Transkei. As such, he is the senior Black official of the territory and the leader of the ruling Party—the Transkei National Independence Party (TNIP). Under authority of the Transkei Constitution Act (No. 48) of 1963, passed by the South African Parliament, and the first election in the homeland (November, 20, 1963), Matanzima assumed his post as chief minister. He and his party won a second election in 1968, retaining control of the Legislative Assembly. These constitutional steps also brought into existence a "Transkei citizenship," embracing all Transkeians (numbering 2 million) domiciled in the territory and, as well, all Xhosa-speaking Blacks (estimated at 1.8 million) living and working elsewhere in the Republic.

The territory has universal suffrage for adults. The Legislative Assembly is composed of 65 traditional chiefs (these nominated by the South African government), plus 45 elected members. Matanzima's ruling proapartheid party holds a heavy majority of the elective membership and controls most of the traditional chiefs. An antiapartheid opposition party, the New Democratic Party, holding only a few seats, is led by a Methodist churchman, Knowledge Guzana. Bills passed by the Legislative Assembly must have the approval of the state president of South Africa, who has the power to refer them back to the Legislative Assembly if the South African government disapproves of the legislation. At present, executive power is vested in the chief minister and several other ministers. These presently hold portfolios of finance, justice (lower courts only), agriculture and forestry, roads and public works, and education and health. White South African senior civil servants still actively assist in administering the foregoing departments. These remain on the Republic's payroll but are seconded to the Transkei and, reportedly, are responsible to the Transkei government alone. White civil servants are gradually being withdrawn as Blacks assume positions of responsibility and gain experience. Thus, in 1963, when the transfer of authority first occurred, 1,900 White civil servants were immediately replaced by Blacks, leaving 567 Whites. By 1969 that number had been reduced to 324 White civil servants out of 3,460 positions.

The 1970/71 budget of the Transkei approximated Rand 24 million ($33.6 million).[2] Some $25 million came as a South African "grant." The remainder was raised by local taxation. The ministries of education, agriculture, and forestry are recipients of one-half the budget. A large percentage of the budget goes for day-to-day administration rather than for basic development.

Chief Matanzima, who is in a strong position politically as the result of winning two separate elections in the past, has ordinarily been considered a "Black separatist" and a proponent of the apartheid concept. He is not, however, a government "stooge." In April 1971, for example, he shocked South African officialdom by insisting that the Black majority of 15 million in South Africa was forced to live on only one-eighth of the Republic's land, whereas the White minority of 3 million was "ashamed" at its occupation of seven-eighths of the country's land. Matanzima has bluntly demanded more land, more cities presently considered White spots, additional governmental departments, and additional financial help from the Republic. Thus far, the South African government has refused to accede to these demands. Late in 1971, Matanzima, returning from an official visit to Britain, spoke out cryptically against apartheid. He is quoted by The New York Times of November 10, 1971, as saying: "If South Africa refuses to accept non-Whites on the basis of equality, a day of reckoning is coming. Sooner or later destruction will befall the country. . . ."

Chief Matanzima has been reported by the South African press as being against independence for the Transkei at this stage, even though South African authorities would probably give it to him for propaganda purposes.[3] Matanzima had said that the Transkei should be more developed before separation from the Republic and certain existing land questions should be settled.

KWA ZULU

One of the most populous of the Bantustans, yet the most disparate geographically, is Kwa Zulu. It is composed of 29 separate pieces, these located mainly in northern Natal. The historically warlike Zulu tribe numbers nearly 4 million persons, including those still living in reserves and those migrant worker-residents of the metropolitan White areas. In 1970, this Bantustan received central government approval for creation of a territorial authority and executive body.

The territory's chief executive, Chief Gatsha Buthelezi, has indicated that the second-stage legislative assembly will come into being late in 1972. At that time internal control will be assumed over finance, community affairs, roads and works, agriculture, education, justice, economic affairs, and forestry. It is expected that Kwa Zulu will differ somewhat from the other Bantustans, in that it will be the only such territory to have a constitutional monarchy. When the legislative assembly comes into being, it is expected that Chief Buthelezi will assume the post of chief minister and, eventually, prime minister. The Zulu national capital is to be sited at Ulundi, a city not yet in being. Until it is built, the temporary capital is sited at Nongoma.

Political independence of the Kwa Zulu seems almost unattainable without resolution of some of its present imponderable economic and geographic problems. As noted elsewhere, the Zulu tribal reserves dot the face of Natal in 29 noncontiguous spots, like a leopard's coat. These reserves are lacking in sufficient rainfall and, in general, are heavily eroded and overstocked. Subsistence farming of corn and the raising of cattle constitute the lifeblood of the tribal economy. There are few cash crops. The main problems therefore, are those of land sufficiently contiguous to be administered properly, land sufficiently rich to be able to feed its people, land with enough infrastructure to become economically viable, and land with sufficient labor to man itself. The central government admits the necessity of consolidating reserves into not more than ten relatively adjacent areas. No formal action on this problem has yet been taken.

The problem of labor is an especially difficult one. These poverty stricken reserves are constantly being drained of their able-bodied workers by the industrial demands of the Republic. Nearly 2 million Zulus are presently employed outside the reserves, with 2.1 million Zulus, mostly women and children, remaining in the reserves. The latter would be unable to carry on the administrative, economic, and labor burdens of a developing and disparate economy. Though it is claimed that the work of the migrant Zulu labor assures survival of the malnourished families remaining in the reserves, it has been estimated that only 20 percent of migrant income is remitted to these reserves. Thus funds, so necessary for subsistence, are insufficient for capital formation.

The Financial Mail (Johannesburg) reported on March 3, 1972, that

> roughly 70 percent of Kwa Zulu is not ideally suited to crop production in terms of either rainfall, gradient or other factors. Arable land is overcrowded and overstocked. A traditional land tenure system is in force which inhibits agricultural production, coupled with a lack of agricultural expertise. . . .

Most knowledgeable observers have concluded that the only hope for Zululand rests in a large-scale consolidation of its many reserves into a single land mass, which would include the potential of Richards Bay. Training of manpower, industrialization, establishment of cooperatives, and massive improvement of agriculture and livestock would also be essential. It is generally agreed that politico-economic development of Kwa Zulu as it stands and without major financial-technical assistance from Pretoria or elsewhere cannot suffice. While the Zulu Territorial Authority, led by Buthelezi, has requested Pretoria to permit search for foreign aid as a means of alleviating Zululand's economic troubles, this request has not yet been approved. Until attainment of full independence that prospect of foreign aid for Kwa Zulu seems most unlikely.

The present political leader of the Zulu homeland, Chief Buthelezi, a university graduate and a devout Anglican, was born in 1928. He is considered a leader to be reckoned with. The London Sunday Times of March 19, 1972, writing of "The Zulu who could be South Africa's Luther King," characterized Buthelezi as "the most formidable Black politician in South Africa." Unlike Matanzima of the Transkei, Buthelezi is antiapartheid and nonracial, an avowed nonviolent integrationist. He has agreed to work within the Bantustan framework only because he has no other choice, no alternative. Buthelezi, in the words of the Sunday Times correspondent, does not "remotely accept [the Republic's] racialist premises . . . he sees Kwa Zulu as an interim means of enabling him to create a climate in which change may become slightly less avoidable. . . ." Buthelezi has fought the central government at various stages—first on a national day for his Zulu "nation"; more recently on the oath of allegiance to South Africa, on the position of the Zulu monarchy, and on the use of the Zulu language as vernacular [Buthelezi insists on English] in the homeland schools. He also insists on the need of consolidating his tribal reserves and on the need of additional arable land for his people. He has also asked openly for capital and foreign economic aid for his territory. Like Luthuli, his famed Zulu predecessor and mentor, Buthelezi clearly does not favor Bantustans and the almost inevitable partition of South Africa. However, he believes, if it must come, it must be fair to all races.

According to The Economist of January 22, 1972, the South African government is already finding that some of the tribal Bantustans are "turning out less docile than . . . expected. . . ." The magazine states of the South African goverment that,

> by basing these [Bantustans] firmly on tribalism, it hoped to keep them both quiet and conservative . . . these mini-states . . . in [South Africa and . . . South-West Africa] . . . are all, supposedly, being led towards independence by the paternal hand of Pretoria. . . . It all looked like a classic piece of colonial bluffmanship. But now some African leaders are managing to use the Bantustans as platforms for voicing Black grievances and aspirations.
>
> Foremost among these leaders is Zululand's Chief Gatsha Buthelezi . . . Chief Executive Officer of the Zulu Territorial Authority . . . [who] has become a focal point of Black attention far beyond his own tribe. Worried by his growing prestige and out-spokenness, the Government has been trying lately to clip his wings. It sought to exploit the resentment that some members of the Zulu Royal Family felt towards the Chief, and to divert most of the political power in the Bantustan into the hands of young King Zwelithini Goodwill. . . . Chief Buthelezi, in a remarkable display of political adroitness, outmaneuvered the Government, King and all. He persuaded his fellow Councillors unanimously to expunge all vestiges of Royal power from [Zululand's] draft constitution . . . [and] urged them to give Zululand a constitutional, not a medieval, monarchy—and this they enthusiastically did. As a final snub to Pretoria they also rejected an oath of loyalty to the South African Government: Chief Buthelezi boldly declared that he could not swear fealty to a Government "which has many laws I am bound to disagree with". The Government's dilemma now is whether to let the Chief go his own anti-apartheid way, or to force Zululand to toe the line, and in doing so publicly expose the hollowness of the Bantustan programme. . . .
>
> The [South African] Government is beginning to experience similar difficulties in the main South-West

> African Bantustan of Ovamboland [See Chapter 7.]. . . . On January 14th . . . Ovambo work contract demands were backed by the Ovambo Bantustan administration . . . [and] a perplexed [Minister of Bantu Administration] . . . headed for the negotiating table—itself a piece of history in this part of the world.

APPRAISAL OF THE BANTUSTAN PROGRAM

The Bantustan program has been criticized by Afrikaner intellectuals and by parliamentary opponents of the Nationalists as being naive in its presumptions and probable results, serving only to tear the Republic apart. The Bantustan plan has also been criticized by right-wing members of the Afrikaner community as "doing too much for the Blacks." The program is attacked by both White opposition and by Black leaders as being both too hazy in its political goals and too uncertain as to its economic results. As noted previously, some Black leaders, however, view the Bantustan concept as the only means by which they can attain even a minimum of social, economic, and political objectives for their peoples under a forced apartheid program. Yet other Black leaders, these mainly in urban centers, believe that their tribal counterparts should have nothing whatever to do with the program. In addition to being itself a cornerstone of the South African doctrine of apartheid, the Bantustan idea has been utilized heavily by the South African government for international propaganda purposes. South African officials have emphasized that the Bantustan thesis embodies the doctrine "separate but equal." If so, then the economic underpinnings and developmental features of the Bantustans become even more important.

It will be essential for observers to make an assessment, at a later stage, as to whether it draws Blacks back into the homelands from the White urban areas as South African authorities presume it will. On the basis of the record thus far, however, it must be assumed that the Bantustan doctrine provides only a temporary rural palliative for what is essentially a permanent urban cum rural problem. It may also be a delaying tool of the government, which seeks to impede the unsatisfied abiding drives of Black African nationalism. It also fails to make the case for "separate but equal facilities" in either economic or social spheres. Nor is it clear that these mini states or de facto colonies will ever attain real autonomy, internal and external. Finally, the future relationship of these Bantustans with the White South African autarchy remains in doubt, even if all promises of autonomy are fulfilled.

One apparently unexpected result appears certain. The Bantustan program now seems to have reawakened African nationalism, reinvigorated tribalism, and created, under the very aegis of the central government, an entire new, highly motivated, and sophisticated Black African leadership. Should these Black leaders be successful in uniting all the Bantustans (with their urban and rural wings) on a nationwide scale, then South African Whites may find that the Bantustan doctrine has recreated and unleased the very Black power that they unwittingly sought to isolate and submerge.

Based on the intensive examination of the Bantustans made in preceding pages, and the evidence of their evolution thus far, there follows a summary appraisal of these tribal "homelands":

The Bantustan program, as developed to date, seems to be an effort to provide a rural solution for what is essentially an urban cum rural problem. It is an attempt at damming the flow of Blacks from reserves to cities in the hope of drying up the numbers of Black workers in the towns and eventually forcing them back into the homelands.

The Bantustan program provides no basic social, economic, and racial reforms. Instead, by arbitrarily dividing the Black races and isolating them in the tribal reserves, the program creates new rifts between tribes and between racial groups.

The South African government has not yet seemed to have faced up to the full implications of the Bantustan program in economic, political, or financial arenas. In particular, it does not yet seem to have analyzed the requisite changes in the Republic's own infrastructure, the necessary redistribution of the country's natural resources, the financial obligations involved in making the mini states viable, and the movement toward federation, confederation, or partition that are bound to eventuate. This reluctance to talk out the future nature of the Republic may stem as much from a philosophical reticence to break up the country as from an unwillingness to put into the program the planning, the direction, and the funding required to make the program work.

The Bantustan program does not appear to have the wholehearted support of leaders and citizenry of White South Africa. Among these Whites, there appears to be a real conflict of viewpoint with respect to the Bantustans on administrative, political, and financial grounds. To assure even a modicum of success for the Bantustans, it would appear that majority support by the Whites would be required.

Blueprints for moving these territories forward to real autonomy and to independence, to political as well as economic viability, are still not clear-cut. Pressures are mounting in Pretoria, in Capetown, and in the Bantustan capitals, all seeking clarification of the central government's plans. Thus far, it appears that the South African government desires to retain central direction of essential powers—security, foreign affairs, defense, finance, and education. As yet, there has not even been a settlement of basic land disputes—consolidation of reserves or determination of boundaries of these "nations."

Efforts of central government and Bantustan authorities to encourage the flow of White capital into the homelands on a licensing basis have proved meager. There is insufficient capital flowing from central government coffers and insufficient indigenous Black capital to provide even a basic infrastructure for these areas. Even those wages sent back to the reserves by absentee migrant workers are minuscule in comparison to territorial needs and are essential for family subsistence and education. A way must be found for massive infusion of capital and of know-how (such as agricultural and animal husbandry, soil and water conservation, cottage industries, mineral exploitation, and health and educational services) to insure some possibility of local capital formation and economic viability.

Efforts by the central government to establish "border industries" have been only moderately successful thus far. To achieve even a minimal economic base for these territories, it would appear that much greater effort must be expended. Special concern is required for the problems of the Black African work force, these including housing, transport, wages, job security, and training. Attention must also be given to the thousands of new workers coming forward in the Bantustans each year. If these territories are to become "nations," as much attention must be given by the government to the foregoing problems as is currently being given by the government to the problems of border-area entrepreneurs.

If the tribal homelands are not to be merely empty shells holding pools of unused labor, and if South African public and private sources do not provide the necessary capital, then ways must be found for the Bantustan leaders to obtain that capital and technical assistance from international sources such as the World Bank or the UN Development Program.

By creating the Bantustans, the South African government, unwittingly, may have set up a Trojan horse of "colonies" and of rejuvenated Black nationalism. Though it may not willingly admit to the existence of the "colonies," Pretoria must surely admit to the creation of a host of new Black nationalist leaders. In fact, some of the leaders have achieved both national and international fame. That fame has been achieved under the aegis of Pretoria, with the Bantustans their political platforms. Within South Africa there is also emerging a new Black African character and new Black power. These leaders and these political factors may be the most important products of the Bantustan program. If her credibility is to be maintained, Pretoria must not only accept these leaders and factors but must give them the opportunity (and the support) to operate constructively.

CHAPTER

6

THE NATION'S ECONOMY

GENERAL

As a result of her rich supply of natural resources, her favorable climate and geographic location astride two oceans, her extraordinary supply of cheap labor, her determined spirit of economic nationalism, and her extraordinary foreign investments, South Africa is reaching toward economic self-sufficiency. The discovery of large deposits of diamonds, gold, and coal late in the nineteenth century, followed by large-scale British and U.S. investments, gave the first major impetus to her development. Her strategic situation at the junction of Atlantic and Indian Ocean sea lanes during World Wars I and II also hastened her industrial, agricultural, and general economic growth. Her industry and manufactures now represent 21 percent of her GDP, while mining represents 12 percent and agriculture 11 percent of GDP. Her economic strength now compares favorably with those of other "middle powers," such as Canada, Australia, and Sweden.

The Republic is highly developed compared with the rest of the African continent. Her GNP is said to approximate 20 percent of the continent's GNP, though she has only 6 percent of its population. Her steel production is equivalent to two-thirds of the continental African total, and her electric power production approximates 40 percent thereof.

South Africa's great economic strength lies in her mineral resources. It is well known that she produces more than 60 percent of the world's gold and approximately 50 percent of the world's diamonds. Less well known is the fact that she produces commercially, for internal use and for export, some 45 other valuable minerals. These include uranium, coal (from the world's largest known reserves), platinum, copper, iron ore, manganese, chrome, asbestos, and so forth.

Less than 2 percent of her food supplies are imported today. These are in the range of meats, rice, wheat, butter, and some luxury goods. Except in drought years, South Africa is a net exporter of foodstuffs—including sugar, corn, fruits, wool, hides and skins, and fish. She now stands fifth among nations in production of sugar and sixth in fisheries.

In her drive for export markets South Africa has been highly successful over the past ten years. Despite the international drive for economic sanctions and boycotts against her, her trade pattern has expanded in every sector of the world, even including the African continent. Her principal trading partners have been Britain, Germany, Japan, and the United States. Her trade with Japan and with Communist China has recently been increasing. Two-way trade with the United States has recently been running in the range of $700 million annually, with South Africa buying more from the United States than the United States purchases from her. South Africa's trade with Europe is subject to considerable potential damage, given the expansion of the Common Market. However, it is assumed that the Republic will seek to balance this potential loss by expanding her trade with Latin America, with the Far East, and with the rest of Africa.

South Africa's economic growth over the past 25 years has been little short of phenomenal. Between 1946 and 1960 the country's national income doubled. Her GDP in 1948 was Rand 2.17 billion, increasing to Rand 10.28 billion in 1968.* The average rate of growth was over 8 percent per year for those two decades. This average was reached despite a dull period of growth between 1957 and 1962. That dullness was overcome by a subsequent period (1962-68), where a growth of nearly 9.5 percent was attained annually. During those years South Africa's rate of growth was exceeded only by Germany and Japan. However, the strains on the economy and conditions overseas brought about an inflationary price increase of some 3 percent over these latter years. Adjusting for inflated prices, the real growth over these two decades still ran above 4.8 percent annually.

Until World War II the South African economy was based primarily on agricultural production—and on the production of her gold, diamond, and coal mines. Since 1945, however, there has been a spurt in primary and secondary manufacturing. This sector of the national economy, in fact, now accounts for a larger proportion of the national income than does either agriculture or mining.

---

*South African rand 1 equaled approximately U.S. $1.30 in 1972.

During this period the South African economy was much influenced by external factors. The devaluation of the British pound (followed by South African devaluation) combined with new gold finds brought about unusual increases in South African gold production and upward movements of the entire economy. The demands of the Korean war were also influential. The higher commodity prices resulting from this war gave new impetus to South African exports of raw materials.

The slower South African growth during 1957-62 resulted from the recession in the United States, dullness in other export markets, and the massive capital outflow that occurred as a result of the internal political developments of 1960-61. These developments included the Sharpeville (1960) disturbances, the withdrawal of South Africa from the British Commonwealth (1961), and the creation of South Africa's own coinage (rand replacing the pound in 1961).

Following upon imposition of an embargo upon outflow of foreign investments, and a renewal of foreign investors' interest in South Africa, the economy took a new spurt upward during the period 1962-68. This period, by every economic indicator, was more expansive than any previous period in South Africa's national history. Diversification of industrial production and of export (especially of minerals) was exceptional. Development of new domestic industries, such as automotive, petrochemical, and pharmaceutical, were prime examples of the new growth.

Foreign investment in the South African economy has been extremely heavy. Present U.K. investment there is estimated at more than $3.5 billion. The direct investment from the United States (in some 300 or more corporations and corporate branches) exceeds $800 million and may add up to an additional $500 million in portfolio holdings and deposits. Foreign businessmen have been encouraged into the South African field by the extraordinary returns on their investments in an expanding market. It has been estimated by the U.S. Department of Commerce and other reliable sources that net profits on these foreign investments have been ranging from 12 percent to 30 percent after taxes. The median net return on U.S. investment in the Republic is said to have run at 19 percent for each of the past five years. Thus, these "golden prospects" for foreign investors in South Africa have provided material impetus for the Republic's drive toward self-sufficiency and have provided a kind of psychological defense for her policies internationally as well.

South Africa has not been immune from the usual inflationary pressures. Prices of all commodities, domestic and imported, have risen steadily. The consumer index for the nation as a whole increased some 4 percent in 1970 and moved to 5 percent in 1971. It is expected to show an even sharper increase in 1972 as a result of revaluation of foreign currencies and devaluation of the rand. Also

FIGURE 1

Key Economic Indicators for the Republic of South Africa, 1970

GNP	$16.7 billion	9.6% over 1969
GDP (Constant 1963 Prices)	$13.7 billion	5.2% over 1969
Per Capita (Current Prices)	$784 million	6.1% over 1969
Nonagricultural Employment	35% above 1963	5.8% over 1969
Average Monthly Wages—Whites (in manufacturing)	$496	14.6% over 1969
Average Monthly Wages—Blacks (in manufacturing)	$85	10.9% over 1969
Total Government Debt	$7.5 billion	5.4% over 1969
External Debt	$321 million	116% over 1969
Retail Index (100 in 1961)	207.4	9.4% over 1969
Wholesale Index (100 in 1963)	111.2	2.2% over 1969
Gold and Foreign Exchange	$1.1 billion	24.6% down from 1969
Balance of Payments: Total Change in Gold and Foreign Exchange	minus $368 million	353.4% down from 1969
Balance of Trade Deficit	minus $1.4 billion	41% down from 1969
	(not including gold sales)	
Exports (fob)	$2.1 billion	3.2% over 1969
Exports (U.S. share)	$181 million, or 8.4% of total	19% over 1969
Imports (fob)	$3.5 billion	19% over 1969
Imports (U.S. share)	$593 million, or 16.7% of total	14.5% over 1969

Note: In 1970 South African rand 1 equaled U.S. $1.41.

Source: Foreign Economic Trends, U.S. Department of Commerce (Washington, D.C., June 1971).

influential have been higher labor costs and freight charges, new controls on installment buying, and various excise taxes levied by the South African government during 1970 and 1971.

For the past several years critical shortages have existed in areas of capital, labor, and transport. These shortages are likely to continue for several years to come. Not surprisingly, shortages in each of these areas are closely related to South Africa's race problem, and some result from the barriers and constrictions that apartheid itself creates.

Shortages of capital for South African needs has been a compound of several factors. Major among these has been the sharp industrial and general economic growth that the country has experienced over the past decade. As a result the economy, like so many others worldwide, became overheated, and domestic inflationary pressures built up. Shortages of capital were not wholly alleviated by domestic sources, and it was necessary to continue to look abroad for more funds, public and private. Though there was occasional reluctance of private investors to lend to South Africa (including some American banks and business firms), there appeared to be little difficulty in floating public loans on the various European money markets, especially in France, Switzerland, and Germany. New capital needs arose not only from the swift expansion of the country's economy, but also because of her preparations for the Bantustan program, including the drives for decentralization of industry. The Bantustan policy represents a new financial load, which does not yet appear to have been fully assessed by South African budget makers in terms of new infrastructure needs.

Capital shortages resulted also from the pressing demands of importers for foreign capital goods and for ordinary overseas luxuries and essentials. The massive amount of these imports put South Africa's foreign trade figures into serious imbalance. This shortage could not have been overcome had it not been for an extraordinarily good showing of South Africa's gold producers—an element that, thus far, has always been able to bridge the Republic's foreign trade deficits. In this connection, with the official rate of gold now (1972) newly pegged at $38 per ounce and with the free market price in the range of $70 per ounce, both South African gold producers and the South African Treasury stand to benefit materially. The new price levels free them from the stringencies imposed by the controlled gold markets ($35 per ounce) of the last decade. Gold and foreign exchange reserves were at a high point of Rand 1.2 billion—a decline as of May 1971—which in 1969 had been at a figure of Rand 600 million. At that stage they were declining at a rate of about Rand 15 million monthly. This decline appears to have been arrested completely as of early 1972 as a result of the stringent new governmental controls (import and exchange) and the improved situation with respect to gold prices.

In addition to cutting into those reserves, however, it has been necessary for South Africa, over recent years, to introduce various import curbs and other fiscal and monetary controls, all designed to reduce consumption and to reduce the overheated condition of the country's economy. In recent years, as the financial temperature went up or down, the central government successfully imposed, relaxed, and reimposed a series of these measures. It is to be expected that this program will continue for some years into the future, as there appears to be no doubt, at this stage, that the South African economy will continue to grow. Outside demand for the wide range of South African minerals and the recent increases of official and unofficial prices for gold would seem to assure a continuing upward economic trend for South Africa, despite potential threats of internal strife over the race issue.

Despite the favorable upward price of gold in recent months, it should be pointed out that some of South Africa's other main export items—notably diamonds, wool, and platinum—have been suffering from depressed international market conditions. Some of these markets are bound to be resilient, however, and the fact of South Africa's great diversity of natural resources available for export cannot be overlooked. Thus, in the near-term and mid-term the outlook for South African economy is favorable. It could be even more favorable should there be a satisfactory containment of the domestic inflationary pressures, a moderation of internal race frictions, and elimination of inhibiting labor policies. The general projections of South African government sources are for a continuing upward movement of the economy at an annual rate exceeding 5 percent.

In spite of the exceptionally rapid changes in South Africa's economy in recent years, her national economic profile today casts dual shadows. One of these represents urban South Africa as highly industrialized, sophisticated, and wealthy. The other profile represents rural South Africa, undeveloped or only partially developed, poverty stricken, and often drought ridden. The duality of the profile splits the population, without regard to color lines, into rich urban and poor rural facets.

MINERALS

Editors of the London Times once observed that, without its possession of vast quantities of gold and diamonds, South Africa would never have acceded to the hierarchy of nations. That flat assertion might be questioned on at least two grounds: (a) the peculiar reputation South Africa has earned as a result of its race policies, which would inevitably have brought it to the forefront of world attention; and (b) the broad array of the Republic's commercially exploitable minerals required for modern technology, which, combined with its geographic position, gives her a special strategic value.

South Africa is endowed with at least 60 commercially exploitable minerals. No less than 45 of these are sold abroad today. The Republic is the world's foremost gold producer, today mining about 80 percent of the free world's annual production. She is also a producer of diamonds, uranium, coal, platinum, copper, iron ore, manganese, chrome, and asbestos. (Each of these foregoing is given individual treatment below.) Other important minerals produced commercially include antimony, feldspar, fluorspar, graphite, gypsum, kaolin, lead, limestone, marble, mercury, mica, nickel, phosphates, salt, silver, sulphur, titanium, tungsten, vanadium, wolfram, and zinc.

Total production from the mining industry as a whole in 1970 was Rand 1.56 billion. Of this total gold production accounted for nearly 58 percent. In the national economic picture the mining industry represents 11.7 percent of South Africa's GDP. This figure is down from 20 percent in 1940. The mining industry's earnings, including gold, represent more than one-half of the country's total export values. Employment in all mining of the Republic in 1970 totaled 703,459, of which Blacks numbered 612,140 and Whites 83,734.

The historic influences of South Africa's possession of immense quantities of gold (first discovered in 1870) and diamonds (first discovered in 1867) cannot, however, be overlooked. These two products have provided the financial strength for the creation of South Africa's now highly diverse infrastructure. Furthermore, the foreign exchange they earn has invariably provided a bridge for any foreign trade gaps. Thus, in the development of South Africa's economy, they must be considered pivotal.

Gold

Annual gold production has been averaging 30 million ounces in recent years, valued at more than $1 billion yearly at the former official rate of $35 per ounce. With that official rate now $38 per ounce and with the unofficial rate of the free market running well above $70 per ounce, South African producers should be able to cope with increased production costs for perhaps several decades to come. Most of the gold mines have been marginal producers of large bodies of low-grade ore. Because of these characteristics it would be impossible to have operated most of those gold-bearing ore bodies without a constant supply of low-cost Black labor.

Production of gold increased yearly between 1950 and 1965 at the rate of 7 percent. During the years 1955-65, production ran fairly steadily at about 25 million fine ounces. Development of rich new mines in the western Transvaal and improved productivity have again increased production. This has now leveled off at above 30 million ounces yearly. (Production in 1970 was valued at Rand 830 million.) Further increases in production would depend not only on the maintenance of marginal mines but, as well, on new finds and the continued inflow of cheap Black labor. The gold, produced mainly in the Transvaal and Orange Free State, requires employment of the country's largest single work force, next to manufacturing and agriculture. In 1970 some 39,386 White workers and 386,113 Black workers were employed in the gold fields. Their wages and subsistence exceed $300 million annually.

Several years ago officials of the U.S. Bureau of Mines had estimated that the peak of South African gold production would occur between 1968 and 1970—leveling off thereafter at about 30 million ounces annually. This judgment was conservatively correct. They estimated as well that this level would probably be the all-time peak for the Republic, barring major new discoveries. They expressed the view as well that this high rate of production could be continued for another 40 to 50 years if operating conditions continued to be as favorable as at present.

White labor on the mines is fairly steady and long resident. Black labor for gold and other mining activity, however, has historically been recruited on a contractual basis from rural areas of the Republic (especially the Bantustans, such as Transkei and Kwa Zulu). Black workers are also imported from the former British High Commission territories—now the independent nations of Swaziland, Botswana, and Lesotho—as well as from Malawi, Mozambique, Rhodesia, and tropical Africa. Contracts with these Black laborers, recruited in large groups, are generally for an 18-month period. Recent changes in immigration policies restricting recruitment of Black African labor from countries north of the Zambezi River have begun to limit Black mine labor to workers of indigenous origin. This has caused the mining companies some concern, especially in the face of competitive industrial demands for workers elsewhere in the Republic. A major shortage of Black workers has not yet developed, however, and such shortages as have existed are being offset by increased automation.

In long-term anticipation of a run-out of the gold-mining properties and given the large financial outlays required to open new mines, there has resulted a horizontal expansion and vertical integration of the industry through use of the conglomerate and holding company. In South Africa this is known as the "group system." These groups maintain control of major gold producers and allied diversified concerns through large stockholdings and interlocking directorates. Largest of these groups is the Anglo-American Corporation, headed by the internationally known tycoon Harry Oppenheimer. The Anglo-American conglomerate controls gold, diamonds, coal, and copper mines; the DeBeers diamond sales cartel; and investment companies; and so forth. Its mining ventures are worldwide. It is also heavily invested in production of explosives, sugar, tin, cement, manufacturing, and engineering. General Mining, Anglo-Transvaal, Rand Mines, and Union Corporation are among the other large South African conglomerates.

Until recently South African gold sales were made through London, in association with the Bank of England. Now, however, the Republic sells much of its gold in France, Switzerland, and Germany.

It is known that the South African Reserve Bank, which controls all marketing, has sold considerable amounts of gold recently in both official and unofficial markets, but total sales thereof have not been revealed. Given the new offical rate of $38 per ounce and the higher free market rate, $70 ounce, South African gold sales abroad are expected to continue at a level that will not seriously depress the free market. The regular production of South African gold and its orderly sale in both official and unofficial markets has helped in a measure to stabilize currencies and to alleviate major swings of gold prices worldwide. Thus, the Republic's production has given some stability to both world monetary structures and the world gold pool. South African production in recent years may well have contributed somewhat to lessening pressures against the dollar and against dwindling U.S. gold reserves. Since the 1971 decision by the U.S. government to remove the partial gold backing of its currency and no longer to sell gold abroad, this factor of South African gold production has become of less importance to the U.S. Treasury.

Rising costs of production without a concurrent increase in the price of gold (from 1934 until late 1971 that price remained fixed at $35 per ounce) had been a major concern to the gold-mining industry of South Africa. While the recent official increase to $38 per ounce was welcomed by South African gold producers, they had expected an even higher revaluation. Today, South African gold producers receive a premium rebate from the South African government on that part of their gold production sold on the free market above the official price level of $38 per ounce. Thus, it is in their interest to see that the free market price is sustained. It is assumed that as long as the free market price remains above the official gold price, South Africa's gold producers will continue to receive their premium. Further, both gold producers and South African Reserve Bank authorities agree that industrial demands for gold, added to continuing demand of speculators and hoarders, should keep the free market price of gold well above $40 per ounce in the foreseeable future. It is estimated that today less than 5 percent of total world output flows into official monetary reserves. Official gold stocks reportedly account for no more than one-third of all monetary reserves under the control of the International Monetary Fund and central banks. Industrial demands for gold, which now are said to account for nearly 95 percent of all free market dealings, are expected to continue to be high. Fears that speculators or hoarders would place sufficient amounts of gold on the free market to break it are usually discounted by financial authorities, including South African sources.

In support of the foregoing, an interesting article appeared in the Durban Sunday Tribune on October 3, 1971. The article entitled "No Worry Over Gold Price," quoted South African financial authorities as saying that "in the opinion of Reserve Bank [South African] experts, speculators have played little part in the free gold market since 1968 and their holdings today are minimal." Estimates of South Africa's actual gold production for 1971 range up to Rand 890 million, compared with production of Rand 830 million in 1970. With South Africa's balance of trade deficit running at about Rand 900 million for 1971 (compared with a deficit of Rand 860 in 1970), any increase of gold production in coming months will be of special value in bridging the foreign trade gap.

As further indication of gold's special ability to bridge the Republic's recent foreign trade gap, The New York Times of November 4, 1971, carried the following:

> The South African Reserve Bank's gold holdings fell 800,000 to 325.8 million rand last week while total gold and foreign assets dropped 17.4 million rand to 460.1 million rand. Total gold and foreign assets have fallen by 221.1 million rand since the beginning of this year and 736 million rand since the all-time high on April 18, 1969, the bank said today. . . .

Given the existing world currency situation and the recent revaluation of gold in official and free markets, South Africa appears to be in a fairly strong position as regards her gold output for the mid-term future. Most reputable South African financial and mining sources agree that, despite inflationary pressures, labor shortages (White and Black), and other production difficulties, the recent international monetary developments have proved a bonanza for South African mines, the South African economy, and the South African government.

Diamonds

Rich deposits of diamonds occur both in South Africa and in South-West Africa. Those in the Republic, mainly in the Cape and the Transvaal, occur in the form of kimberlite pipe, which requires mining underground. Those in South-West Africa are alluvial, occurring in ocean beach gravels, situated along the Atlantic Ocean shoreline and at the confluence of the Orange River with the sea. A majority of the South-West African finds are gemstone; those of South Africa are primarily industrial. South Africa and South-West Africa together produce more gem diamonds than any other country. Only Zaire produces more industrial diamonds.

The right to mine diamonds is strictly controlled by the government. Production and sales are strictly controlled by the DeBeers syndicate, a subsidiary of the Anglo-American Corporation, already mentioned as the country's major gold producer. DeBeers is reputed to handle the marketing of over 80 percent of all the world's diamonds (gem and industrial), including those from other African nations and from the Soviet Union. The United States and the United Kingdom are DeBeers' prime customers. Prices of diamonds are subject to considerable fluctuation, dependent heavily on world economic conditions.

As reported in the Durban Sunday Tribune of January 16, 1972, total free world sales of diamonds through the DeBeers cartel amounted to Rand 446.4 million in 1971. It is assumed that more than 50 percent of this free world total came from South Africa and South-West African sources. An official breakdown of diamond sales from those sources is not made available to the public. It is understood, however, that 1967 production from South African sources alone exceeded 6 million carats, these valued at Rand 62 million.[1] Assuming that the 1971 production from South African sources remained at or above the same level, it must then be inferred that diamond production and combined sales from South and South-West Africa must have been considerably higher.

Uranium

For two decades South Africa has been one of the major producers of uranium, following closely upon Canada, the United States, and Russia. On the African continent it is now being challenged by other producers, notably Niger, the Central African Republic, and Zaire. Known uranium reserves in the Republic are estimated at well over 1 billion tons, with an oxide content exceeding 370,000 tons. Uranium recovery is also being effected from the slag dumps of the country's gold mines and as a by-product of newly produced gold-bearing ore. Much of the country's uranium production was spurred by long-time buying contracts extended by the United States and the United Kingdom. Though the United States is no longer purchasing uranium from South Africa, sales of the ore continue to Britain, to France, and reportedly to Israel. The Republic is also looking for new markets in the Far East. Much of the financing of the uranium production and recovery from gold-bearing ores was underwritten by loans from the U.S. Eximbank, operating in teamwork with the U.S. Atomic Energy Commission. Loans from the United States during the past two decades are reported to have exceeded $1.25 billion. Most of these loans have since been repaid.

The United States withdrew from purchase of South African uranium primarily because world production (including U.S. domestic production) rose beyond all expectations in the first years of the last decade. The United States found that it was buying South African uranium oxide at rates considerably higher than it could be mined within the United States ($11.75 per pound fob South Africa versus $9.35 per pound in the United States). The United States has not received uranium from South Africa since 1966.

South Africa has recently developed a large nuclear reactor—Palundaba—which became operative in 1965. As a result of recent internal scientific development associated with the new reactor, South Africa's own capabilities and potential for use of her uranium have been considerably expanded. This has reportedly been possible because of the discovery, by South African atomic scientists, of new and cheaper methods of producing the enriched uranium ores. In passing, it should be noted that atomic energy power plants are planned for both Cape Province and Natal within the next several years. Thus far, all governmental and scientific claims have been that its domestic uranium production is only for peaceful purposes. It seems evident, however, that given its scientific know-how, South Africa has definite capabilities for atomic energy uses in the military fields.

Coal

Coal is South Africa's third biggest mining industry in terms of annual output value. Only gold and copper bring more return. Known reserves are estimated at 2 billion tons. It is also the second largest employer (after gold) in terms of manpower needs. Employment in the coal mines in 1970 totaled 75,742. Of these Blacks numbered 67,349 and Whites 8,173. An additional 78,000 are employed in related industries. The output of coal in 1970 was 63 million short tons, valued at Rand 109.9 million.

The main bodies of coal are located in the eastern Transvaal, Orange Free State, and northern Natal. The coal includes bituminous, coking, and anthracite types. Chief producers are General Mining and Anglo-American Corporation. The Electricity Supply Commission (ESCOM) is the Republic's largest coal user, buying one-third of all coal mined in the country. Only anthracite is exported beyond Africa, this mainly to the Far East.[2]

While world demand for energy is rising, the use of coal for energy requirements is diminishing proportionately, contracting at about 1 percent annually. With alternative sources of energy cutting into the market, the long-term outlook for coal is cloudy.

Platinum

South Africa is the world's prime producer of platinum, mining 70 percent of the global total. Most of that production comes from the Merensky Rift in the Transvaal. Sales of platinum have been averaging 1 million troy ounces annually in recent years. The price of platinum has been ranging from $100 to $140 per ounce. Production from the platinum mines has increased 500 percent since 1963, and the mines report a gross annual yield of 6 percent.

Chief use of the mineral has been in production of nitric acid. There is increasing use of platinum in the jewelry market. Platinum is also being seriously considered as an antipollution emission catalyst (for removal of carbon monoxide and hydrocarbons) for automobile exhausts.

Major users of South African platinum are Britain, Japan, continental Europe, and the United States. The latter takes about 20 percent of South African production yearly. It is reported that recent production of platinum has been piling up in South African stockpiles, owing in part to a falling market and in part to increased sales of platinum from the U.S.S.R.

Copper

The principal sources of copper are located in the northern Transvaal, Cape Province, and South-West Africa. About four-fifths of all copper produced is exported. Until recently the United States was the chief buyer, but Japan is now taking an increasing share. More than 149,000 tons of blister copper were produced in 1970, this valued at Rand 139 million. Additional amounts of electrolytic copper are produced in sufficient quantity to satisfy domestic needs. The new mine in the northern Transvaal, Phalaborwa, contains one of the world's most extensive reserves of copper-phosphoric and vermiculite. One-third of the $100 million capital for that new and important development reportedly has come from U.S. sources. U.S. mining companies, including American Metals Climax and Newmount, are active in the Phalaborwa partnership, along with British and South African concerns.

Iron Ore

There are exceptionally large deposits of iron ore in South Africa, these mainly located in the Transvaal and the northern Cape. Estimates of ore reserves are said to exceed 5.5 billion tons.

Increasing industrialization in South Africa and the expansion of the government-owned Iron and Steel Corporation of South Africa (ISCOR) assure a growing domestic demand for this commodity. It is important to note that South Africa is able to produce iron and steel products at costs ranging among the lowest in the world.

There has been special interest in large-scale buying of South African iron ore exhibited on the part of Japan. That nation has recently considered purchase of up to 100 million tons of the ore. Large-scale exploitation of the iron ore has been delayed, however, owing to particular transport and port-handling problems. Proposed new rail and port facilities in the Cape Province (including Saldanha Bay and Port Elizabeth) are expected to overcome these deficiencies. It is estimated by South African official sources that exports of iron ore from the Republic over the next 30 years could reach a total of 500 million tons, valued at Rand 4 billion.

Chrome

South Africa's chrome ore bodies are said to represent over 75 percent of the world's known reserves. However, in 1970, the Republic produced only 20 percent of the total global production, or 1.42 million tons, valued at Rand 10.6 million. The most extensive deposits are in the Transvaal. There are several basic grades of chrome ore available. Some 95 percent of the country's ferrochrome is exported—mainly to the United States, the United Kingdom, Japan, and West Germany.

Manganese

One of the world's largest producers of manganese, South African production reached 3 million tons in 1970, valued at Rand

26.6 million. One-half the annual production is exported, mainly to the United States, Germany, France, and Japan. These exports were valued in excess of Rand 19 million in 1968.

Asbestos

Four types of asbestos are commercially exploited in South Africa. Shipments thereof are made to virtually every industrial country in the world, including the Soviet bloc. Particularly important is the South African production and export of one variety, amosite, which is in great demand for the lining of satellite and rocket engines. Total asbestos production in 1970 was valued at Rand 34 million and totaled 287,000 tons in 1970. The Republic is the world's largest producer of asbestos after Canada and the U.S.S.R.

Petroleum

To date no commercially exploitable petroleum fields have been located within the Republic or South-West Africa. This is the single major lack in the Republic's self-sufficiency picture. That lack is of utmost concern to senior Governmental officials and defense officials. Until 1955 all petroleum requirements had to be imported. In that year the government sponsored production of oil from coal.

South Africa has tackled the problem of her petroleum needs in five different ways.

1. She is encouraging both onshore and offshore drilling for petroleum. Thus far, explorations have provided only small traces of oil and larger traces of natural gas. The activities have engaged a number of international oil concerns, including Americans.

2. There has been stepped-up import of crude oil, principally from Iran and the Persian Gulf states. Storage facilities for these imports have been increased. It is conservatively estimated that South Africa today possesses a full three-year supply of her refined and unrefined petroleum needs.

3. To meet increased civilian demand and to insure her defense needs, South Africa has been expanding her refinery capabilities, even to production of high octane fuels and specialized lubricants. American refineries include Mobil and Caltex. British Petroleum, Shell, and the French company Total are also involved.

4. In order to insure fast distribution of her petroleum to the highly industrialized areas of the Transvaal, two pipelines from the Natal coastline to the Transvaal are now in operation. Each of these runs parallel to existing rail facilities—one pipeline from Durban to Johannesburg (440 miles), the second from Richards Bay-Empangeni

to the eastern Rand. This latter will take petroleum in crude form from the supertanker docks planned for Richards Bay. It is estimated these facilities will be in operation by 1976.

5. As a final hedge against its lack of petroleum, the Republic has concentrated on producing fuel oil and lubricants from its vast supplies of coal.

This government-owned South African Coal, Oil and Gas Corporation (SASOL) now produces about 10 percent of the country's fuel needs. That production is expected to double within the next decade. It is of special interest to note that the government's planning has even involved the possible flooding of unused sealed mining shafts as a means of achieving safe underground storage. SASOL, with a capital investment exceeding Rand 100 million, is said to be the largest "oil from coal" plant in the world. The plant produces a wide variety of commodities, ranging from petrol and diesel oil and industrial gas to a variety of chemicals, including nitrogenous fertilizers and materials for synthetic rubber. It is estimated that SASOL activities save the Republic more than Rand 50 million annually in foreign exchange. The corporation also exports products valued at Rand 3 million.

AGRICULTURE

During most of South Africa's history, even since gold was discovered, agriculture has been a mainstay of the country's economy and one of its prime producers of foreign exchange. Only in the postwar years have industry and mining outstripped agriculture in the national economic picture. Today, though still highly important, agriculture only contributes 10 percent to 12 percent of the GDP. Of even more importance, however, is the fact that agriculture provides a living for 40 percent of the entire population (62 percent of the non-Whites and 16 percent of the Whites). The South African minister of agriculture, speaking in Parliament in March 1971, reported that the gross value of all agricultural products produced by White farmers in the Republic and South-West Africa during fiscal year 1969/70 was estimated at Rand 1.28 billion (no income figures were announced for Black agriculturalists, who are mainly subsistence farmers). A 1969 survey by the South African Agricultural Union reported that a total of nearly 4 million persons are involved in agriculture. Of these 3.15 million are Blacks, with Whites numbering 381,000. The Black population on farms is reported to be growing at the rate of over 4 percent annually, while White population on farms is decreasing by 1 percent annually.

As noted, the country's total agricultural production by White farmers reached Rand 1.28 billion in 1969/70. This represented a massive rise from the production total of Rand 396 million in 1947. Cash crop production by Blacks is estimated at Rand 80 million annually, in addition to unknown values of subsistence production. It is also estimated that domestic food consumption, White and non-White, has increased by 20 percent in the past two decades, this apparently reflecting improved health standards for all racial groups. The central government is doing much to assist the nation's agricultural stability through crop quota systems, agricultural subsidies, and producer marketing arrangements.[3]

The Republic is a major producer and exporter of sugar; corn; deciduous, citrus, and canned fruits; wool, hides, and skins; and tobacco. In value her agricultural exports are second only to gold. Proponents of potential trade boycotts and sanctions against South Africa should be aware that she is virtually independent of the outside world for her food needs, importing only 2 percent of her foodstuff requirements. She imports in quantity only rice, wheat, meat, dairy products, coffee, and tea. She is increasing her domestic production of both wheat and tea. Only in drought periods does she import dairy products and meats.

Drought in South Africa is pervasive, almost a malignancy. As a result the government has had to concentrate on soil and water conservation programs on an extensive scale. Special arrangements have, at times, been required for massive fodder lift and food transport programs, especially to the tribal reserves. As only 15 percent of the land is arable, the Republic is unusually dependent on rainfall and irrigation. Large irrigation schemes have been developed recently, these including the giant Orange River scheme now underway. However, at least 10 percent of the country's highly uneven rainfall is still lost by erosive runoff into the sea. Farming is becoming more intensive as one means of combating weather imponderables.

Sugarcane

South Africa's sugarcane production should be especially noted, since she is now reported to be fifth in line as a major world supplier. She operates under the international sugar agreement and thus strictly controls domestic production and export sales. South Africa's sugar production for the 1971/72 season was 1,864,000 tons, with exports representing 52 percent of production. Export earnings therefrom represented Rand $85.2 million, placing sugar at the head of the country's agricultural foreign exchange earners.* If need be, she

---

*Financial Mail (Johannesburg), August 4, 1972, p. 380.

could easily expand her production. Her domestic use of sugar has risen sharply in recent years and appears likely to continue to rise. The Republic is reportedly amongst the first three world producers in profitability per acre grown. Most of the cane is grown and refined in a rich strip of land stretching 250 miles along the shoreline of Natal and Zululand and into the eastern Transvaal. Total sugarcane lands in production exceed 800,000 acres. On these, some 2,200 White farmers, 3,500 Black farmers, and 1,800 Asian farmers are in operation. (The White farms and estates embrace about 92 percent of the sugar crop.) There are 20 sugar mills and refineries in operation.

Handling of both domestic production and export of sugar is by consortium action taken by associations, growers, refiners, and the South African Sugar Association. The work of these groups is highly automated. Storage and loading operations in Durban Harbor can care for more than 500,000 tons of refined sugar.

The Republic sells most of her sugar exports to Japan, the United Kingdom, Canada, and the United States. South Africa exports some 50,000 to 60,000 tons of refined sugar to the United States annually under U.S. import quotas. For this South Africa receives remuneration well above the world sugar price. This premium results from the protective feature of domestic U.S. sugar subsidies. The fact of this high payment, plus the international agitation against South African race laws and cheap labor, keeps South African trade lobbies in contact with the U.S. Congress to guard against cancellation of the South African share of U.S. sugar imports.

Corn

Corn (white corn) continues to be a vital domestic foodstuff and export item. Corn is still the most important staple of the Black African diet. In good years production of corn is said to run above 100 million bags (of 200 pounds each). In 1970, however, corn production was estimated to have reached only 6.4 million tons[4] (or 64 million bags). Over 55 million bags are required for domestic consumption annually. The remainder is available for dietary supplements to Black African needs in the Bantustans or for nearby countries, particularly Lesotho and Botswana.

Deciduous and Citrus Fruits

Production of deciduous and citrus fruits has been a fast-growing sector of South African agricultural development and export. Much of the fruit, fresh or canned, is consigned to Britain and to continental European countries. It seems likely that these exports will suffer somewhat from British and Scandinavian movement into the Common Market. Recent devaluation of the rand, however, may offset some of that loss by opening other markets. During the past decade the export of deciduous fruits has increased by more than 113 percent. The United Kingdom takes over 50 percent of that fruit crop. Production of citrus fruit has more than doubled in the past two decades. Citrus fruits, exported to more than 30 countries, were valued at more than Rand 42 million in 1971. The United Kingdom and continental Europe are the principal markets. In the past two decades the production of canned fruits has quadrupled. Canned fruit exports now create Rand 60 million yearly and utilize over 70,000 tons of domestic sugar in processing. Exports representing two-thirds of the production total are made to more than 70 countries.

Wine

Yet another South African agricultural export—that of its wineries—is also likely to suffer from British entry into the Common Market—with replacement of the Republic's wines by those of France and Italy. Annual production of South African wines now exceeds 100 million gallons, with values ranging above Rand 35 million. Less than 10 percent of the total production is exported—Britain taking more than one-third of all exports.

Wool

South Africa is the fifth largest producer of wool in the world and with its allied lines gives a livelihood to more than 750,000 persons. Annual production from 42 million sheep exceeds 300 million pounds. The value of wool exports exceeds Rand 111 million annually.[5] Mohair is also an important allied export, this valued at about Rand 6.5 million yearly. Export of another allied product, karakul skins (mainly from South-West Africa), ranges in value about Rand 11 million annually. Some 60 percent of the total production of other types of hides and skins were also exported, these valued at Rand 17.5 million. Principal buyers of South African wool, hides, and skins are the United Kingdom, Japan, Italy, France, the United States, Germany, and Belgium. The United States had been an important wool buyer from South Africa until United States production of synthetic textiles cut seriously into that market.

Tobacco

Tobacco has been an expanding sector of the agricultural picture in South Africa. A highly organized producer-marketing cooperative group controls this activity. Of production averaging 60 million pounds annually, some 20 million pounds of leaf tobacco are exported. Net sales revenues exceed Rand 35 million annually. The country is still dependent on imports of cigars and cigarettes for the remainder of its domestic needs.

FISHING

One of the most controversial and potentially pessimistic of South Africa's foodstuffs production is that of fisheries.[6] As with other of her economic activities, commercial fishing from the Republic and South-West Africa has grown swiftly. Production has risen twentyfold in the past 25 years, now running at some 2 million tons annually. This rate of production has placed South Africa (and South-West Africa) sixth among nations of the world in fisheries, ranking her behind Peru, Japan, Russia, Norway, and the United States. South Africa also ranks second in worldwide production of fishmeal.

The main reason for the controversy is whether conservationist politics of the high seas and the richness of the fishing grounds will offset the technological advantages of factory-ships and massive catches, which cut down future production. There is considerable fear that the rich fishing grounds of the South Atlantic may soon be depleted. Efforts to husband these natural resources are few, now applying only to waters within the Republic's 12-mile limit. It has been clear for some time that commercial fishing licenses were granted by the government with little regard for the consequences. It has now been decided by concerned Cabinet ministers that certain factory ships, especially those operating off South-West Africa, be limited as to intake.

Nearly 80 separate fishing companies are now engaged in the trade, these operating 22 factory ships and nearly 1,000 other vessels. These all operate out of 16 ports and harbors in South and South-West Africa. The principal varieties they gather include anchovies, pilchards, rock lobster (crayfish), mackerel, and hake. The industry's total earnings are estimated to be in excess of Rand 105 million annually, with two-thirds thereof earned from exports. Domestic sales have tripled in the past decade. This reflects the fact that Black Africans are beginning to accept fish in their diet. Principal foreign markets have been France, the Netherlands, the United States, the United Kingdom, Rhodesia, and West Germany. The crayfish industry alone earned Rand 16 million in 1968, with the United States reportedly taking 90 percent of that production.

FORESTRY

The forested surface of South Africa occupies about 3 million acres, or 1 percent of the Republic's total land area. About 20 percent of this area is covered by indigenous growth; the remainder of 80 percent is planted with the more useful fir, gum, and wattle. Capital value of forests is about Rand 420 million, with an additional Rand 180 million invested in the timber-processing industry. Total timber production is estimated at Rand 700 million annually, including both domestic and export returns. Value of exports in 1970 exceeded Rand 35 million. Furniture, timber, hardboard, and paper products are included in the timber-processing picture.

Employment in the forestry industry is about 100,000. The country is now able to satisfy about 90 percent of its own timber needs and 100 percent of its paper-making needs. Export of timber and related products (especially paper and hardboard) is swiftly increasing. The United States has recently become a major importer of South African hardboard.

INDUSTRY

The industrial preeminence of the Republic on the African continent is unchallenged. It produces and uses more steel, electricity, automotive products, textiles, and clothing than the rest of the continent combined. Manufacturing is, today, the largest single sector of the economy, creating 23 percent of the country's GDP. Her total manufacturing output is now in excess of Rand 2.4 billion, produced in more than 20,000 factories by a work force of 1.2 million persons.

Both GDP and industrial output more than quadrupled between 1940 and 1958 and doubled again in the next decade. Industrial investment increased threefold over the past ten years. The country's industrial progress and processing has been based on utilization of her own diverse natural resources and raw materials. Her relatively low-cost power (coal), her reservoirs of unskilled labor, her relatively low taxation, her encouragement of private foreign investment earning high returns, and her long-standing program of tariff protection for new industry have all been major contributing factors in her industrial growth. While import and exchange controls have been a recent feature of the South African economy, these have been strengthened or weakened as the current economic situation dictates. These have not proved impossible factors for the growth of manufactures but rather have only delayed expansion and, thus, have probably contributed to stability of the economy by creating pent-up demand.

The Republic's major private industrial activities range through agricultural machinery, automobiles, fertilizers, paper, plastics, cement, pharmaceuticals, textiles, clothing, shoes, explosives, chemicals, match manufactures, and so forth. Her quasi-public industrial sector ranges from the activities of ISCOR to the diverse activities of ESCOM and the Armaments Board.

One of the major sectors of industry that has grown enormously in South Africa in recent years has been the production of automobiles and automotive parts. General Motors, Ford, Chrysler, Volkswagen, Mercedes-Benz, and several other U.S., German, British, Japanese, and French manufacturers all have factories or assembly plants operating within the country. South Africa now has more than 1.8 million motor vehicles in operation, with an average of 200,000 new registrations made annually. In order to expand domestic self-sufficiency, the government has insisted on a gradual increase of the percentage of local content or components of these vehicles. Passenger cars manufactured in South Africa now have a 52 percent local content. This is scheduled to rise to 66 percent by 1977. Commercial vehicles have only 20 percent local content as yet. These local content requirements have necessitated investment of over Rand 400 million in manufacturing plants thus far. It appears that the new requirements will necessitate investment of an additional Rand 160 million. If localization is to succeed financially, it is likely that it will be necessary to reduce both domestic model ranges and imports of finished automobiles.

One of the fastest-growing industrial areas has been that of production of chemicals, including pharmaceuticals and fertilizers. With an annual turnover now in excess of Rand 350 million, chemicals are now rated as the fourth largest sector of secondary industry. Within the next five years, the country is expected to be virtually self-sufficient in its heavy chemical needs, its fertilizers (especially phosphates), its synthetic rubber, its plastics, and its pharmaceuticals.

The five major governmental enterprises operating in the industrial, power, investment, and transport of the Republic are ESCOM, ISCOR, the IDC, SASOL, and SAR&H. (There are other state-sponsored commercial-industrial corporations but these five demand special attention.)

ESCOM

The government-owned and operated ESCOM was begun in 1922. The activities of this corporation have made South Africa the major powerhouse of the African continent. The Republic, spanning only 4 percent of the land area of Africa, with a population representing only 7 percent of the continent, is now reputed to generate more than 50 percent of the continent's power. More than 80 percent of the country's power comes from ESCOM sources, in the form of thermal power from coal. ESCOM now operates 20 major power stations throughout the Republic. These stations have an aggregate capacity of 6,500 megavolts. Annual increases in power production have been running at about 8 percent—a total of 28 billion kilowatt-hours generated in 1968. Hydroelectric developments in the Republic have been slow. At present, however, there are several major water-power schemes in planning stages or underway. These include the gigantic Orange River project in the North Cape, the Ox-Bow project in Lesotho (scheduled to furnish power to the Transvaal), and the Ruacama scheme in South-West Africa. Lacking major opportunities for expansion of its own hydroelectric power, the Republic has turned to two other sources of power for future needs. The first of these is association with the gigantic Cabora-Bassa power plant in central Mozambique. When this hydroelectric harnessing of the Zambezi River is achieved, probably by about 1978, South Africa is expected to be the major customer.

Alternatively, however, she is planning at least two nuclear power plants. The first will be located in the western Cape (to be in use about 1976). The second will be located in Natal. The country has its own nuclear reactor—Palundaba—brought into operation in 1966. Its use is presumably peaceful thus far. As noted elsewhere, South Africa recently developed a new (reportedly inexpensive) system of uranium enrichment process. Though still remaining secret it is said to have reached the state of pilot plant production. According to A. J. A. Roux, head of South Africa's Atomic Energy Board, the country's uranium developments must eventually prove self-sufficient.[7]

ISCOR

The Republic produces three times as much steel as the rest of Africa combined. The main producer is ISCOR. That entity produced more than 39 million ingot tons of steel between its founding in 1934 and 1968. Since 1960 ISCOR has been engaged in an expansion program costing more than Rand 1 billion. ISCOR now produces 77 percent of the country's iron and steel requirements. ISCOR presently operates two works, one at Pretoria and the other at Vanderbijlpark, in addition to seven mines and quarries that furnish it raw materials. A third steel works is underway at Newcastle, in Natal, due to be in operation in 1974. The Newcastle operation is expected to add

1.5 million ingot tons to ISCOR's present production of 3.7 million ingot tons of steel. Two other new mill sites are projected. Total assets of the corporation now exceed Rand 500 million, with sales at Rand 250 million annually.[8]

The IDC

As one means of spreading its economic nationalism and increasing its self-sufficiency, South Africa has created the IDC. This entity has the prime task of helping establish new undertakings and promoting existing corporations where the capital involved is so large or the profit return likely to be so delayed that private enterprise is unable to take the lead. The corporation has the right to establish industrial undertakings on its own. The IDC ordinarily assumes only a minority sharehold. It has sought to limit its participation in full management, but combines roles of development banker, entrepreneur, and management consultant. Since it was established in 1940 with a capital of Rand 10 million, it has increased to Rand 204 million (by 1969).[9] The IDC is considered a "mainspring" of the Republic's economic growth. Among the projects that it has aided are SASOL, phosphates developments, many border industries, a new underseas cable linking South Africa and Europe, the South African Marine Corporation Limited (Safmarine), the oil search consortium, and a new aluminum smelter at Richards Bay.

(The Bantu Investment Corporation was established in 1958 to promote industrial undertakings and investment possibilities in the tribal reserves or Bantustans. This government entity is presently capitalized at Rand 2 million. By the end of 1967 the Bantu Investment Corporation had made a total of Rand 4 million available through some 800 separate loans to Bantu businessmen and potential industrialists, with an additional Rand 4.7 million made available for housing developments. The Xhosa Development Corporation, established in 1965, has the object of providing similar capital stimulus, particularly for the Transkei homeland. [See Chapter 5 on Bantustans.] A similar-type Coloured Development Corporation was launched in 1962, with capital of Rand 500,000. That share capital now exceeds Rand 3 million. These capitalizations are very small amounts, considering the capital needs of those endeavors.)

(For discussion of the activities of SASOL, see preceding section on petroleum.)

SAR&H

SAR&H is a diverse and sprawling state-controlled giant on the Republic's economic scene. It is the Republic's largest single employer (222,750 employees) and has a capital investment exceeding Rand 2.6 billion. It operates in South and South-West Africa, controling rail, air, and road transport services; two oil pipe lines; and the entire system of commercial harbors. Because of its anachronistic labor policies (especially as regards employment of non-Whites in skilled or supervisory roles), because of its tendency to lag far behind in planning for essential expansion (especially port facilities and rolling stock), and because its hierarchy is composed almost entirely of Afrikaner nationalists, SAR&H has been under heavy criticism in recent years, especially from importers, exporters, shipping firms, and the English vernacular press.

According to the Standard Bank Review of March 1971, "the view has been expressed that this administration is not so efficient as it could be and drastic reorganization is necessary to meet the demands of an expanding economy." However, the Review makes a qualified defence of SAR&H, pointing out that criticisms tend to overshadow the historic achievements of this organization. The Review points out, for example, that in the 60 years of its existence, SAR&H has "grown remarkably despite the difficulties which are peculiar to Southern Africa." Certainly SAR&H has played, and will continue to play, a vital role in the development of the country.

Transport growth in the Republic has obviously been hampered by the fact of great distances, of diverse and mountainous terrain, and lack of internal water transport. Transport is thus confined to costly rail, air, road, coastal shipping, and pipelines. The greatest industrial-mining complex is situated far from the seacoast. Further, the standard guage of the South African railways is three feet by six inches—a relatively narrow guage. Furthermore, most rail construction was pre-World War II—a time far less demanding on transport needs than now. There has been little postwar expansion of trackage. In 1921 rail trackage totaled 7,500 miles. By 1970 that trackage was 13,700 miles, of which one-third was electrified. Each year the railways carry more than 490 million suburban and 30 million main line passengers, as well as 114 million tons of goods. Total revenue in 1967 was Rand 741 million. Expenditure in the same year was Rand 706 million. Railway earnings annually are normally meant to cover outlay for working, maintenance, betterment, depreciation, and the payment of interest due on capital borrowings. The net surplus in 1967 was nevertheless Rand 35.3 million. Capital valuation of SAR&H, was in excess of Rand 2.6 billion in 1970, and in that year revenue totaled Rand 889 million.

South African Railways also maintains some 32,000 miles of diverse road transport services. These include bus lines, interurban van lines, and farm-to-market trucking services, which link practically every village and hamlet to the railway system. In 1967 SAR&H motor buses carried more than 10.8 million passengers and 3.6 million tons of goods.

Commercial airline service began in the Republic in 1929 and, in 1931, SAR&H began its own commercial airmail and passenger-carrying facilities. An international consortium airline arrangement was entered into with the British Overseas Airways Corporation in 1945. Concurrent airport development (now operated by the Department of Transport) was begun for major centers. Airways development, both domestic and international, has expanded very rapidly over the past decade, in addition to South African Airways service, to all major areas of the free world, including North America. The Republic is served by 21 foreign air-carriers. South African Airways, operating under SAR&H jurisdiction, also operates an extensive domestic, passenger, and freight network, using Boeing-type aircraft almost exclusively. In 1969 more than 1 million passengers were carried on internal and external flights by South African Airways. These and air-freight brought the South African Airways a profit exceeding Rand 4 million.

Most observers would admit that the building and expansion of South Africa's major harbors at Durban, Capetown, Port Elizabeth, East London, and Walvis Bay has been spectacular during the past 40 years. Even so, it has not been possible for the railways administration to keep up with the demand in these areas. The port of Durban, which handles ships and tonnage equal to all other South African seaports combined, is now rated the largest on the African continent, possibly the twelfth busiest in the world. Recent expansion of South African harbor facilities have included new berths, deepened channels and turning basins, cargo handling equipment, repair graving docks, and storage facilities. It has been determined that the pressures on existing facilities can now only be relieved by building two new deep-water ports. One at Richards Bay, north of Durban, will specialize in the handling of petroleum products from deep-sea supertankers. The second, at Saldanha Bay, near Capetown, will specialize in the export of iron ore and other minerals. Though it is operated as a separate corporate entity, some mention should here be made of the South African merchant fleet. These activities represent an important adjunct of the South African harbors.

In the past decade the number of South African-owned ships has more than trebled. The leading overseas shipping company carrying the Republic's flag is Safmarine. It owns, operates, and charters some 50 vessels, including several large tankers, six refrigerated cargo ships, and two large passenger liners. Another three ships are under construction. The establishment of an oil tanker fleet is being considered by the state and private companies. There are also a number of private coastal shipping lines.

The SAR&H combine represents a highly important element of South Africa's economy in other categories as well—particularly in the purchase of goods and as an employer of major consequence. Whereas in 1910 SAR&H purchased about Rand 17 million in "stores," those purchases amounted to more than Rand 360 million annually by 1970. The purchase of rolling stock alone has helped South Africa to build up ancillary industries. Before World War II virtually all such stock came from Europe. Today, virtually all needs, excepting heavy locomotives, are built within the Republic. Other similar ancillary industries strengthened by SAR&H needs include cranes, tugs, dining car food supplies and other catering services, and paper. Construction in ports and along railways has involved heavy building equipment as well. The ancillary private industry thus created has, in itself, become a prime defense contractor (tanks and armored cars) and an exporter of railway rolling stock for industrial uses.

As a governmental entity aimed at spreading benefits to the agricultural interior, as well as to the coastal and interior industrial complexes, SAR&H has been operated as a nonprofit undertaking. Many branch lines were constructed into rural areas, and many of these have never been economically justifiable. Parallel road development transport has forced the curtailment or abandonment of many of these lines. However, insofar as urban areas are concerned, traffic density has built up so quickly that both existing rail and trucking facilities of SAR&H have been insufficient to carry the traffic, and serious bottlenecks have resulted both at ports and along internal transport routes. The refusal of the government to permit long-haul private trucking except in emergency situations has protected the monopoly position of SAR&H and has increased bottlenecks. The job reservation policy of the government, made applicable to both port and railway labor, has served to worsen these bottlenecks.

As the largest single employer of labor in the country, SAR&H plays a major economic and social role. In March 1970 total employment by SAR&H was estimated at 222,750. This included some 111,000 Whites and just over 111,000 non-Whites. Total wages paid in 1970 were Rand 416 million. Staff shortages have been an increasingly difficult problem for SAR&H, these shortages created in part by the government's own restrictive job reservation and apartheid policies. Staff losses in all categories have been heavy in recent years, this occurring because of industrial-labor demands elsewhere. It has been particularly difficult to recruit engineers and skilled railwaymen. While training periods are being curtailed, age requirements relaxed, and women and students utilized wherever possible, the major need is for relaxation of "Whites only" standard. This could be most profitably applied in the categories of engineer, brakeman, crane driver, fork lift operator, shunter, and the like. If the government permitted broad employment of Coloureds, Asians, and Blacks in these categories, most of the staff shortages could be alleviated.

Two other major shortages of South African railways facilities must be mentioned. The first is in the transport of its commuter passengers (especially Blacks). The largest proportion of these are carried between township locations to cities—such as from Soweto to Johannesburg or from Umlazi to Durban. The crush on these commuter trains for non-Whites and the large number of train accidents involving numerous deaths and serious injuries have become something of a national scandal. Such incidents, involving so many non-Whites, could easily spark major race riots and, in recent years, have several times threatened to do so. Passengers carried on commuter lines are now reported to be nearing 500 million annually—a figure that has doubled in the past two decades. (Some 230 trains daily handle 225,000 passengers traveling between Soweto and Johannesburg alone.) The SAR&H administration has promised improvements, but such improvements come slowly for non-Whites in South Africa, especially in the face of industrial-commercial priorities.

A final shortage on SAR&H facilities is the lack of rolling stock—particularly bulk ore and tank cars. The petroleum distribution shortages have been relieved by installation of pipelines from Durban to Johannesburg and from Richards Bay to the eastern Transvaal. Large-scale export of minerals in bulk is, at the moment, almost impossible for the railways to handle. Foreign trade sales of this type to prospective customers, such as Japan, have actually been lost in recent months, owing to transport and port shortages. Progress here, too, is limited by lack of both capital and labor. South African ports also face the problem of containerization and specialized handling. This type of freight handling is constantly increasing, and special arrangements are being made at Durban and Capetown for container berths. Present problems can only be solved by long-term planning.

FINANCE

State financial activity and private sector financial activity are a blend in the country's financial institutions, just as they are in the public and private composites of industry. The main concerns of the Republic's financiers are the following: (a) satisfying loan requirements for capital development of both state and private corporations, (b) the maintenance of satisfactory terms of trade to insure a first-class creditworthiness at home and abroad, (c) the maintenance of adequate financial reserves, and (d) if need be, the application of adequate, but not self-defeating, controls. Among these financiers, there is mutual concern over inflation, taxation, investment, and general economic growth. These matters are touched upon in the paragraphs following.

South Africa's monetary system is based on the rand and cents (100 to the rand). The value of the rand (1972) is Rand 1 equals U.S. $1.30. South Africa is a member of the sterling bloc. Her international exchange activities are based primarily on London, Paris, and Zurich. The South African Reserve Bank is the principal central banking institution. In addition to supervising interest and credit and currency requirements, it handles all gold transactions, including sales of bullion abroad.

Although there are some 60 different banking corporations in operation within the country, including commercial and merchant banks, most of the business is done by five large chain banks—Standard, Barclay's, Netherlands, Volkskas, and Trust Bank. Building societies dominate the home-building mortgage market. There has recently been a pronounced increase in the number and size of Afrikaner-owned and -managed financial institutions, ranging from banks to insurance firms and building societies.

Taxation in South Africa is moderate compared with many countries, including Britain and the United States. Rates of taxation in the upper brackets are considerably lower than in those nations. Primary taxes come from customs and excise and from income levies (national and provincial). The withholding tax concept was introduced in 1963, with employers collecting and remitting these taxes and the self-employed making provisional returns.

As with other sectors of her economy, South Africa's financial sector experienced dynamic growth during the past decade. Illustrative has been the growth of the South African Stock Exchange, now listing over 750 stocks. Of these only 20 percent are mining stocks. The greater proportion of quotations are on straight industrials.

During the past decade South African reserves of gold and foreign exchange have been subject to considerable outside attack. One of these hiatus periods occurred after the notorious Sharpeville troubles of March 1960. Immediately thereafter, net outflow of some $270 million occurred as a result of temporary loss of external confidence in the South African internal security. Exchange balances further declined following the South African withdrawal from the British Commonwealth in 1961. More recently, pressure against the Republic's exchange reserves has occurred as a result of international monetary crises, major stock market fluctuations, and uncertainty over the future of gold. The growing imbalance between South Africa's imports and exports has also occasioned a heavy drain on her reserves.

Following upon the sharp but temporary flights of capital experienced in the early 1960's, South Africa had a heavy inflow of foreign investment capital. By 1968 total reserves exceeded $900 million. Thereafter, the so-called two-tier gold system was established by the free world's leading central banks. This action separated the official gold market from the free market for gold. For more than a year South Africa had withheld most of its gold production from the market in anticipation of increased gold prices, then re-entered the market and took advantage of higher free market prices. The Republic's reserves reached a high of $1.7 billion by mid-1969. Later that year the Republic reached an arrangement with the IMF for sales of its gold on both free market and official market. With increased imports and heavy sales of gold on the free market to take advantage of higher prices, the Republic's reserves fell to about $1.2 billion by the end of 1970 and to $750 million by the end of 1971. The country has since reimposed import controls to alleviate the foreign exchange drain and has established heavy excise taxes on luxury imports. Restrictions regarding full repatriation of foreign investment capital (though not of profits) remain in force.

Officials of the South African Reserve Bank, in their annual report on the Republic's economy for fiscal year 1970/71, stated that the economy had suffered a slowdown from the preceding boomtime. They reported a rate of growth in the GDP of 9 percent in 1970/71, as compared with a rate of growth of 12 percent in the preceding year. Despite this slowdown government economists foresee a continuing overall growth rate of 5.5 percent annually for the first half of the 1970-80 decade.[10] They also reported a countervailing factor, this being an all-time high inflow of foreign capital for the year 1970/71. This inflow amounted to Rand 725 million and helped to overcome the high balance of payments deficit being encountered by the Republic's economy. The trade deficit had exceeded Rand 1.084 billion in that year. Even so, some Rand 359 million of gold and foreign reserves had to be used to meet the overall deficit. In late 1971 and 1972, however, there appears to have been some moderation in the situation. Chief causes of the trade gap, as noted elsewhere, have been the combination of high capital goods investment by public and private sectors and high consumer spending. The foreign exchange inflow can be accounted for, in part, by establishment of new business ventures (including the preparations for the yet-to-be-opened TV market). It resulted, also, from reinvestment of some of the high profits accruing to foreign investors in recent years.

The country's adjusted GDP in 1969 exceeded $15 billion, this representing the major inputs of manufacturing, mining, and agriculture. The country's per capita income in the same year was said to be $770. This figure, however, conceals a great disparity between White and non-White personal income. The Financial Mail has estimated that actual annual per capita income in 1969 amounted to $120 for Blacks, while White income was nearly $1,600 in that year. In this connection, it should be noted that the country's cost of living increase, which ran between 3 percent and 4 percent in early years of the last decade, took a sharper rise in recent years. The cost of living increase was reported to have exceeded 6 percent annually in 1970 and 1971 and was expected to be even higher in 1972.

According to the Financial Mail of December 24, 1971, while devaluation gives indication of past mismanagement, that devaluation could also provide a basis for new growth. The magazine contends that internal fiscal measures no longer curtail growth to solve South Africa's balance of payments problems. With the rand now cheaper in terms of all major trading partners, South Africa's adverse trade balance is reduced, and new export prospects are good. In terms of local substitutes, too, imports are less competitive. This provides new opportunities for domestic industry. The main problems here are in controlling wages, inflation, and excessive capital demands. Control of consumer spending, of wages, and an increased use of Black workers is "essential . . ."

FOREIGN INVESTMENT

For the past century South Africa has been the scene of heavy foreign investment. Mining booms, industrial development, and commercial opportunities—all with rich profit margins in comparison to the long-developed nations (such as the United States and the United Kingdom) have encouraged foreign capital movement to the Republic. The facts of her international abrasiveness and broad external criticism to her internal policies have not seriously weakened this inward investment flow, though events such as Sharpeville (1960) and creation of the Republic (1961) have temporarily interrupted that flow.

It is difficult to obtain accurate and up-to-date figures on foreign investment, since the South African government no longer releases them. The most conservative and reliable estimates would place present foreign investment in South Africa in excess of $7 billion. This figure has more than doubled since 1960. The United Kingdom and the United States are the largest investors in the Republic. In 1966 the United Kingdom was reported to total 57 percent of all foreign investments in South Africa, that total then estimated at $2 billion (now estimated at $3.5 billion). At that time the United States was reported to hold about 13 percent of the total. The U.K. share of such investment is reported to be falling, but that of the United States is rising, along with investments of France, West Germany, and Japan. The proportion of U.K. investments is now estimated at roughly 50 percent of the total, with those of the United States about 15 percent. Today, France, West Germany, Switzerland, Italy, the Netherlands, Japan, and Canada are each reputed to own from 3 percent to 5 percent of the pie of South African foreign investments.

There has been a notable rise in the holdings of continental European nations within the Republic. In 1966 the combined holdings of France, Switzerland, and West Germany were approximately $640 million. By 1968 South Africa's total foreign investment liabilities to Western Europe were said to have reached $1.2 billion.

In this connection the South African government has had to seek new capital for its utilities group, for its iron and steel enlargements, and for its local authorities' needs. Foreign loan demands were estimated to be 40 percent higher in 1972 than in the previous year. Recently, ISCOR obtained $200 million from a group of international banks by way of a nine-year loan. Several major American banks declined to participate in this loan syndicate. Of South Africa's outstanding foreign loans most are tied to the European money market and to countries that have recently revalued their currencies. Excluding foreign investments South Africa's total foreign liabilities, public and private, are said to have risen from Rand 3.4 billion in 1965 to Rand 5 billion in 1970. Costs of servicing these debts have risen from Rand 226 million in 1965 to Rand 371 million in 1970. There can be no suspicion that the country might not be able to afford to service its foreign debt, though there is some impression that foreign currency rationing will be essential in the years ahead. Foreign exchange controls are likely if the current rate of growth is to be maintained, and import controls, especially consumer goods, are always in danger of being extended.

Much of the increased direct investment within the Republic under U.S. and U.K. flags comes from profits plowed back. With South Africa going through a period of rapid economic expansion, profit levels have been high, encouraging expansion of old operations and inauguration of new ones. The original major field for foreign investment was, of course, mining. By 1960 the proportion of foreign investment still invested in mining was 33 percent. Investments during recent years, however, have concentrated on manufactures, especially consumer goods. Both public and private sectors have been recipients of foreign capital. In recent years loans have been floated by the South African government corporations and municipalities in West Germany, Switzerland, Italy, the United Kingdom, the United States, the Netherlands, and France. Repayment on these investments obviously constitutes an important burden for South Africa in the context of her balance of payment problem. Of the more than $440 million paid out by South Africa in 1968 to meet these obligations, the United Kingdom and the United States together probably received about two-thirds.

British financial and commercial influences in South Africa are not what they were immediately post-World War II or even prior to formation of the Republic in 1961. However, given the magnitude of her investment, the fact that she is reported to have more than 500 concerns in operation in the country, the fact that she controls two of the largest banking chains (Standard and Barclay's), and uses South Africa as the central distribution point for much of her interAfrican trade gives Britain a continuing powerful financial leverage in the Republic. Thus, Britain still continues to be the most influential of the Republic's foreign investors. It is estimated that about 10 percent of all U.K. investment abroad is in South Africa. Only Australia and Canada rank ahead of South Africa for the British investor. In the mid-1960's UN sources reported that average earnings for Britain from South Africa were running above $170 million annually. Net earnings on U.K. investments in the Republic have been reported as running above 12 percent. This return is said to be 50 percent higher than on other British investments overseas. Mining investment returns to Britain are said to have been averaging 25 percent or more and manufacturing returns about 10 percent.

The New York Times of April 2, 1972, quotes U.S. Department of State sources as saying that some 300 U.S. corporations (including 12 of the 20 largest) now operating in South Africa have investments valued between $750 million and $1 billion. The average yearly return is now running at 17 percent "and contributes handsomely to the plus column of the United States' balance of payments." Private American holdings in the Republic are said to have increased by 80 percent between 1963 and 1969. Indirect investments held by the United States may represent an additional $500 million, this including loans, stockholdings, and deposits.

American investors in the Republic have done extremely well. During the past decade U.S. investments in the mining industry alone have averaged a net return of 16 percent annually. Returns on manufacturing and commercial enterprises are said to run considerably higher, ranging from 12 percent to 30 percent annual net profits, depending on the field of activity. Some 50 percent of U.S. holdings in South Africa are in manufacturing, with 30 percent in mining. The principal American industrial investments are in the field of automobile assembly and manufacture, agricultural equipment, mining equipment, electrical goods, chemicals, oil refining, food processing, and drugs.

In 1968 the United States held in South Africa only 1.1 percent of her total foreign investments. However, this represented more than 40 percent of U.S. investments on the African continent. Rates of return for U.S. investments in the Republic are extraordinarily high compared with U.S. domestic profit margins. It is estimated that during the decade 1960-70, rates of return for all U.S. investment in the Republic averaged 19 percent annually and, as noted previously, are today averaging 17 percent. The average return for the United

States in all its other foreign investments abroad was not above 11 percent annually for the last decade. The African continent as a whole is now reported to produce nearly 10 percent of all U.S. earnings overseas—compared with only 1 percent in 1961.[11]

Until recently, management of American firms in South Africa had been largely in the hands of U.S. citizens. There is an increasing tendency to use South Africans as managers. To date, there are no non-Whites in managerial positions. Among special management problems have been those imposed by the country's aim toward economic self-sufficiency, production of defense items, and general economic nationalism. These developments have been particularly exemplified by demands that certain manufacturers produce bulletproof tires or armored vehicles and that automotive firms swiftly increase their component percentages of domestically produced vehicles of all types.

There is a standing UN arms embargo against South Africa. There is also a standing UN embargo against exports to Rhodesia, this contrasting with the close economic ties existing between Rhodesia and South Africa. These situations raise questions in the UN and elsewhere as to whether U.S. investments in South Africa actually improve or worsen economic and social conditions within the Republic, especially for non-Whites. The claim of benefits for all South Africans, including non-Whites, is often made by U.S. officials in defense of U.S. private investment within the Republic. Until now, the official U.S. view on investment in South Africa has been somewhat ambivalent. The contention has been made that, while neither encouraging nor discouraging such investment, there is a presumption on the part of U.S. officialdom that such investment gives impetus to economic integration, to potential political ferment, and to social change. This "benevolent neutralism" of U.S. officials has become more difficult to defend in recent months in the face of the increasingly harsh apartheid measures of the Republic, the prejudicial job reservations policies, South Africa's drive toward economic nationalism, the divisiveness of the Bantustan program, and the condemnatory attitude of the South African government toward American churchmen, academics, and newsmen. Thus, any defense or even tacit acceptance of additional American investment in South Africa on the part of U.S. officials is becoming less credible.

Indicative of the new situation that U.S. officialdom faces on this matter have been the recent American church-sponsored investigations of labor conditions in American industries in South Africa; the intense criticism of labor policies of U.S. mining houses operating in South-West Africa; and demands by some American clerics, laymen, and students for this officialdom to divest itself of all portfolio stock of U.S. concerns doing business in South Africa. (There are similar demands emanating from Black intellectuals and political circles.) Other challenges may soon come from a series of bills pending in Congress. Some of these call for denial of tax credits to American companies operating in South-West Africa and call for an extension of fair employment practices to non-White South African employees of American companies operating in the Republic. A few American Black leaders state that they would agree to U.S. firms remaining in South Africa but only if they improve the working conditions and social situation of their non-White employees. All this debate centers about the thesis of whether foreign investment in South Africa is capable of moderating apartheid policies there or whether that investment simply bolsters the status quo. The debate may also represent the larger thesis of increasing public demand for social criteria to be met and applied by big business. Thus far, within South Africa it would seem that there has been an official tendency to downgrade both the extent and the power of these outside demands.

Until now, U.S. firms, seeking to improve the situation of their non-White workers in fields of work, pay, and fringe benefits, have operated under the South African constraints of social custom, labor legislation, and apartheid laws—including job reservations. A very few U.S. firms have been progressive in their efforts. Certain firms, in order to advance their own prospects within that country, have not been as progressive as they might possibly be, some through managerial ignorance of any leeway.

The Wall Street Journal of September 22, 1971, makes a telling point on this subject, stating inter alia that

> (US) companies sometimes blame the South African Government for the wide differences in pay between White and non-White employees. This is one of the misconceptions often cited about South Africa. These facts emerge from a study of government regulations, trade union rules and labor-management agreements: There is no limit what a company may pay a Black or any other non-White for a job. A company is free to decide to pay equal wages for equal work. The Government does insist, however, that Blacks not supervise Whites. There are Government job reservations that save certain posts for Whites . . . no legal machinery prevents a company from establishing in-service training to help non-White workers advance . . . Managements are free to establish Black productivity committees that can serve as valuable channels between Executives and Black workers. . . .

An example of what can be done is the so-called Polaroid case. The American manufacturing firm of Polaroid, bowing to demands of its stateside American employees, instructed its South African distributor to upgrade the wages, working conditions, and employment opportunities of its Black workers. The distributor was also instructed to establish an annual sum (from profits) to be used for Black African education.

According to The New York Times of October 31, 1971, the Polaroid effort to "counteract apartheid in South Africa from within the system . . . is a success." Polaroid's distributor, Helmut M. Hirsch, claims the experiment of improving the wages and the job-training prospects of Polaroid's non-White workers has done far more to bring about a civilizing relaxation of prejudice than withdrawal would have done. Hirsch said that his company would attempt, insofar as possible, to pay "the rate for the job . . . but would not contravene Government regulations by placing Blacks in position of authority over Whites. . . ." Polaroid in South Africa is reported to have a work force of about 300, one-half of whom are Blacks.

The Financial Mail of January 14, 1972, reports Polaroid has increased Black workers' salaries by about 21 percent, going up from Rand 75 monthly to Rand 91 monthly. During 1971 eight Black foremen were appointed, these supervising Blacks only. The fund from profits established to train Black workers, as well as to educate young Blacks and to provide cultural exchanges, had an original endowment of Rand 75,000. Early applications for benefits from this fund were said to total nearly 700. The South African government has made no attempt to sabotage the experiment.

It was hoped by many Americans that the Polaroid experience would become a pilot project, inducing other American firms operating in South Africa to follow suit. Thus far, only a few American concerns have done so. Among these are reported to be Ford, General Motors, Chrysler, Norton Abrasives, J. R. Watkins, Chase-Manhattan Bank, Pepsi-Cola, Coca-Cola Corporation, International Business Machines, and Minnesota Mining.[12]

FOREIGN TRADE

South Africa's principal trading partners are the United Kingdom, Rhodesia, Germany, the United States, and Japan. The United Kingdom has ordinarily accounted for about 25 percent of exports from, and imports into, South Africa. In 1970 South Africa imported from the United Kingdom goods valued at Rand 560 million, and exports to the United Kingdom totaled Rand 446 million. These figures are likely to be seriously affected by entry of Britain into the Common Market. In fact, recent statistics on South African exports to Britain have already shown a considerable decline. Some accounting for the decline in export value bound for Britain is represented by declining prices in primary goods, such as wool and metals. Some, too, is accounted for by the recent South African devaluation. Of some consequence, however, is the fact that the United Kingdom sent 52 trade missions to South Africa between 1966 and 1971 in order to boost U.K. exports. These efforts have obviously paid off, as Britain is planning an additional 20 missions during 1972 alone.

The United States has consistently supplied about 17 percent of South Africa's imports in recent years and takes 7 percent of her exports. South Africa's trade with Germany and Japan is increasing. In 1970 two-way trade with these nations was Rand 480 million and Rand 400 million, respectively. On the African continent Rhodesia is by all odds South Africa's best customer. In the face of UN economic sanctions against Rhodesia and South Africa's undercover help to her neighbor, up-to-date figures on this trade are difficult to come by. In 1968 South Africa reportedly exported to Rhodesia Rand 103.5 million and imported from that country goods valued at Rand 81 million. In anticipation of losses of exports in the Common Market area and as a means of building her political position internationally, South Africa has recently been making stringent efforts to expand her trading relationships in Latin America, in the Far East, and on the African continent.

In 1970 South Africa's total imports were valued at $3.6 billion, and her exports were valued at $2.1 billion in the same year. The export figures exclude gold sales that are used to offset unfavorable trade balances. The foregoing trade figures represent the total for the southern African customs zone. This zone includes South-West Africa and the independent ministates of Botswana, Lesotho, and Swaziland. The Republic's share of the trade figures, export and import, regularly runs about 80 percent of the total.

Major exports include minerals, precious and semiprecious stones, fruit and vegetable products, prepared foodstuffs, tobacco, textiles, machinery, chemical and allied products, animal products, paper, and so forth.

Major imports include machinery; electrical equipment; transport equipment; textiles; mineral products, including petroleum; chemicals; optical, photographic, and musical equipment; plastics; and so forth.

Main U.S. exports to South Africa and South-West Africa totaled $563 million in 1970, rising from $506 million in 1969 and $456 million in 1968. These goods included machinery, textiles, rice, and petroleum products. The 1970 figure represented one-third of all U.S. exports (1.4 billion) to the African continent.[13]

U.S. imports from South Africa and South-West Africa in 1970 totaled $288 million, compared with $243 million in 1969 and $256 million in 1968. These goods included minerals, diamonds, wool, hides, sugar, and fish.[14]

The United States had an increasingly favorable balance of trade with South Africa through 1970. In that year the net balance favoring the United States exceeded $275 million. It is likely that final 1971 and 1972 figures will not prove so favorable to the United States, mainly because of the American East and West Coast dock strikes. However, long-term trade prospects between the two nations remain favorable. This results from the fact that American industry is in need of South African metals (manganese, chrome, copper, gold, diamonds, and platinum), as well as animal products (hides, skins, and wool) and fish (especially crayfish, or South African rock lobster). In turn, South Africa needs from the U.S. heavy machinery, electronic goods (particularly computers), components for the South African branches of American car manufacturers, and high-quality petroleum products, such as lubricants. With respect to future U.S.-South African trade, the effects of devaluation, of consumer curbs on imports into South Africa, and the influence of the European Common Market are unknown quantities. Despite trade impediments on both sides of the Atlantic, with government-sponsored expansion in the capital sector (in fields such as iron and steel expansion), American manufacturers should continue to find good markets in South Africa for some time to come.

In the controversial business-political atmosphere of South Africa, U.S. commercial interests and efforts have been ambivalent. Given the recent economic dynamism of the South African scene, the United States could undoubtedly have sold additional exports of industrial-commercial goods. However, in the face of UN pressures, church pressures, political pressures, and the U.S. domestic race situation, the United States has not always pursued an agressive program (including government-sponsored trade fairs) to insure expansion of U.S. sales to the Republic. In the past two years, however, given the massive increase in the U.S. foreign trade deficit, that position vis-à-vis South Africa seems to have been tacitly modified. Until recently, given the difficult racial tensions within the Republic and their influence on the American domestic scene, U.S. government officials viewed critically any long-term Eximbank loan applications from American producers selling to South Africa. It is, therefore, extremely interesting to note a recent change in U.S. policy as regards Eximbank credits for South Africa. In January 1972 U.S. government approval was given for an Eximbank loan guarantee of $48.6 million, covering the purchase of American diesel locomotives, this payable over a ten-year period.[15]

It should be noted that trade boycotts by other nations have been more of an irritant to South Africa than a real menace. Until now,

African continental nations (excluding Rhodesia) have accounted for less than 10 percent of all South Africa's foreign trade. However, this trade has been increasing, especially that with Malawi, Ivory Coast, Ghana, and Gabon. Total South African exports to Africa in 1970 were Rand 264 million, and her exports therefrom were Rand 131 million.

Thus, primary boycotts seem to be of little avail. However, secondary boycotts of airline (airport transit) and shipping facilities have sometimes been effective, necessitating costly rerouting of South African Airways flights around African countries where overflight rights are unavailable. However, even in this area, those countries that could be most effective in secondary boycotts (Kenya and Ivory Coast, among others) are reluctant to lose good revenue from South Africa.

CHAPTER

7

THE LABOR SCENE

Despite apartheid claims and legislation to the contrary, there has been a steady movement toward economic integration of White and non-White workers in South Africa during the past decade. More than one-third of all South Africans are employed. Some 70 percent of all nonagricultural workers and 85 percent of all agricultural workers are non-White. The largest group of workers (2.96 million) are in agriculture, forestry, and fishing, followed by services (2.86 million), manufacturing (1.16 million), mining (650,000), and construction (412,000). Excluding agriculture there were 987,000 White and 2.561 million non-White workers employed in the nation in 1960. By 1970 Whites employed totaled 1.283 million and non-Whites 3.733 million. Thus, in 1960 Whites totaled 36 percent of the nonagricultural working force. In 1970, however, the proportion of Whites had fallen to 30 percent in that category. This drop occurred despite governmental efforts to maintain job reservations curbs, despite administrative efforts to reverse the influx of Blacks into urban areas, and despite the general increased levels of both population and employment.

Employment in agricultural pursuits in 1969 totaled Whites, 20,566; Coloureds, 227,050; Asians, 6,410, and Blacks, 1.352 million, including owners who worked. In the same year farm population (including owners who worked) totaled 3.9 million. Of that figure Whites numbered 381,000; Coloureds numbered 452,000; Asians, 9,000; and Blacks, 3.147 million.

A detailed analysis of the country's labor situation appearing in Johannesburg's Sunday Times (January 31, 1971) contended that the apartheid thesis is obsolete in the face of the economic facts. It cited services, manufacturing, mining etc. as examples, to wit:

In services (railways, government departments, banking, finance, commerce, wholesale and retail, professions) Whites employed in 1960 totaled 642,290 and non-Whites 1.370 million. In 1970 Whites so employed totaled 871,000 and non-Whites 1.992 million. (Thus, the proportion of White employees declined from 33 percent to 30 percent, despite the additional employment of some 800,000 new workers.)

In 1960 the clothing industry employed 7,240 Whites and 36,687 non-Whites. By 1970 it employed 10,577 Whites and 104,365 non-Whites. (The ratio of Whites here decreased from one-sixth of the working force to less than one-tenth.)

In the metal products industry Whites employed in 1960 numbered 23,253, rising to 34,322 in 1970. In the same decade non-Whites so employed rose from 36,913 to 102,588.

In the construction industry White employees numbered 72,461 in 1960 and non-Whites 203,683. In 1970 the number of Whites had dwindled to 59,400 but non-White employment had grown to 353,000.

In mining and quarrying the number of Whites employed increased from 61,748 in 1960 to 62,689 in 1970. Non-Whites so employed increased from 553,401 in 1960 to 588,742 in 1970.

In textiles Whites employed numbered 5,150 in 1960, rising to 8,100 in 1970. Non-White employees numbered 29,185 in 1960, rising to 73,909 in 1970. There, the proportion of White employees fell from 16 percent to ten percent of the total.

In the electrical machinery field White employees numbered 13,224 in 1960, rising to 18,100 in 1970. During the same decade the numbers of non-White employees rose from 11,669 to 25,610.

In the transport equipment field White employees numbered 32,970 in 1960, dropping to 29,511 in 1970. During the same decade non-White employment rose from 22,587 to 51,332.

In paper products employees, numbering 4,526 Whites in 1960, rose to 7,388 in 1970. During the same decade non-White employees rose from 10,987 to 22,298. (Here, the proportion of White employees fell from 30 percent to 24 percent of the total.)

In the printing trade Whites employed in 1960 numbered 16,151. That figure rose to 17,722 in 1970. During the same period non-White employment rose from 8,745 to 16,110 in 1970. (In 1960 Whites represented about 66 percent of the total. By 1970 the percentage of Whites to non-Whites was almost equal.)

In 1960 Whites so employed in the furniture industry numbered 5,153, rising to 5,366 in 1970. Non-Whites employed in the field numbered 12,502 in 1960, rising to 28,999 in 1970. (Thus, the proportion of Whites to non-Whites fell from 30 percent to less than 14 percent.)

One of the few industries showing a decline in numbers of both White and non-White workers was the tobacco industry. This clearly reflected results of automation.

In the manufacturing field generally, overall employment figures also present a clear picture. White employment in 1960 totaled 210,702, rising to 277,288 in 1970. During the same decade non-White employment more than doubled, rising from 433,407 to 883,078.

Beyond the usual problem of economic growth, adequate capital, inflation, increasingly high wage and price levels, skilled manpower shortages, and unstable markets—problems that beset all capitalist countries—South Africa has yet one more problem, that of "job reservations." This problem is self-imposed and is considered an essential underpinning of the apartheid concept. Job reservations legislation, embodied in a number of acts described in subsequent pages, provides differing scales of wages and working conditions for Whites, in contrast to those applicable to non-Whites. The same legislation reserves certain types of work for Whites alone, prohibiting intrusion into these work categories of non-Whites, particularly Blacks. It also prohibits supervision of Whites by non-Whites. These prohibitions constitute a major limiting factor to normal growth in many industries. It has already demonstrated its harmful effect in such areas as transport, stevedoring, manufacturing, commerce and mining. Thus, it provides special protection to lower-echelon White workers, such as railwaymen, shop foremen, mechanics, truck drivers, fork-lift operators, and crane drivers. This group of workers, being mainly Afrikaner in background, has successfully protected itself in this way from the emergence, rising expectations, and rising capabilities of Blacks, Asians, and Coloureds. It has been estimated by reputable observers that only 3 percent to 5 percent of the total labor force of the country has been affected by legal exemptions and illegal circumvention of the job reservation legislation. Job reservations are invariably designed to protect White workers from non-White competition. However, labor shortages, especially in skilled and semiskilled fields, have brought on a rising demand from industry and commerce for relaxation of governmental curbs on employment of non-White laborers. Though the government appears to be making some spotty and hesitant adaptations to these demands, there is, as yet, no overall remedy to this situation in sight. The government has permitted employment of a few Asian and Black fork-lift drivers on South African docks, but, as yet, it refuses to permit employment of Coloured, Asian, and Black crane operators, railway brakemen, or engineers. The government refuses to permit extensive employment of Black drivers of heavy-duty trucks and refuses to permit employment of Black African barmen or non-White taxi drivers for White customers.

The recent parliamentary revelation that 15,000 railway jobs, previously classified as White, have now been filled by non-Whites, has led to further perplexity among industrialists and bitterness among White railwaymen. The new determination permits Coloureds, Asians, and Blacks to become "train compilers" rather than "shunters." As such, they are under White supervision and paid less than White shunters. (In this work White shunters now receive a minimum of Rand 160 per month. Coloureds and Asians will get Rand 120, and Blacks will receive Rand 100.)[1]

Contrasted with all other factors, race is the most common denominator in employment, promotion, and opportunity to learn a trade. Practically, this has assured that, despite pressures to open labor ranks because of shortage of labor, higher-paying jobs, skilled jobs, and all supervisory jobs are reserved for Whites. Different pay scales also prevail, with higher pay going to Whites, intermediate wage levels set for Coloureds and Asians, and lowest pay scales for Blacks. Working conditions for non-Whites, but especially Blacks, are considerably inferior. This comes, in part, from the fact that the Blacks do not have the right to strike or bargain collectively. Working conditions, including pay and fringe benefits for Whites, compare favorably with those of the most highly industrialized European countries.

Thus far, only ten percent of the entire working force of South Africa is unionized. Of the total union membership over 70 percent are Whites. Most of the remainder are Coloureds and Asians, there being no recognized Black unions. The 1971 Survey of Race Relations reports a total of 182 unions. Of that number 90 are White unions, 49 are Coloured unions, and 43 are mixed (White, Coloured, and Asian) unions. Membership in Whites-only unions numbers 350,191. Membership of Whites in mixed unions numbers 54,841. Total White union membership is 405,032. Coloured union membership 71,481; Coloureds and Asians combined in mixed unions number 110,729. Total union membership of Coloureds and Asians is 182,210.

The slow growth and relatively passive history of labor unions in South Africa since the end of World War II results in large measure from the fact that workers seek to gain protection from intrusion and upgrading of non-White members by governmental action. For this, they sacrifice some of their own militancy. Though, to date, trade union officials are forbidden by law to engage openly in national political activity, trade union leaders are bound to become an increasingly important political force within the Republic.

All Blacks are prohibited from collective union organization and the right to strike or to bargain collectively. It should be added that curtailment of educational opportunities for Blacks, including lack of free compulsory education, governmental insistence on the vernacular (tribal dialect) teaching in lower grades, and closure of White universities and professional schools to Blacks all create additional unnatural barriers to natural growth of Black labor forces and skills. (These barriers are described in detail in chapters on apartheid, Bantustans, and the cultural scene in this book.)

Some trade unions assist on negotiating wage levels on behalf of the Blacks. In general, however, in lieu of unions, the work complaints of Blacks are legally handled only by central, regional, or local labor boards or committees composed only of Whites. The Workmen's Compensation Act, major social security legislation, and retirement or hospitalization schemes also generally exclude Blacks. Welfare measures, when applicable to Blacks, are usually handled through central government departments, as, for example, departments of Bantu Administration or Community Services.

Until recently there were four main trade union groupings in South Africa. Two of these have been forced out of existence, and only two remain. (A number of other powerful independent trade unions are operative, but they are not actively associated with the trade union councils.) The two trade union groups now disbanded were the racially mixed, left-wing South African Congress of Trade Unions (SACTU) and the all-Black Federation of Free African Trade Unions of South Africa (FOFATSA).

The largest and most active of trade union groupings is the Trade Union Council of South Africa (TUCSA). Its membership in 1970 was reported to be 193,000. Its membership comprises Whites, Coloureds, and Asians, but no Blacks. TUCSA opposes governmental political interference in the labor movement, and TUCSA officials are dedicated anti-Communists. TUCSA has been anxious to keep up affiliations with international and American labor organizations, but this has been difficult because of the international drive for sanctions against South Africa and its domestic organizations.

TUCSA succeeded in remaining multiracial (including Blacks) until 1969, when it finally bowed to governmental and public and internal pressures and dropped its Black affiliates. Many TUCSA leaders still support the rate for the job and object to the industrial color bar and job reservations. However, advocacy of certain of these programs on behalf of Blacks has brought some of the more progressive TUCSA leaders into open conflict with the central government. The government has consistently opposed formation of Black unions and, in fact, has been hostile to the growth and power of organized labor.

The second large trade union grouping, the South Africa Confederation of Labour, is made up of the Co-ordinating Council of South African Trade Unions, the South African Federation of Trade Unions, and the Federal Consultative Committee of SAR&H staff associations. In 1969 this grouping was reported to represent 27 different unions, numbering 183,781 members, all Whites. The strength of the South Africa Council of Labour has increased considerably in recent years, especially through its association with the South

African Iron and Steel and Allied Industries' Union and Federation of Mine Production Workers. The grouping has gained additional members by altering its constitution to permit affiliation of individual trade unions, as well as federations. This move had the apparent goal of picking up individual unions that had broken away from TUCSA over the issue of Black African membership in that body. This exclusively White confederation supports the Nationalist government and its policies. There is some divergence of views among members, including conciliations and political powers. Most members, however, agree on the thesis of job reservations.

Labor relations and management-labor associations are controlled by three major legislative enactments—the Industrial Conciliation Act of 1924, the Wages Act of 1925, and the Mines and Work Amendment Act of 1926. All these were passed in the 1920's but have since been amended. The first of these set up consultation machinery between trade unions and employers. Providing for settlement of wage disputes, it gives White unionists the right to engage in negotiation of all wage rates, including those for non-Whites. Blacks are not permitted to engage in these discussions but are bound by final terms. The Wages Act set minimum wage rates for all industries in which workers were insufficiently well-organized to undertake collective bargaining. The Mines and Work Amendment Act set up job reservations policy, entrenching the principle of racial job discrimination in the mines.

The subsequent and highly important amendments to the Industrial Conciliation Act in 1956 provided for enforcement of job reservations for particular racial groups and enforcement of racial separation within trade unions. This legislation created the necessary machinery to reserve partially or fully certain types of work for certain races. Differing stipulations may be made for different industries, trades, or geographic areas. The philosophy of this "job reservation" is stated by South African official information sources as "insuring that in a country where the inhabitants are of differing levels of civilization, there shall not be unfair competition. It is therefore a precaution against inter-racial competition. . . ." Under that legislation a five-member board advises appropriate Cabinet ministers, who can recommend that specific jobs be reserved to members of specific races.

The application of apartheid to labor union membership has prohibited registration and activities of any union open to workers of all races. No mixed unions are permitted, unless special permission is given. Separate meetings are required for White and Non-White (Coloured and Asian) members.

There are yet other important pieces of legislation that constitute major impediments to non-White labor (especially the Blacks) through pass laws, control of migrant labor, and establishment of ceilings or distribution on that labor. Some of these are as follows:

The Bantu Urban Areas Amendment Act of 1956 provided power to local authorities to deport Black workers from areas where their presence was considered detrimental to the maintenance of peace and order.

The Physical Planning and Utilization of Resources Act of 1967 gave ministerial authority to direct siting of industries and allocation of labor.

The Bantu Laws Amendment Act of 1970 (revising earlier legislation of 1964 and 1967) aimed at the prohibition of employment of Blacks in certain jobs that might lead to labor integration and possible racial strife. Under this legislation the minister of Bantu administration may prohibit the performance of work by, or employment of, a Bantu: (a) in a specified area, (b) in a specified class of employment, (c) in a specified trade, or (d) in the service of a specified employer or class of employers. Parliamentary opponents of the bill, notably the Progressive voice, Helen Susman, noted that this bill provided to the minister of Bantu administration even wider powers with respect to job reservations than were already possessed by the minister of labour.

The Bantu Affairs Administration Act of 1971 gave the minister of Bantu administration authority to declare any area outside the homelands a Bantu administration area. Boards operating thereunder (with ministerial guidance) lay out lands, control movement of Bantu laborers between administrative areas, distribute laborers, and establish residence requirements for all Blacks in those areas. This legislation reemphasises the 72-hour limit for "nonresident" and migrant Blacks.

A new Bantu Labour (Contributions) Bill was introduced into Parliament early in 1972. This bill proposes consolidation and raising of present employment levies. Under this bill the government intends to tax all Black African workers outside the homeland the sum of rand 1 monthly from their all too meager wages. At the same time the employers of those Blacks may be required to pay the sum of rand 2.50 monthly for each such Black African on the employers' payrolls. Funds of these taxes will reportedly be used for Bantu development.

South African officials contend that there have been no major strikes in the Republic during the past 20 years. (The recent Ovambo strike in South-West Africa, to which area South African labor legislation has not fully applied, will be discussed in later paragraphs.) The reason for the few strikes can be ascribed to restrictive legislation on the books. For White, Coloured, and Asian workers the maximum penalty for illegal striking is rand 200, plus one year's

TABLE 1

Employment in South African Mines, by Race, 1970

Race	All Mines	Gold Mines Only	Coal Mines Only
Whites	83,734	39,386	8,173
Coloureds	6,956	352	46
Asians	629	20	274
Blacks	612,140	386,113	67,249
Total	703,459	425,871	75,742

Source: South African government news sources and South African Institute of Race Relations.

imprisonment. The maximum penalty for Blacks is rand 1,000, plus three years' imprisonment. Whites, Coloureds, and Asians are permitted to strike legally only within narrow limits. Blacks are not permitted the right to strike legally under any circumstances.

Yet another important element in any discussion of the South African labor scene is that of the great disparity in wages—unequal pay for equal work (wage differentials based on race). It is difficult to obtain up-to-date and comprehensive evidence on this point. However, the composite of available information shown in Tables 1 and 2 presents a fairly clear picture of the disparities.

TABLE 2

Monthly Averages of Salaries, Wages, and Allowances of South African Mine Workers, by Race, 1970 (in rand)

Race	All Mines	Gold Mines Only	Coal Mines Only
Whites	341	354	350
Coloureds	71	90	73
Asians	93	87	79
Blacks	19	17	18

Note: Contradictory statements as to the value of perquisites for Blacks (including food, housing, medical services, recreation, and some clothing) range from rand 7.50 to rand 30 monthly.

TABLE 3

Number of Employees and Salaries in Manufacturing Industry, by Race, South Africa, 1969
(in rand)

Race	Numbers Employed	Average Salaries and Wages per Head
Whites	266,000	262
Coloureds	176,000	64
Asians	66,00	69
Blacks	556,000	48

Source: South African Institute of Race Relations, A Survey of Race Relations in South Africa (Johannesburg: The Institute, 1971).

As a leading light in the gold-mining industry, the Anglo-American Corporation recently reported increases in wages for both White and Black mine workers. The average White miner's wages will now approximate rand 360 monthly. Wages for Black workers, following increases, will approximate rand 21.84 per month, or a basic 84 cents per shift. Boss boys will earn rand 48.36 monthly.[2]

Commenting favorably upon these increases Francis Wilson, expert on South African mine labor, is quoted in the Durban Sunday Tribune of August 15, 1971, as follows:

> . . . welcomes Anglo-American's decision to raise Black miners' pay. . . . He had described as "scandalous" the increasing disparity between White and Black laborers' pay on the mines . . . [claiming] that taking rates of inflation into account, the Black mine worker was today receiving the same pay as that received by his grandfather in 1911. Wilson also said that value of food and lodging paid Black workers combined with their pay makes their income still less than that received by Black workers in government service. . . .

The Guardian of September 25, 1971, reports that manufacturing industry wages for Whites were rand 238, while those for Blacks were rand 44. (See Tables 3 and 4 for numbers of employees and salaries in the manufacturing industry and construction field.)

In the metals and engineering sector figures available for 1968 show 76,000 Whites, 15,000 Coloureds, 3,000 Asians, and 177,000

Blacks employed. Some Blacks are reportedly being paid from 19 cents to 22 cents hourly, averaging rand 37 to rand 43 monthly for a 30-day month. (See Tables 5, 6, 7, 8, and 9 for figures on employment and wages in banks, wholesale trade, and retail trade, as well as for figures on employment and wages paid by the central government and SAR&H.)

In the field of agriculture, employment is currently in a hiatus stage, since the "squatter" and labor-tenant systems are being abandoned by reason of government intervention. Here, the government seeks to return illegal Black workers to tribal reserves, permitting White farmers to retain on their farms only specified and absolutely required workers. For temporary and harvest requirements the White farm employers will be required to arrange for importation from the reserves. In the case of large employers, such as the sugarcane industry, special arrangements for importation of labor on a contract basis are made. According to the South African Institute of Race Relations wages and payments in kind are now reported to average about rand 20 monthly on most private farms. According to South African Sugar Association officials the wages of Black African workers in the sugar fields average rand 38 monthly, including overtime bonuses, but excluding housing, food, and smaller perquisites. The Natal Mercury (Durban) of October 3, 1968, reported that there were at least 150,000 African families on Natal farms who were in danger of eviction as a result of government resettlement policies. The paper reported that these workers were "refusing to accept wages of Rand 6 monthly offered by many farmers for regular work.

TABLE 4

Number of Employees and Salaries in Construction Field, by Race, South Africa, May 1971 (in rand)

Race	Numbers Employed	Gross Salaries and Wages
Whites	60,800	326
Coloureds	47,400	110
Asians	5,300	144
Blacks	272,000	49

Source: South African Institute of Race Relations, A Survey of Race Relations in South Africa (Johannesburg: The Institute, 1971).

TABLE 5

Number of Employees and Salaries in Banks, by Race, South Africa, 1971 (in rand)

Race	Numbers Employed	Monthly Salaries and Wages
Whites	43,778	258
Coloureds	1,303	73
Asians	300	108
Blacks	5,269	61

Labor tenants refusing to accept wages on conditions laid down by farmers were then considered illegal squatters . . ."

Recent parliamentary discussion re apprenticeship training programs for the various races furnish an important sidelight on the preceding industrial-technical labor situation.[3] The following table indicates the number of apprenticeships registered:

Year	Whites	Coloureds	Asians	Blacks
1960	6,426	522	69	—
1971	9,140	1,596	604	—

Wages of domestic servants vary according to geographic locations within the Republic, Johannesburg reporting higher wages than those paid in smaller cities. Such wages are reported to range

TABLE 6

Number of Employees and Salaries in Wholesale Trades, by Race, South Africa, 1971 (in rand)

Race	Numbers Employed	Monthly Salaries and Wages
Whites	76,000	281
Coloureds	18,900	76
Asians	9,200	108
Blacks	80,000	54

TABLE 7

Number of Employees and Salaries in
Retail Trade, by Race, South Africa, 1971
(in rand)

Race	Numbers Employed	Monthly Salaries and Wages
Whites	119,300	151
Coloureds	30,200	59
Asians	16,000	91
Blacks	108,400	43

TABLE 8

Number of Employees and Salaries Paid by
South African Government, by Race, 1971
(in rand)

Race	Numbers Employed	Monthly Salaries and Wages
Whites	102,779	293
Coloureds	32,000	145
Asians	7,578	195
Blacks	145,521	52

TABLE 9

Number of Employees and Salaries Paid by
South African Railways and Harbors, by Race, 1970
(in rand)

Race	Numbers Employed	Monthly Salaries and Wages
White	111,006	295
Coloureds	14,623	71
Asians	1,244	54
Blacks	96,845	52

Note: These figures include valuation of perquisites and allowances for all racial groups.

from rand 10 to rand 40 in metropolitan areas monthly, with wages in kind estimated at rand 20 monthly.

The Sunday Tribune (Durban) September 12, 1971, reported that "a recent study of general employment of Blacks in the Soweto complex of Johannesburg showed that only 32% of Soweto Blacks earned more than rand 60 [US $78] per month . . . and that even a family of five required rand 67 monthly to rise above the poverty subsistence line." One-half of the Black families in Durban metropolitan area are reported to be below the poverty datum line. The present official minimum wage rate for unskilled laborers in Durban is Rand 7.25 per week.

The 1969 Survey of Race Relations reports that recent estimates by market researchers show that Blacks constitute 67 percent of the total populace of the Republic but receive only 18 percent of the cash income. The Whites, constituting 19 percent of the population, received 73 percent of its income. Average monthly income works out at Rand 95 per head for whites and Rand 7 per head for Blacks.

A study of Asian households in Durban showed monthly living costs for each family averaging rand 73.51; however, more than one-half of all Asian households in Durban had incomes below that amount and, therefore, are below the poverty datum line. In Capetown a survey of Coloured families showed 30 percent were below the poverty datum line.

It will be recalled that South Africa's Industrial Conciliation Act excludes Black workers from the definition of workers for the purposes of industrial agreements. In South-West Africa workers in general and Ovambos in particular are reported by recent press stories to be treated as "little better than slaves." Their wages, tenure, housing, and food have been determined wholly by recruiting agencies and their employers. The Blacks have had no say. The U.S. News and World Report of February 7, 1972, stated that the Ovambo miners were earning an average of less than $13 monthly. Many of the workers were employed by the American-operated mining complex at Tsumeb. In South Africa paternalistic White officials attend industrial council negotiations to put in a good word for the Black worker and occasionally succeed in getting some concessions. By and large, however, the South African Black has to be satisfied with what he gets, since it is illegal for him to strike. In South-West Africa, surprisingly, South African antistrike legislation was not applicable. As a result the largest single group of Black employees, the Ovambos (numbering 13,000) recently struck. The strike involved some disturbances and conflicts between police and workers. The South African government has considerably strengthened its security forces in the area.

The dispute showed up glaring inequities in the South-West Africa labor system. The Ovambos sought the following: (a) improvement in their employment contracts, (b) more freedom in doing the kind of work they wanted, (c) freedom to change jobs without fear of landing in jail, (d) freedom to have their families with them (e) payment of the rate for the job irrespective of race, (f) improvement of food and transport, and (g) removal of barricades between Ovamboland and Angola to permit access to families.

As a result of the Ovambo demands the South African government was forced to come to the conference table and to sanction a new deal for the laborers. Anachronistic labor agreements were overturned. In an agreement signed June 20, 1971, the South African government, now acting on behalf of the workers, overthrew a notorious recruiting arrangement and placed labor relations on an official "treaty" basis between the Ovambo-Kavongo tribal governments and the Government of South Africa (operating through the ministry of Bantu administration). The Ovambo government assumed the recruiting function. The new pact will also make it easier for workers to change their jobs. Length of contract was shortened. Working conditions (including food, housing, and wages) are to be improved. Improvements are promised for "maintaining family ties." The South-West African Bantustan authorities accepted the new arrangements, and the strikers returned to work. The new agreement was to go into effect about February 1, 1972.

The strike brought South-West African mining and much of its agricultural work to a virtual halt. Commerce in the capital city of Windhoek was brought to a halt as well. The Ovambo Legislative Council supported the strikers in the face of government action. It was found impossible to recruit other Black workers in the area. With the virtual collapse of the South-West African economy the government was forced to accede to many of the strikers' demands. In this situation, for the first time, Blacks and Whites consulted, and at least tentatively agreed on labor reforms. The precedent is an unusual one for South African White officials.

It might ordinarily be presumed that, lacking sufficient manpower, the government would encourage massive immigration of skilled labor into South and South-West Africa. Asian immigration is prohibited altogether. Black African immigration is permitted only under contractual labor time limits for migrant Africans from nearby territories. Migration is not permitted for the families of those migrants, and when the contract is completed, it must either be renewed or the worker is deported. White immigration is encouraged, and partially subsidized by government, for skilled workers, artisans, and professionals. These come mainly from the United Kingdom, the Netherlands, West Germany, Belgium, Austria, and

Switzerland. White immigration from southern Europe, especially from the Catholic countries, is tacitly or openly discouraged. According to the South African Bulletin of Statistics (South African Government Publication, Pretoria, 1971) 41,523 immigrants entered the Republic in 1970 and more than 300, 000 entered during the past decade. During recent years White immigration has averaged above 3,000 persons (workers and families) monthly. However, there is an offsetting outflow—emigration—of about 1,000 persons monthly. Thus, the net inflow barely exceeds more than 30,000 annually.

In a speech made at the University of Stellenbosch on March 21, 1972, Harry Oppenheimer, chairman of Anglo-American Corporation, made a telling indictment of South Africa's economic and labor policies. Inter alia, he said:

> Inflation can be tackled in two ways: by cutting back demand or by increasing production . . . the second alternative, if it is practical, must be preferable. Why is it then that the authorities in South Africa have had to concentrate their efforts, through credit control and the private sector, on throttling back the economy, rather than on stimulating it? Efforts, incidentally that have been largely ineffective because of the failure to keep public expenditures under control or to finance it in a non-inflationary way.
>
> Inflation in South Africa is characterized by an acute shortage of skilled labour and it is because of this limiting factor that it is proving so difficult to get the economy moving ahead again. Last year, for example, production by private industry grew only 3% against a planned figure of 6 1/2%. . . . We have a huge reservoir of Coloured, Indian and, above all Bantu workers, who, because they cannot obtain the necessary training . . . and because they are prevented by legal or conventional barriers, or by the action of some White trade unions, are unable to make the full contribution of which they are naturally capable to the national growth and the improvement of the standard of living. . . . The basic answer to our economic challenge is to turn to account this huge potential national asset . . . [this] is a plain, obvious truth . . . a country that refuses to allow something like 80% of its labour force to do the best work of which they are capable cannot hope to progress as it should or to hold its place in a highly competitive world. . . .

Commenting on Oppenheimer's statement, the Financial Mail of March 24, 1972, states that what is needed by South African business and labor are the following: (a) availability of Black African workers in established industrial areas; (b) future stability and permanence of Black workers resident in those areas; (c) freedom of industrialists to expand their undertakings, if necessary, by increasing the numbers of their Black employees in response to opportunities; (d) provision of technical training for urban Blacks; and (e) government support of trade union cooperation with management on a program of training for Blacks.

CHAPTER

8

THE CULTURAL-RELIGIOUS SCENE

Earlier pages of this book have sought to analyze the main sectors of the social milieu resulting from apartheid—to describe the racially compartmentalized life-style of South Africa and the disparities in the economic life of Whites as contrasted with non-Whites. This chapter will set forth views of other important South African cultural institutions—educational, religious, and communications.

EDUCATION

Measurements of progress in South African education are somewhat contradictory and confusing. Available statistics[1] clearly show a massive increase in school population over the past 20 years. Figures also show a sharp proportionate growth for non-White students over White students. Not evident in these statistics, however, are the discouraging factors of inferior quality of education for non-Whites and difficulties attendant upon obtaining an education that confront non-Whites. Illustrative is the fact that Blacks alone are required to pay tuition fees and to buy their own books through the elementary and junior secondary levels. Black parents, unlike parents of other race groups, must provide their children with most of their textbooks and writing materials. They are also required to pay small sums monthly for community school construction loan costs and to pay an annual tuition fee in secondary schools.

By contrast, for Whites, Coloureds, and Asians, schooling is free and compulsory, and books are free through secondary levels. Further, mainly for financial reasons, the dropout rate for Black pupils after the first four years of schooling is extraordinarily high. School buildings in non-White communities are grossly overcrowded, and many Black communities are required to build their own schools. Double sessions and platoon classes are common. In addition, as indicated in paragraphs following, the disparity of wages paid to White teachers in contrast to Black teachers is great, despite similar requirements for academic backgrounds. Finally, as a result of the apartheid doctrine requiring separate (and as yet unequal) universities for all racial groups, there have been created separate universities for Blacks, Asians, and Coloureds. The strengths and weaknesses of these separate institutions cannot yet be measured fully.

In 1946 there were approximately 500,000 Whites and 500,000 non-Whites in the country's elementary and secondary schools. This ratio had altered materially by 1970. Nearly 3.5 million non-Whites (including 2.7 million Blacks) and 862,000 Whites were reported in school attendance. General growth of education for all races is also shown in the increased number of teachers, from 46,000 in 1948 to 93,000 in 1970. This last figure includes about 46,000 Black teachers. Teaching staffs of universities and technical schools increased by two and one-half times during the two decades—but this figure is diluted by the establishment of the non-White universities and teacher-training colleges. While White university students trebled between 1948 and 1968, non-White students in higher grades increased by only 50 percent.

The case is made by South African authorities that general education of Whites and non-Whites, as well as overall literacy rates, are now the best in Africa. The South African Institute of Race Relations in its 1971 Survey of Race Relations records UN findings that 49.5 percent of the 8.6 million Blacks over the age of 15 in the Republic were literate. This figure requires comparison with recent educational statistics in some of the more progressive Black African states, such as Ghana, Nigeria, Kenya, and even Lesotho. The comparative literacy rate for Lesotho alone in 1969 was reported to be 75 percent. However, there is no doubt that the proportions of Black African children and the number of literates in the Republic have grown enormously over the past two decades. There remains, however, a real disparity between the amounts being spent by the state on White education per capita in comparison to sums being spent for non-White pupils, particularly the Blacks.

Total educational expenditures for the Republic in 1970 (including the Transkei and all races) amounted to about Rand 371 million. This is estimated at 3.5 percent of GNP and about 12 percent of total governmental expenditures. There are no recent official statistics available for the exact proportion of that budget that is allocated for White students, although an approximation is available from the fact that allocations for non-Whites are known. Thus, it appears that more than Rand 225 million was allocated for education of about 680,000

Whites—a per capita expenditure of rand 260. In comparison allocations for Coloureds was Rand 49.8 million in 1971, including university costs. Student enrollment was 536,000, and per capita expenditure Rand 73. For Asian education funds allocated were Rand 28.3 million for 167,000 students. Per capita allowances were Rand 65 in primary and Rand 105 in secondary schools, averaging Rand 85 per pupil. The expenditures for African education included government allocations of Rand 57 million. (Of this, some Rand 9.6 million was allocated to the Transkei and Rand 3.4 million went to South-West Africa.) Adding certain other income—about Rand 18 million that came from the Black community and contributions from local authorities and private donations through farm and factory schools—the grand total for Black education is estimated at Rand 75 million for 1971. (Of that total it was estimated that parents of Black pupils had raised Rand 1.7 million for costs of buildings and privately paid teachers.) Per capita expenditures for Black pupils reportedly range from Rand 13.55 per year in primary schools to Rand 55 per year in secondary schools. The grand total works out at per capita expenditures approximating Rand 28 annually for Black pupils. Thus, by conservative estimates, expenditures for education of White pupils are about nine times the sums allocated for the education of Black pupils.

A further comparative breakdown shows that in 1970 roughly 26,000 White teachers taught 862,000 White students in about 2,900 schools. For Coloureds there were 16,000 teachers for 536,000 students in an estimated 1,800 schools. Asians had 167,000 students, with 5,800 teachers in 370 schools. For the 2.7 million Blacks there were 45,000 teachers and 9,500 schools.

Recent statistics indicating averages of teachers' salaries (varying slightly according to sex and academic background) also make an interesting comparison. For Whites, beginning annual salaries range upward from Rand 2,010 at primary levels to Rand 3,860 at secondary levels. For Coloured teachers, the average ranges upward from an annual Rand 1,080 at primary levels to Rand 1,875 at secondary levels. For Asians, the averages range upward from an annual Rand 1,080 at primary levels to Rand 1,875 at secondary levels. For Blacks the annual averages range upward from Rand 600 at primary levels to Rand 1,200 at secondary levels.

In contrast to parents of pupils of other races, parents of Black students are required to pay a sum of 38 cents monthly toward costs of construction of school buildings. At secondary levels they are also required to pay tuition costs of rand 4 for each pupil annually. In addition they are required to pay for costs of stationery, most textbooks, and compulsory uniforms. (Uniforms are required for pupils of all races.) Those additional costs for Black pupils average from

Rand 9 to Rand 16 at primary levels, from Rand 25 to Rand 29 at junior secondary levels, and from Rand 32 to Rand 37 at senior secondary levels. It should be kept in mind that these additional costs are borne by a high proportion of Black African families who are under the poverty subsistence line.

The central government has broad administrative control over education, with provincial governments carrying out established guidelines. The central government maintains a tighter control over universities and technical schools, while departments of Coloured Affairs, of Indian Affairs, and of Bantu Administration have extensive direct control over non-White educational functions, including syllabi. The CNE policy is thus developed in accordance with apartheid principles and separateness of races and cultures.

For White students there are Afrikaans-medium and English-medium schools in operation, as well as dual-medium institutions. Enrollment in these is usually dependent on the "mother tongue." To be admitted to a university students must qualify in both Afrikaans and English, as well as other subjects. Vernacular tongues are used for Black children in tribal areas and township schools through the elementary and secondary levels. Thus, it is necessary for the Black pupil to carry on study in his early years using three separate languages (Afrikaans, English, and the tribal dialect) concurrently.

There are 11 universities for Whites in the Republic, four teaching in English, five teaching in Afrikaans, and two bilingual. There are five universities for non-Whites. In 1971 there were 89,000 university students of all races. Of these some 77,000 were Whites, 2,000 were Coloureds, 4,200 were Asians (including 1,000 Chinese), and 5,400 were Blacks. With rare exceptions (only in the University of South Africa, Pretoria) are non-Whites permitted to enroll in White universities. As the University of South Africa is a major correspondence center, it presently enrolls about 2,800 Blacks (who have been included in the foregoing Black university enrollment figure). About 2,400 Black Africans are registered in the three separate Black universities—Fort Hare in Cape Province, University College of Zululand at Ngoya, and University College of the North in the northern Transvaal. Some 200 Blacks are also registered at the non-White medical school associated with the University of Natal. The Coloured higher-level students attend University College of the Western Cape. The Asians attend the University College of Durban-Westville.

There are reported to be some 4,000 Black university graduates now in the Republic. In 1969 a total of 250 university degrees were awarded to Blacks. This compares with 9,472 degrees earned by Whites, 113 degrees earned by Coloureds, and 306 degrees earned by Asians in the same year. The central government subsidizes a high percentage of university costs for non-Whites.

While universities provide teacher-training courses, most technical and vocational teachers are taught at separate technical colleges. In 1969 there were 15 teacher-training institutions for Whites, as well as 12 technical colleges. There were four teacher-training institutions for Coloureds. There was one technical school and one teacher-training institution for Asians. There were 43 teacher-training, technical, and agricultural schools for Blacks. Several new technical colleges are being developed for Blacks in the homelands.

The influence of the universities on South African political life and social structure has long been weakened by the dichotomy of Afrikaans- and English-speaking groups, by cleavages of race and tribe, by the closure of White universities to non-White students and faculty, and by the dependence of the universities on central government for their finances. Thus, university thought and action is kept separate and weakened by the same influences that are present in other sectors of society. Weakening, too, has been the constant emigration of many of the more brilliant and progressive faculty members of all races—these seeking academic freedom in the outside world. This outflow of brain power from South African universities has, in turn, created a problem for those university administrators who have remained. It has proved difficult for those administrators to hire reputable academics from overseas in the face of strict immigration policies and governmental stifling of liberal academic thought. Yet, despite closing of the White universities to non-Whites by statute and the generally repressive influences over intellectual life, there remain some courageous academics who seek to keep freedom of speech and thought alive. It is of special significance to see this courage exhibited more and more openly in the Afrikaner institutions of higher learning.

The three White political parties of the Republic each have their youth groups. In general, these are active only during periods of political campaigning, and they are centered about the universities. More important, by far, in the youth leadership and civil rights fields have been the activities of organized university student groups. Like labor and politics, however, they have been split along cultural and ethnic lines. Thus, they have been repressed and weakened and have become increasingly ineffective. Two representative White student groups are the English-oriented National Union of South African Students (NUSAS) and the Afrikaans-speaking Studenter Bond (ASB). Though several non-White student groups have appeared and disappeared in the various Coloured, Asian, and Black universities, only one existing Black student group—the South African Student Organization (SASO) seems to be of consequence. This group is centered in the non-White medical school of the University of Natal and has affiliations with Fort Hare and the University of Zululand (Ngoya). SASO emphasizes the concept "Black is beautiful." SASO has discouraged open affiliation with liberal White groupings. Leaders of NUSAS, however, try to keep a personalized association with the Black leaders of SASO.

According to its constitution and its activities ASB emphasizes that its membership is for White Afrikaners, believing in Christian national concepts of education. It has sought, however, to enroll as members some of the more conservative students of English-oriented universities. The ASB has consistently supported Nationalist government politics. However, fissures are appearing in these cultural dikes, as student group chapters in more liberal Afrikaner-oriented institutions, like the University of Stellenbosch, have openly questioned the politics of apartheid and have openly entertained such Black leaders as President Banda of Malawi and the Zulu chief, Gatsha Buthelezi.

NUSAS has sought constantly to keep a liberal and open approach on questions of race. It has never barred non-Whites from local university chapters, and it has courageously opposed closing of the White universities to non-White students. Its leaders have encouraged NUSAS members to participate in public protests against apartheid, sometimes to the point where the NUSAS leaders themselves were either banned or exiled. In fact, today, a number of former national officers of NUSAS are political exiles and are lecturing or studying in British or American universities. NUSAS has worked against Afrikaner and English cleavages and has sought to form a single student body in South African universities. These efforts have been unsuccessful, and, in fact, NUSAS has been hard put to maintain its existing membership of about 25,000. It remains to be seen, in the face of external pressures against South Africa and internal pressures for conformity on political and race issues, whether these student body groups can play an effective role in both student and national affairs.

RELIGION

At least 22 major world religions claim adherents in South Africa, but the bulk of the people are members of five Christian faiths. Of 3.8 million Whites, just under 2 million are members of the DRC (Nederduits Gereformeerde Kerk—NGK) and its sister churches. More than 400,000 Coloureds are also members of this church, as are 550,000 Blacks and a few Asians. Methodists number 1.7 million adherents, of whom 1.3 million are Blacks. The Anglican Church claims just under 1.5 million adherents of all races, of whom 750,000 are Blacks. There are more than 1.25 million Roman Catholics of all races, of whom 760,000 are Blacks. Lutheran membership exceeds 700,000, of whom 500,000 are Blacks. Other large Christian communions include Presbyterians, Congregationalists, Apostolics and Christian Scientists.

Membership in non-Christian sects is also large. About 500,000 Asians are associated with Hinduism. Most of the remainder of the Asian community follows Islam. (Some Blacks are now embracing Islam). There are some 150,000 Whites associated with the Jewish faith.

An important recent religious phenomenon has been the extraordinary growth of the Black African "independent churches." These are now reported to number in excess of 3,000 religious bodies, most of which have splintered off from more orthodox Christian groupings. Adherents to these independent churches are now reported to number in excess of 3 million. An African Independent Churches' Association, comprising 358 units of the more than 3,000 independent churches, now has full membership in the interdenominational South African Council of Churches (SACOC). Growth of these independent churches has resulted in loss of membership of a number of Christian sects, including Anglicans and Methodists. Black membership in Presbyterian and Congregationalist bodies, among others, has remained fairly steady in recent years, while Black membership in Dutch Reformed, Roman Catholic, and Lutheran churches has increased. It is assumed that much of the membership in the independent churches comes from Africans who were formerly animist or who held only nominal membership in Christian communities. Development of the independent church movement in South Africa and elsewhere in Africa deserves more intensive study than can be attempted here. It is conceded among White churchmen and Black intellectuals that one major reason for this development has been the fact that White churches have failed to set up adequate channels of communication with their Black congregations. Concern for one another is considered by Blacks to be either absent or hypocritical among Whites. Black Christian churchmen are also asking for more say in church affairs. Says one Catholic priest succinctly, "The Church in Africa must become more African, rather than remaining a foreign club."

There has been increasing conflict between church and state in South Africa during the past two decades. This conflict brings into the open the contradictions between the politically conservative, Calvinist ethics of Afrikaner apartheid ideology and the far more liberal ethics of the "foreign" Christian churches. In recent months this conflict has been heightened, resulting from statements and actions antagonistic to apartheid from Christian churchmen. These have been condemned, in turn, by high officials of the Republic's government, particularly the prime minister. Foremost in this debate on the side of the church have been clerics and laymen of Anglican, Roman Catholic, Methodist, Congregationalist, and Lutheran faiths. Even a few members of the DRC ranks have participated. As open criticism of apartheid has come from the pulpits, government officials have responded by taking direct action against church leaders. These actions have resulted in a number of searches, detentions, and deportations of British, American, and German clergymen, both Protestant and Catholic. Government officials, defending these actions, have also vilified "liberal" foreign and South African clerics and laymen.

In this debate liberal Christian spokesmen contend that they are the only effective opponents of apartheid at home and abroad. They state that, by forcing their members to examine their consciences and to take personal actions against apartheid, they are requiring those members to decide what they "must render to Caesar and what they render to God."

SACOC is composed of 28 different religious bodies and church-related organizations. (The DRC withdrew from the World Council of Churches [WCC] and SACOC some years ago.) In its association with the antiapartheid WCC and in its criticisms of the repressive racial situation within the Republic, SACOC has come into direct conflict with high Nationalist officials, including the prime minister himself. Illustrative of this conflict was the action taken in 1968, when SACOC and the Christian Institute jointly convened in Capetown a national conference dealing with the relationship between church and society. The SACOC meeting had stressed the need of all men, regardless of race, to find the means of living together in peace. It also sought to define the individual realms of church and state, of Caesar and God.

Early in September 1968 a "Message to the People of South Africa," drawn up by an interdenominational commission was published in the name of SACOC. The message stated, inter alia, that it is the right of the church to concern itself with political systems. It stressed that, in South Africa, Christians were involved in repressive policies of racial separation that were increasingly characterized as being "the South African Way of Life." The letter stated that this doctrine was hostile to Christianity and based only on preservation of racial identity. It thus contravened the Gospel command that one should love his neighbor as himself. There were signs, the letter continued, that the doctrine of racial separation had become for many South Africans a "false faith." The message called on citizens to distinguish between what was demanded of them as citizens of South Africa and what was demanded of them as disciples of Christ. Approximately 7,000 copies of this document were circulated to church leaders throughout the Republic who read it to their congregations from pulpits. The document was given wide attention in South Africa and abroad.

Obviously touched to the quick by this letter, Prime Minister Vorster gave it his personal attention. In a speech delivered September 24, 1968, before the National Party Congress in Natal, Vorster said that the job of the clergy was "not to turn your pulpits into political platforms . . . to do the work of the United Party, the Progressive Party and the Liberal Party." The following day the executive council of SACOC responded, insisting that it was necessary for church leaders to speak courageously on issues of the day and, if necessary, to criticize the government.

At a party meeting in Brakpan on September 27, 1968, Prime Minister Vorster returned to the attack, insisting that the pulpit should not be used for political ends. He said that there were "clerics toying with the ideas of doing the sort of work in South Africa that Martin Luther King had done in America." Vorster then issued a threat against the churchmen: - "Cut it out . . . the cloth you are wearing will not protect you in South Africa . . . " Leading members of SACOC, in a subsequent open letter to the prime minister, submitted that the pulpit should not be used to support political parties, that the government was not simply the instrument of a party, that the church had the calling to involve itself in politics in the broad sense of the word, and the policy of apartheid was not in accordance with the word of God.

On October 26, 1968, in Klerksdorp, Vorster again referred to the church-state controversy, stating that the pious talk of the church leaders did not impress him. He added that they were attacking the government from the pulpit under the cloak of religion. A few days later, in Capetown, a group of more than 100 clergymen issued a statement deploring the prime minister's Klerksdorp remarks and renewed their support of the SACOC message.

In June 1970 a new issue arose to fan the flames of antagonism between church and state in South Africa. SACOC had been actively associated with the WCC and its executive directorate in Geneva. Some years before the WCC had instituted an active program to combat racism worldwide. In 1970 it increased its efforts in that field, inspired by its American executive, Eugene Carson Blake. As a part of its new antiracist efforts, the WCC set up a $500,000 fund to give to organized groups of exiles from racialist regimes (especially from southern Africa). The only stipulations made were that these funds were to be used for humanitarian and not military purposes and that the political objectives of the exile groups must not be opposed to the general purposes of the WCC.

There was an immediate protest from South African government officials and citizens who contended that the WCC was thereby contributing to, and espousing, "terrorism." The WCC responded that these actions did not endorse or sanction terrorism but rather the long-term goals of racial justice and self-determination. The WCC followed these actions by asking that member church groups check their portfolios of investment to see whether these, in turn, were supporting South Africa's apartheid policies and whether such investments were perpetuating racism in countries elsewhere. One result of this action was preparation of a report on American church-owned stockholdings in South African branches of American corporations. The American National Council of Churches and individual church bodies in America found that they had millions of dollars invested in such operations within the Republic. Some groups sought to divest themselves of these holdings.

While there was definite approval of the WCC action in Britain and Scandinavia, there was considerable conflict over the issue in Germany and the United States. A widely distributed set of articles in Reader's Digest was particularly condemnatory of the WCC action, as were some American TV and radio commentaries. The main argument was made against support of violent change under Christian church aegis.

The greatest chagrin was demonstrated in South Africa, where Prime Minister Vorster at once took issue with the WCC. He immediately denounced the grants to terrorist organizations. English-speaking churches still operating in South Africa were placed under new pressure, and there were demands made that they withdraw from the WCC altogether. Despite the widening conflict SACOC continued its membership in the WCC. As one astute observer put it the Christian church in South Africa, "after so many years of service to the oppressors it . . . has returned to the Christian role of service to the oppressed. . . ."*

The church-state conflict continued to rage during 1971 and into 1972. In August 1971 Theo Gerdener, minister of interior, accused South African churches of being unduly influenced by overseas forces trying to bring "a massive onslaught on the government's political beliefs—even if it ultimately led to violence . . . "[2] By implication Gerdener made it clear that he and other government leaders believed a real gap was developing between certain of the church leaders and groups of their own congregations, the latter becoming increasingly disturbed about a confrontation on matters not considered to be the church's responsibility. Gerdener warned that government and church-goers of the Republic would never allow growing attempts to create a clash between church and state to succeed.

---

*Quoted from "The Activist Church" by Jon Woronoff, appearing in Africa Report, February 1972 (Washington, D.C.).

The churchmen again reacted, insisting that a dialogue be instituted with church leaders at Cabinet level. The well-known and courageous Roman Catholic Archbishop of Durban, the Most Reverend Denis Hurley, stated:

> Many of us want . . . to contribute to the making of South Africa . . . eradication of racism is integral to the communication of the Christian gospel . . . we are beginning to see this now. . . . If this means a clash with government policy, we just have to face it and take the consequences, but I think there is much we could discuss if we could get together. . . .[3]

At the same time Natal's Anglican Bishop Vernon Inman said the government's attacks, bannings, and deportations of so many clergy made it hard to believe the state wanted to avoid a confrontation.

In another powerful statement on the same subject, Archbishop Hurley said that a significant section of the church body has moved from silent support of the establishment toward social reform. He stated that the church must be concerned about the situation in which 20 percent of the world's population, mainly Whites, enjoy great opulence, while the remaining 80 percent are deprived, often starving. The political domination is such that the undeveloped four-fifths can not free itself from the affluent one-fifth. If religion means anything at all, it means this situation cannot be allowed to continue . . . religion must play its part in redressing the balance . . . religion has the duty to be involved in the righting of such enormous wrongs . . . if this is bringing religion into politics, so be it. . . .[4]

Illustrative of this new mood of the churches was the action taken by the Anglican synod of South Africa in November 1971. This conclave took formal action to assist people banned by the government and determined to work actively against apartheid as a doctrine that "violates Christian principles."

Late in November 1971 the South African press reported on crucial talks on deteriorating church-state relations and recent detentions and actions taken against church leaders. These talks took place in Pretoria between the prime minister and church leaders. Also present were the three Cabinet ministers most concerned—Gerdener (interior), Moller (police), and Pelser (justice). After the discussions, described as "very frank," church leaders were reluctant to discuss details, although they acknowledged that there had been wide differences on some subjects. They were anxious to keep the door open and not jeopardize further top-level talks. Among churchmen present were the Reverend Alex Boraine, president of the Methodist Church of South Africa; Roman Catholic Cardinal Owen McCann;

Anglican Archbishop, the Most Reverend R. Selby-Taylor; Congregationalist Reverend Allen Hendrickson, and the Reverend August W. Habilgaarn, president of Lutheran Churches and present head of SACOC.

In 1971, shortly after the last World Court advisory opinion on South Africa was handed down, this recognizing the supervisory UN rights over the territory, the churches of South-West Africa also reacted. Two major Lutheran groups disclosed the contents of an open letter from Lutheran Church leaders to Prime Minister Vorster. This letter censured South Africa for withholding basic human rights from the inhabitants of the territory and asked that South-West Africa be permitted its independence. This was the first major stand against the Republic government taken by the Lutheran Church on its own. It was important, also, because the Lutheran sect is the largest in South-West Africa, representing more than a half the Black populace. Prime Minister Vorster met with a Lutheran delegation but insisted that South-West Africa must be developed separately along Bantustan and wholly South African lines. Church leaders, still in opposition, insisted on a unitary state and full independence for the territory.

One recent governmental action in the church-state controversy that attracted international attention was the arrest, trial, and conviction of the dean of the Anglican Cathedral in Johannesburg, the Very Reverend Gonville Aubie ffrench-Beytagh. Late in 1971 the Anglican dean was convicted in a Johannesburg court for alleged terrorism and violation of the Terrorism Act. The main charges centered about his alleged support of revolutionary activities by distributing antigovernment literature and antiapartheid funds. He was sentenced to five years' imprisonment. The sentence was appealed. In April 1972 the South African Appellate High Court overturned the conviction. In a lengthy written judgment the court ruled unanimously that the mere intemperate expression of antigovernment views could not be equated with terrorism or subversion. The dean, who is a British subject, was subsequently deported. Despite this unusual judgment in favor of the church, it seems certain that the controversy over religious condemnation of apartheid in South Africa is bound to continue.

It is important to note that, operating within the race relations field, but impinging upon both educational and religious sectors, are four important independent organizations. These are the Christian Institute of Southern Africa, the University Christian Movement (UCM), the South African Bureau of Racial Affairs (SABRA), and the South African Institute of Race Relations.

Membership of the Christian Institute, established in 1963, is multiracial and interdenominational. It represents persons rather than particular church groups, but the body has had great influence in SACOC. Its primary aim has been to build bridges of understanding between members of differing racial groups, regardless of religious denomination. The institute has been particularly successful in maintaining contact with Black African independent church groups. An important voice of this body is the monthly magazine, Pro Veritate. Its present director is the Reverend Beyers Naude, a minister of the DRC. Naude insists that such opposition to racism is a "Christian duty." Naude has been an outspoken opponent of apartheid, as have certain other Dutch Reformed clergymen who are members of the institute. As a result this body has come under vehement attack from the established DRC, which, in recent synods, has insisted that its own members must withdraw from institute membership.

The UCM is also a multiracial organization. It emphasizes study of women's liberation, literacy and adult education, and Christian theology, Black and White. Because of its aims the group has special associations with South African churches, seminaries, and universities. It has sponsored ideas of ecumenism on various university campuses and operates under the special guidance of Roman Catholic, Methodist, Anglican, Presbyterian, and Congregationalist churches.

SABRA is of conservative Nationalist outlook and has a membership policy of Whites only. It has the special backing of the government's Department of Education. The group supports the principle of separate development of Bantustans. It was established particularly to counter the race relations activities of other independent groups, such as the Christian Institute and the Institute of Race Relations. It has served, more or less, as an academic propaganda wing for the National party. In recent years it has been relatively quiescent. Though it has attempted to be a forum for free discussion, the discipline of the Nationalist philosophy and Afrikanerdom has usually prevailed.

The South African Institute of Race Relations is a highly respected, independent, privately financed organization. It has several main functions. It provides an active and scholarly association for those interested in improvement of race relations within the Republic. It sponsors academic research and symposia on various fields of race relations, community development, and constructive social change. It maintains a bursary (scholarship) program for non-Whites. It publishes valuable pamhlets and books on the South African racial scene. The authoritative annual, A Survey of Race Relations in South Africa, quoted often in this book, is one of these. Finally, the institute, to support its own activities and to cherish the continuation of authentic Black South African handicrafts, maintains a selling organization for these artistic products.

Despite their valuable contributions to the South African cultural and racial scenes, three of the foregoing organizations (along with NUSAS)—the Christian Institute, the UCM, and the Institute of Race Relations—have come under governmental scrutiny. During the 1972 parliamentary session, Prime Minister Vorster established a select committee to investigate these groups. Reasons for so doing, he contended, were the following: (a) these organizations had unduly associated themselves with the church-state controversy, (b) they had improperly opposed the government's race policies, (c) they had allegedly and improperly received foreign financial help (including support from the Ford Foundation) and (d) they had thus served as agents of outside "liberal" influences.

COMMUNICATIONS

As noted elsewhere, the Republic has two official languages—Afrikaans and English—in addition to a number of tribal languages and Asian dialects. Afrikaans is a derivative of seventeenth-century Dutch and is now spoken by 70 percent of the Whites, 90 percent of the Coloureds, and by numbers of Blacks and Asians. The lingua franca of the Blacks and Asians is English, though amongst the Asians Tamil, Hindi, Urdu, Telegu, and Gujarati are also utilized. Many Blacks speak either English, or Afrikaans, or both, and in reserves and townships they use mother tongues, including Zulu, Xhosa, Venda, Sotho, and Tswana, and so forth. Governmental efforts to push the Bantustan program and to extend the use of Afrikaans have obviously impeded what might otherwise have been the general use of English as a lingua franca of the country.

Within the Republic there are 19 daily newspapers and five Sunday newspapers. There are also a large number of weekly, biweekly, and monthly professional and trade publications. The estimated combined daily readership of English-language newspapers and other periodicals is over 2 million, while Afrikaans-medium journals exceed a 1.75 million readership.

There has been a consistent growth in the number of publications directed to the Black Africans. During the past two decades over 300 such publications have arisen—these using English, Afrikaans, and tribal dialects in some combination. One Black-oriented daily newspaper published in Johannesburg is reputed to have a daily circulation approaching 200,000.

Fear of incurring government attention and displeasure keeps the non-White press (both Black and Asian) from engaging in strong editorial stands or criticism of government policies. Editors of these periodicals find themselves under heavy constraint in portraying the realities of daily life among non-White South Africans. In addition to routine governmental obstacles to development of the non-White press, there have been other difficulties. These include the economic factor—so many potential readers being below the poverty datum line and, therefore, unable to pay the cost of even a daily newspaper. The high illiteracy rate (still estimated at about 50 percent for the Blacks above the age of 15) and the multiplicity of Black African dialects have also been impediments, as, until recently, has been the lack of advertising revenue. This last barrier is being overcome as some White-owned consumer industries are coming to recognize the potential value of the Black consumer market.

Though somewhat provincial in outlook, most of the English-language newspapers, and even some of the Afrikaans-medium periodicals, are highly literate. Some editors are also courageous in criticism of obtuse or racist government policies and actions. All newspapers are subject to restrictive libel laws, "Suppression of Communism" legislation, restrictions on publication of statements on writings by banned persons, and general censorship fiat. Editors operate under constant constraint of their owners and advertisers. Legal firms are retained by the largest of the daily and weekly papers to insure that they do not come into open conflict with the government on the maze of restrictive legislation on political issues. Even so, some newspapers, English and Afrikaans, manage to maintain an extraordinary amount of press freedom at risk of governmental action. Most newspapers and magazines, however, continue to reflect the great disparities of thought between English and Afrikaner, between White and non-White, between racism and nonracialism.

There are a number of foreign news agencies represented in the country—chief among them being the Associated Press, United Press International, Reuters, Agence France Presse, and Deutsche Presse Agentur. Associated with these is the government-backed South African Press Association, of which the country's leading newspapers and government-owned broadcasting services are members. A number of foreign newspapers, magazines, and television companies have staffers or stringers operating within the country. It should be noted, however, that on occasion certain liberal American and British newspapers have had difficulty in securing residence visas or temporary entry permits for their newsmen.

South Africa ranks high in book importation and domestic book publishing. These latter publish more than 500 locally authored books yearly. Of these about two-thirds are written in Afrikaans and one-third in English and tribal vernaculars. Both local publications and overseas imports have recently been hampered by the increasingly stringent activities of the central government's Publications Control Board. That body has powers of censorship and import control and can ban publications. (Many books by recognized South African authors of world repute have come under scrutiny and action by the Publications Board. Many world-reputed White, Black, and Coloured South African writers have gone into exile, realizing that their works could not gain a foothold in South Africa.)

The Publications Control Board has power to examine all publications (except newspapers) and films, domestic or imported. Its power lies in its instructions "to insure that offence will not be given to religious convictions or feelings of any section of the population and to prevent any section being brought into ridicule or contempt. . . ."* (Films shown to non-Whites are usually censored even beyond those cuts prescribed for Whites.) Illustrative of the extent of this board's censorship are the following statistics. Since 1956 the Board of Censors and its follow-up body, the Board of Publications Control (established 1963), banned from importation and/or distribution 12,651 publications, films, and records. Since 1963 the board has prohibited 5,785 publications, of which 5,771 remain prohibited. During 1970 alone, 801 films were submitted to the board for approval. Of these 49 films were banned and 273 were excised—244 approved for exhibition only to persons of a particular race or class and 235 approved unconditionally.[5]

Lacking television, South Africa remains a prime target for movie showing and for domestic movie production. At one time it was reported that the Republic contained one-fourth of all movie theaters in Africa. About one-half of the more than 500 movie houses in South Africa are for Whites only; the remainder are solely for non-Whites. Importation of foreign films—American, British, French, Italian, and Indian films—has been heavy, though these imports have all been subject to banning or excision by the Publications Control Board. As a result of this censorship, production of Afrikaans-medium films has been encouraged by the government in documentary, newsreel, and feature-length arenas.

The South African Broadcasting Corporation (SABC) is a governmental entity. Its policies are set and executed by a nine-man board of governors, members of which are appointed by the state president, with approval of the prime minister. The present chairman of the board is Piet Meyer, an ultraconservative Afrikaner, who was long head of the Broederbond. (See Chapters 3 and 4.) Alleged to be free of political bias in its programming, SABC is actually one of the Nationalist government's most potent propaganda arms in both domestic

---

*South African Quiz, pamphlet published by South African Information Service, Pretoria, 1969, p. 75.

and international areas. SABC program content and staff membership are generally recognized as being heavily biased in favor of the National party and Afrikanerdom. SABC funds are mainly derived from annual licence fees paid by owners of radio receivers, as well as from income of its commercial channel, Springbok Radio.

Domestically, SABC operates 14 separate national and regional program services. Principal among these are Afrikaans, English, Bantu vernacular, and combined Afrikaans-English commercial services. It carries on these domestic activities with a network of 12 medium-wave and over 50 FM transmitters. Institution of its FM network has been in part a technical advance and in part a psychological tool aimed at curtailment of overseas short-wave and medium-wave listening habits of South Africans of all races.

SABC also handles transcription dissemination to many countries and production of international broadcasts over high-powered short-wave transmitters called RSA. The external transmissions of RSA are beamed worldwide. Broadcast languages are in Afrikaans, English, Portuguese, German, Dutch, Spanish, Zulu, and Swahili. These broadcasts convey news and entertainment, with propaganda slants defending South Africa against international criticism and justification of the "South African way of life."

South Africa currently has no television operations, being one of the few developed countries in the world not yet so equipped. It has been contended by some domestic opponents and by some outside critics of the Nationalists that government and DRC leaders actually fear the challenges to Afrikaner culture that television is bound to introduce into the country. Their fear also appears to be that these intrusions from a multiracial world will have an incalculable and destructive effect on the disparate elements of South African society. The lack of availability of Afrikaans-language materials from overseas television sources may be an important factor in this argumentation. It is obvious that it would be costly to provide more than a minimum of Afrikaans-medium programming for the "tube." SABC will eventually become the agency of control for television production, destined to go into operation about 1975.

The Republic conducts a sizable propaganda and information program both at home and abroad. Chief among the South African targets are the United States, the United Kingdom, France, Germany, the Netherlands, Portugal, Brazil, Australia, Japan, and Rhodesia. The Republic's propaganda position among "Western democracies" is difficult. South Africa is the only one among these countries that legally, customarily, and effectively denies to its non-Whites the attainment of some economic, social, and political equality. In the face of constant criticism of its apartheid policies, the South African propaganda channels are aimed at offsetting foreign criticism, this by free distribution of slick-paper publications, by extensive contact with overseas leaders and media, and by government sponsorship of tours of South Africa for overseas leaders and media personnel. In these efforts to defend itself against UN and other international antiapartheid critics, it stresses its pro-Western, anti-Communist stance; its strategic and economic importance to the West; its present internal order; and its Bantustan program. It cites the last named as a visible sign of the Republic's good faith in allowing the Blacks to move toward self-determination and independence.

CHAPTER

9

INTERNAL SECURITY AND DEFENSE

An objective assessment of South Africa's defense and internal security capabilities would tend toward the following conclusions:

As of today South African Police, backed up by the various military arms, including civilian White reserves, can contain and wipe out any foreseeable internal disorder, riot, or insurrection not associated with major external force.

South African Police and military authorities today appear to have the capability of curtailing, controlling, or preventing widespread sabotage.

Internal security authorities cannot prevent small-scale or occasional large-scale sabotage efforts, passive resistance and protest demonstrations, or other minor disturbances.

At the present time South Africa's air, ground, and naval forces cannot completely seal the country's borders and seacoasts. Therefore, the movement of potential exiles outward or of potential saboteurs inward cannot be completely checked.

South Africa should be able to repel almost any foreseeable military cum naval action mounted against her, except one fully supported by a major Western or Communist nation, by a highly motivated and well-prepared UN task force, or by a combination of major powers mounting nuclear attack.

No combination of forces, solely derived from the African continent, appears capable of challenging South Africa militarily today. Logistics, firepower, air power, and trained manpower are weighted in favor of South Africa.

A calculated and unexpected offensive strike against Zambia and/or Tanzania by South African forces cannot be ruled out. Military actions by South African forces within Rhodesia and/or the Portuguese provinces of Mozambique and Angola also cannot be ruled out. International reactions to these potentials are difficult to assess.

In terms of its population, its isolation, its geographic location, and its ever-present internal security problems, South Africa possesses armed might fully sufficient for its immediate needs and foreseeable eventualities. While there may be in public and private circles of the Republic an implicit fear of an eventual UN task force (with major Communist or even Western military backing) mounted against her, the real fear is always one of potential internal violence. That internal violence, of course, could also be associated with action by "freedom fighters" from the north. Whether justified or unjustified, immediate or far-removed, it has been these widespread fears of terrorism and invasion that have enabled the Nationalist government to increase its defense and security budgets constantly. These costs have increased from 6 percent to 18 percent of the total national budget within the past decade. The Republic's defense budget for 1968/69 was Rand 252 million. In 1971/72 it rose to Rand 316 million.[1]

Qualified observers have long expressed the view that South Africa has been preserved from a massive internal uprising thus far only because the large non-White population has been disorganized, disarmed, extraordinarily patient, and, until now, virtually leaderless in national terms. Until now, non-Whites have also been unskilled in industrial techniques, in the use of modern weaponry, and in sabotage techniques. Further, until recently, most potential or effective non-White leadership has been swiftly exiled, jailed, or banned by South African White authorities. Some observers believe that the Bantustan programs and other apartheid policies, in themselves, provide a kind of security insurance for White South Africans through their divisiveness. However, those very policies seem now to be creating a new brand of non-Whites leadership and nationalist thought. These new leaders and new thoughts arising under the very aegis of the Republic's White government may become powerful nationalistic forces later to be reckoned with.

It will be recalled that the UN took action in 1963 to impose an arms embargo against South Africa on grounds that her increasing buildup of armaments seemed destined to make her dominant White regime only more harshly repressive against the Republic's (and South-West Africa's) non-Whites. UN action against sale of further arms for South Africa was supported by both the United States and Britain. Until that time South Africa's armaments were largely of British origin or design. Her military components and organization and training were also of British tradition. South Africa's reaction to the UN action was predictable. It intensified demands for self-sufficiency, enhanced her feelings of economic nationalism, and made her seek other sources for her arms needs.

Then U.S. ambassador to the UN, Adlai Stevenson, speaking in the Security Council on August 2, 1963, and in the General Assembly on December 4, 1963, announced that the United States had voluntarily and unilaterally brought an end to all sales and shipments of military equipment from the United States to South Africa. This action was taken, said Ambassador Stevenson, as a sign of U.S. displeasure toward South Africa's race policies and as a U.S. contribution toward lessening tensions in that area. To this embargo statement, however, Stevenson appended a caveat that existing contracts would be honored and that the United States reserved its rights, in future, to supply South Africa with strategic materials when common defense and international threats to peace so required it.

Since the imposition of the arms embargo at least seven major changes have occurred on the South African defense scene:

The Republic has made herself self-sufficient in certain armaments categories, including small arms, automatic weapons, light tanks, motorized weapons, personnel carriers, and so forth. She has developed capabilities in small aircraft and small ship production. She is now developing some capacity in production of short and medium-range surface-to-air missiles of the "Cactus" variety. (This system is being developed with French technical support.)[2]

France has become the Republic's prime arms supplier, receiving orders for at least $500 million in arms over the past eight years.[3]

South Africa is developing her own nuclear capabilities. Combining her large resources of uranium with her present scientific capabilities (and relationships with France et al), she could easily join the nuclear arms "club" if she chose to do so.

She has developed an effective conscription and militia system. With these and her permanent forces, she could probably field a force of some 200,000 men within 90 days.

An effective early warning radar system is already in operation in the Republic. It is being further extended and should be fully operative by the end of 1972. The system will satisfy both air and maritime surveillance needs.[4]

An Armaments Corporation has been established to coordinate and control production and sale of all arms in the Republic. The Corporation also has power to establish new arms undertakings, to review raw materials needs, and to govern labor in the arms industry.

The Republic is insuring that she has adequate stores of petroleum products sufficient to all her defense and civilian needs for two to three years.

A resumé of the various components of the South African defense-security structure follows (with all figures approximate).

ARMY

Though the prime mission of the South African Army is always to insure defense of the Republic, its offensive capabilities are becoming increasingly evident. This can be assumed, in part, by presumed written or oral agreements for military association with Rhodesia and Portugal if major defense-security action were required in neighboring territories. Thus, army training and planning is oriented first toward reinforcement of the police for internal security, but secondarily, with informal or formal alliances with friendly neighboring states in the event of broader hostilities or external security threats. The army is organized into a number of regional commands covering the four provinces of the Republic and South-West Africa. Personnel is estimated at 15,000 regular army, plus 30,000 one-year conscripts. An additional standby reserve group of 50,000 men receives annual training. A backup group of civilians who have previously seen service, these numbering 150,000 men, could probably be called to service within three months. The army contains a paratroop group and has access to air force helicopters. It also has a large number of convoy trucks, armored cars, and tanks.

NAVY

The prime purpose of the South African Navy, till recently, has been to serve as a coastal defense force. Historically, it has assisted the British Navy in policing the sea lanes between the Atlantic and Indian oceans. More recently, however, as the result of the closure of the Suez Canal and the intrusion of the Russian fleet into the Indian Ocean, the navy has undertaken observation-surveillance functions over Communist shipping, ranging from Angola to Madagascar. Otherwise, navy capabilities are limited to patrol, minesweeping, and detection in coastal waters. It could operate as an adjunct of a larger fleet in event of major hostilities when its submarine arm becomes operative and its capabilities have been thus extended. The navy operates the important naval base at Simonstown and smaller naval units at Durban, Port Elizabeth, and Walvis Bay. Its total complement numbers about 750 officers and 2,500 enlisted or conscripted men. There is a naval reserve force of about 1,500 men. It presently maintains two destroyers, six frigates, a number of minesweepers, and three Daphne-class submarines, newly arrived from France. It has recently placed orders for six new Corvettes. These are to be built in Portugal. Electronic apparatus and surface-to-air missile equipment for these will probably be obtained from France and Britain.[5]

Like other South African defense arms, the navy is also assigned internal-security support roles. Naval dockyards do not have shipbuilding facilities, but major repairs can be accomplished. Shipbuilding at Durban, South Africa's largest seaport, can be accomplished only for vessels ranging up to 6,000 tons and for the repair of larger vessels. The government has under active consideration the expansion of port, shipbuilding, and drydock facilities.

Under the so-called Simonstown Agreement, concluded in 1955 between the United Kingdom and South Africa, the two nations agreed to associate their naval activities in time of war. The agreement gives the United Kingdom continuing use of Simonstown for its fleet, under the presumption that South Africa has access to British arms and naval equipment. This agreement has been a source of some controversy between the Republic and the United Kingdom in recent years.

AIR FORCE

The South African Air Force appears to have three major roles. It assists the police in maintaining internal security by providing air support. Likewise, it backs up army and navy personnel if and when those military arms become involved in internal or external action. It also has special defense and surveillance tasks along South Africa's extensive coastline and land borders. There are about 300 landing fields and airstrips in the Republic and South-West Africa, but only some 20 of these are of international military and jet passenger standards. The air force is reported to have a total manpower of about 5,500, including 300 active pilots. Reserves are estimated at some 10,000, including some 2,500 who have had flight training. Aircraft are said to exceed 400 in number. These include some 75 jets of fighter or fighter-bomber variety, including new Mirages. The airfleet contains transports, trainers, and helicopters (Wasp and Alouette).

POLICE

The South African Police, in addition to routine criminal and civilian control responsibilities, are also responsible for internal security, overt and covert. The police cadre is said to number 31,770 persons, of whom about one-half are non-White.[6] There are a few non-White officers of commissioned and noncommissioned rank, but none of high rank. A police reserve force of some 24,500 (two-thirds White) is available on call.[7] (Units of the South African Police were dispatched to Rhodesia in September 1967 and subsequently sent to to join in operations against "freedom fighters" from the north and to assist Rhodesian forces in maintaining internal security. No units of the Defense Force were sent at that time. However, joint South African-Rhodesian police action is continuing.)

The Security Branch of the police is headed by an assistant commissioner, who is directly responsible to the commissioner and to the appropriate minister. The group also has close liaison with the minister of justice and with the prime minister's office. This branch is charged with the following: (a) detection and suppression of "subversion" in its broadest meaning, (b) protection against Communist infiltration of White and non-White organizations, and (c) protection against "terrorism" and sabotage. It is impossible to ascertain what proportion of the South African Police Force is engaged in special branch activities or how many informers of all races are on its payroll. Estimates range upward from 2,000 regular employees, with at least 15,000 informers, paid and unpaid, alleged to be working in the Transvaal alone. In any event, this police-informer network is vast and effective. The combination of numbers, of adequate budgets, of highly scientific surveillance techniques, of stringent laws, and of special access to the prime minister (himself a former minister of justice) make the South African Special Branch an unusually capable organization.

Recent legislation, termed BOSS, (Bureau of State Security), has created a new highlevel State Security Board. This body is headed by Major General R. J. Van den Bergh, former head of the Security Branch. BOSS holds a special liaison position with the prime minister's office coordinating all security functions in the country. Van den Bergh holds rank virtually equivalent to that of Cabinet minister. He chairs a Security Forces Conference Group, which appears to amalgamate or, at least, coordinate military intelligence, general police functions, the external secret service, and the internal Security Branch.

CHAPTER

10

INTERNATIONAL RELATIONS

In the period between Union in 1910 and creation of the Republic in 1961, South Africa's foreign relations were intimately bound up with Britain and the Commonwealth. After her departure from the Commonwealth in 1961, however, South Africa became disenchanted with, and independent of, Britain's foreign policy lines. While Britain remained an important trading partner, South Africa began to develop a foreign policy that was strictly her own. The Nationalist government was anxious to demonstrate to the world that it represented a preponderantly Afrikaner nation and was not simply a satellite of Britain. It was also anxious to show that it was not a "White colonialist" government of Africa as were Britain and France, for it had no intention of removing its White citizenry from that continent. South Africans, both English-speakers and Afrikaans-speaking, intended to remain permanently in Africa.

The defeat of Jan Smuts, champion of Commonwealth, in 1948, had been followed by the long renaissance (1948-72) of Afrikanerdom and South African nationalism. This nationalism brought into the Republic a new chauvinism, a new patriotism, a paramountcy for all things South African. The chauvinism was only enhanced by external criticisms and pressures of the antiapartheid campaigns mounted against South Africa in Britain, on the continents of Europe and Africa, and in the United States. The various anti-South African resolutions and bombast coming from the UN, the UN arms embargo of 1963, the various foreign efforts to impose sanctions and boycotts on sports and trade with the Republic, and similar actions taken by foreigners against Rhodesia—all these gave South Africa the impetus for seeking new alignments and trade relationships on the African continent and elsewhere. Among the more important of these were her new, and still growing, relations with Rhodesia, with Portugal, and with Malawi.

There were other new strands in South Africa's foreign relations. She began to expand her associations with European nations—with France, Germany, Switzerland, and Italy. Furthermore, with the emergence of so many new nations on the African continent, she began to turn away from those former colonial trading partners whom she now found militantly set against her—Zambia and Tanzania among these. She sought out new trading relationships with the more conservative of African nations—Ivory Coast, Gabon, and Madagascar. Finally, with the 1967 closure of the Suez Canal, yet another strand in her expanded foreign policy has appeared. That has come from redirection of South African markets toward the Far East—to Japan and China, to Australia and New Zealand. With these and more recent associations oriented toward certain Latin American states, South Africa appears to have moved her major foreign policy activities into a southern hemisphere orbit. This new orientation appears to include concepts of defense as well as of commerce. Thus, it can be seen that before 1961 South Africa's foreign policy was somewhat circumscribed by her special associations with the United Kingdom. Today, however, her foreign policy associations are far broader—ranging from Japan through Iran (with which nation she is developing special petroleum relationships); through Portugal, Rhodesia and Malawi on the African continent; and westward to Argentina and Brazil. It seems likely that all these relationships may grow as the European Common Market forces further redirection of South Africa's former trading patterns with the United Kingdom and the European continent.

The strategic relationship of South Africa to the Western powers, particularly the United Kingdom and the United States, has resulted in part from the peculiar geographic placement of South Africa at the base of the African continent. There, the Republic stands beside the sea lanes connecting the Atlantic and Indian oceans. Her strategic location there was amplified in World War years and in times when, as today, the Suez Canal is closed by regional hostilities.

In the same context South Africa holds a vast array of natural resources essential to modern world economy—coal, iron, uranium, chrome, copper, and so forth—as well as the well-known gold and diamonds. So, too, does she hold a place of logistical superiority over most of the rest of sub-Saharan Africa. Control is attained over a vast area of land and sea from her seaports and her airfields. Her geographic situation, too, offers special capabilities for satellite and missile tracking. All these "resource" associations, combined with the major private investment and trading relationships maintained with the United States and the United Kingdom place those latter nations in a special dilemma vis-à-vis the Republic, as contrasted with various Black African states to the north.

THE UNITED STATES

South Africa's relationships with the United States, public and private, have been in a kind of "love-hate" category for some years. Americans are personally popular with South Africans, and the latter have not, until now, resented the influx of American capital or personnel. South Africa, until now, has always accepted willingly the import of American technology, tourists, music, movies, and related cultural innovations. While South Africans do not concur in many American political aims, they appear to admire America's anti-Communist determination, American attainments in science and industry, and the fact that Americans, like South Africans, arose as a nation out of pioneering, decolonized stock.

However, with the passage of several recent U.S. national administrations, notably those of Presidents Roosevelt, Truman, Kennedy, and Johnson, South Africans have begun to look more questioningly on American foreign policy, especially as it relates to Africa and to problems of colonialism and of race. Public and private South African antagonism to the United States was compounded by the American civil rights drive for integration, by American acceptance of the UN arms embargo against Pretoria, and especially by former UN Ambassador Arthur Goldberg's famous statement in Turtle Bay that South Africa had "forfeited" her right of occupation and administration in South-West Africa. The peregrinations of high American officials through Africa during the past decade brought cold comfort to South Africans, but political leaders in Pretoria used these junkets as justification for their apartheid programs and as rebuttal to any thought of introducing into the Republic the political concept of "one man, one vote." Yet, despite all the political flailing of South African segregationists against American integrationists—and of American humanists against South Africa's racialists—the ordinary, day-to-day relationships between the United States and South Africa have actually grown closer in recent years.

Thus, in the 25 years of Nationalist rule in Pretoria, the United States has increased its investment in the Republic from less than $100 million to a total now approaching or exceeding $1.25 billion (direct and portfolio). Furthermore, trade between the two nations during the same period has quadrupled—two-way trade now exceeding $700 million yearly. As well, there have been developed the new aerospace relationships, with the NASA satellite-tracking station and related facilities located in the Transvaal. There have also been unusually close atomic energy relationships, in which a good deal of American know-how has been shared with South African expertise and resources to the profit of both nations.

Until 1968 there was a clear-cut yet confusing ambivalent relationship existing between the United States and South Africa in official circles. However, the advent of the Nixon Administration appears to have brought into U.S.-South African relationships at official levels a somewhat softer association. On the one hand there remains the U.S. contention that apartheid is "abhorrent." Too, South-West Africa is still recognized by the United States as being an "international trust." Yet, on the other hand, there is continuing explicit and tacit assertion by U.S. officials that we must continue to live with, to trade with, and to invest in, South Africa. Secretary of State William Rogers has expressed the hope that the constructive interplay of political, economic, and social forces will inevitably lead to peaceful change and racial equality in South Africa. Meanwhile, in terms of President Nixon's "low-profile" concept, there appears to be a lessening of strictures and a muffling of official condemnation of the South African regime. This "softening" of official U.S. attitudes against all White-supremacy southern African regimes is demonstrated in administrative action—the recent U.S. decision to buy Rhodesian chrome, the offer of a new $435 million "aid" package to Portugal and her African provinces, the new, long-term Ex-imbank loans covering locomotives sold to South Africa, and the quiet acceptance by the United States of recent deportations of U.S. churchmen from South Africa. All these actions betoken a general official U.S. "softening" of official U.S. attitudes toward "the White redoubt."

In measuring the extent of this official U.S. "softening" of attitudes against South Africa and the other White-ruled regimes of southern Africa, former UN Ambassador Charles Yost makes some telling points. An article of his, appearing in The Washington Post of January 27, 1972, states inter alia:

> None of these [UN] actions seem to have had the slightest effect. The White regimes are as firmly entrenched as ever, and as determined to remain so. It is, on the contrary, the United Nations countermeasures which are falling apart. Even Britain and the United States seem about to abandon the sanctions against Rhodesia. France makes no bones about selling arms in large quantities to South Africa. The United States, for the sake of the Azores bases, confers its blessing and economic support on the Portuguese government. All these are easy things to do, but are they wise in the longer run?
>
> It is quite true that economic sanctions against Rhodesia have not worked, that they would be even less likely to work against South Africa, and that no one seriously considers sending a UN military force to overthrow the White regimes.

> What answer, then, are we going to give to the Africans when they ask, "Are violence and bloodshed, Black against White, the only means by which the huge Black majorities in Southern Africa are to obtain equal rights and freedoms?" If the answer is yes, what is the rest of the world going to do when violence and bloodshed actually break out on a large scale? . . . I am convinced that they [the problems] are not going to be solved peacefully and progressively by the Whites of Southern Africa without very strong outside pressure. The status quo is far too comfortable. On the other hand, if the problems are left to be resolved eventually by violence, we may expect to see a ghastly repetition of . . . East Pakistan, except, in this case, with far-reaching and traumatic Black-White overtones.
>
> Frankly, the United States has never seriously addressed itself to this problem, because Africa has not seemed all that urgent or important. We . . . are . . . trying to do the minimum that would appease the 40 African Governments without seriously incommoding our South African and Portuguese friends. We can rock along in that way for some time longer, but in the end it won't work. Some day Africa will be shockingly and hideously on all the front pages. Then we will ask ourselves why we did not, while there was still time, press and drive South Africa and Portugal into the modern world with all the non-military resources at our command.[1]

THE UNITED KINGDOM

South Africa's relationships with Britain during the past decade have also been ambivalent. Public and private attitudes of Britishers differ considerably on the issue of the Republic and apartheid, private criticism being much more forthright. The recent British governments, Labour and Conservative, have also differed radically. Until recently the British press and pulpit have been especially vocal. However, increasing British internal race problems and her movement toward Europe's Common Market have combined to tone down these vocalizations. Even yet, however, there is open resentment in Britain toward South Africa's "Whites only" sports policy.

The UN arms embargo of 1963 and the Rhodesian unilateral declaration of independence (1965), with all their resulting complications for U.K.-South African associations, have proved especially trying to the British governments of Harold Wilson and Edward Heath.

The Labour Party, under Wilson, stood firm in its criticism of internal South African policies and of South African support of the rebel Rhodesian regime. That support seriously weakened U.K. and UN efforts to bring the Rhodesians "to heel." The present Conservative Heath government of Britain, however, has been far softer in its associations with South Africa. Prime Minister Heath has obviously sought to "mend fences" with Pretoria wherever possible, emphasizing trade and giving new assurances on possible sales of British arms counter to the U.K.'s earlier promises of support for the UN arms embargo. Furthermore, despite the fact that a number of her own churchmen-citizens working in South Africa have been deported from the Republic recently, British officialdom has remained singularly quiet. (For a full discussion of U.K. investment in, and trade with, South Africa, see Chapter 6.)

FRANCE

Since the 1963 UN arms embargo against the Republic, relations between South Africa and France have been considerably enhanced. These continue to be good, although they may undergo some tensions as a result of the extension of the European Economic Community. Despite these tensions, it is probably safe to assume that the South African-French rapport will continue. It is worthy of special note that France has virtually taken over from the United Kingdom the role of chief arms supplier to the Republic, that French investment in South Africa is increasing, and that Paris may have been the chief inspiration for the concept of Black African "dialogue" with Pretoria.

BOTSWANA, LESOTHO, AND SWAZILAND

Relations between the Republic and the three Black-ruled ex-British High Commission Territories (now independent)—Botswana, Lesotho, and Swaziland—have generally been good. There have been occasional spats over the operation of the joint customs union and the occasional unexpected forays of South African Police into these territories in search of cattle rustlers or political exiles. There has been some UN and tropical African pressure on these smaller nations to take a more independent line. For example, tropical African leaders have advocated that Botswana, Lesotho, and Swaziland seek an associated role with the European Common Market and take a more militant stand against South Africa within the UN and OAU. Since these nations are all landlocked and highly dependent upon the South African economy and financial structure, the rulers of these three nations are acutely aware of the delicacy of their positions vis-à-vis South Africa. While they keep these roles constantly under review, they are not likely to endanger their present reserved but cordial relationships with Pretoria. It is of particular interest to note that they consider these associations so close that they have not yet seen the need of establishing diplomatic and consular relations with the Republic. They claim that they can conduct most such business with Pretoria informally and effectively by telephone.

NEARBY AFRICAN STATES

South Africa's relations with other nearby African states are also deserving of attention. Pretoria's attitude toward certain of these particularly Malawi, Madagascar, and Gabon—has been friendly. Closer political, diplomatic, and economic ties are being formed with Malawi, which has received some technical and financial aid from Pretoria within the past five years. That financial aid has been concentrated on helping Malawi to erect a new capital city and to increase her tourism facilities. The diplomatic links have included an exchange of ambassadors, the Malawi ambassador to Pretoria being the first Black African ambassador ever accepted by the Republic. The South African ambassador assigned to Malawi is White. (The United States, under Congressional pressure, has considered assignment of a Black diplomat to the American embassy in Pretoria. Reacting informally, the South African government has indicated reluctance about this type of assignment, contending that "the time is not yet opportune."[2] Thus far, the Malawi diplomat remains the only Black official in Pretoria's diplomatic colony.)

OTHER AFRICAN NATIONS

Pretoria's attitude toward other, more militant, Black African nations has been frankly hostile. It is evident that Pretoria fears these nations may be used as major staging areas for offensive military drives (with or without Communist support) against South Africa. South African attention has been particularly riveted on Zambia and Tanzania, which have given sanctuary to South African political exiles and have supported the training of "freedom fighters," or alleged "terrorists." Some of these have infiltrated Rhodesia and South Africa, later to be captured and tried in those countries on charges of sabotage. Pretoria fears that this type of action will increase and might eventually be supported by major Communist allies, especially the mainland Chinese. In view of the logistical situation and the superiority of

South African forces in terms of military groupings on the African continent, there remains considerable question as to the imminence of these external dangers. In any event, the South Africans have made extraordinary propaganda out of those few "terrorist" incursions that have occurred thus far.

Dialogue

Allied to any discussion of South Africa's relations with Africa to the north of the Zambezi River have been the recent debates over "dialogue." Some African leaders, particularly those of former French colonies, such as President Félix Houphouet-Boigny of Ivory Coast, have contended that the only way to effect change within South Africa beneficial to the non-Whites would be to enter into "dialogue" with Pretoria. There has been contention from some knowledgeable quarters that the prime push for this type of discussion actually came from Paris rather than from French Africa. This initiative was apparently in the hopes that an increase in trading relationships between South Africa and parts of French Africa might thereby be accomplished. In any event, the concept of "dialogue" has been discreetly pushed by both moderate French-speaking Black African leaders and by Pretoria, but few results have yet been noted, beyond an exchange of state visits by Prime Minister Vorster and President Hastings Banda of Malawi, plus initiation of trade talks with Madagascar.

As a matter of historical background on the "dialogue" issue, it should be noted that, as far back as 1969, the idea was given attention by Presidents Kenneth Kaunda of Zambia and Julius Nyerere of Tanzania. In April of that year the Chiefs of state of East and Central Africa met in conclave in Lusaka, Zambia. From that meeting was issued a document known as "the Lusaka Manifesto." This document offered to negotiate with South African leaders on the issue of the condition of the Republic's non-Whites. It thus supported the concept of a "dialogue," but specified that failure of such talks would necessitate a reversion to force as the only means of settling the racial problems of the Republic. South African leaders and the country's news media gave scant attention to the manifesto. Subsequently, however, Prime Minister Vorster revealed an unsuccessful chain of correspondence with Kaunda, designed to set up talks between the leaders of those two nations. President Kaunda reacted bitterly to the unilateral release by Vorster of this correspondence.

It is recognized, even by the most ardent proponents of any eventual north-south "dialogue," that two major issues stand in the way of success of these talks. The first is the question of an agenda. For example, would Pretoria agree to discuss its internal political problems under such an international spotlight? The second question would be the position of non-White South African leaders vis-à-vis such talks. For example, would Pretoria be likely to permit participation of acknowledged South African Black leaders in the "dialogue" on the South African side of the table? Responsible South African non-White leaders contend that to make any international "dialogue" effective, preliminary talks should take place within the South African "family."

THE UN

South Africa's relations with the UN are also deserving of special attention. As a prelude to such discussion, it should be recalled that former Prime Minister Smuts was not only a major architect of the UN, but was reputedly responsible for drafting a portion of its charter. In earlier years he had been responsible, too, for South Africa being placed in the supervisory role over the South-West Africa mandate. (That mandate had been assumed by Pretoria at the conclusion of World War I.)

It might thus be assumed that South Africa would have become an arch defender of the world body. From the start in 1945, however, Smuts and his successors tangled so often with various UN bodies that, in the 27 years of South African membership therein, its associations with the UN and its specialized agencies have diminished almost to the vanishing point. In the past quarter-century, there have been almost 100 major resolutions emanating from the UN General Assembly and subsidiary bodies condemnatory of South Africa's policy of apartheid; its treatment of Black, Asian, and Coloured peoples; its manner of administering South-West Africa; Pretoria's violations of the rule of law; and so forth. Some of these matters have recurred on UN agendas for the past two decades. The relatively moderate UN resolutions of earlier years have recently become stronger as the various South African governments have consistently refused to recognize the UN's right to involve itself in matters that Pretoria considers domestic and, thus, not coming within UN jurisdiction. While the UN continues to be concerned about South African matters, the Republic's race laws, in turn, have become increasingly restrictive. Thus, in the face of UN censure, South Africa has refused to moderate its internal policies, applying its apartheid philosophy equally in the Republic and in South-West Africa. Given the present temper of the South African polity, it seems likely that whichever major political party had been in power, that party would have applied and extended South Africa's race laws and social customs more or less stringently. As regards the UN, it would also appear that all South

African political leaders would agree that the country's race laws are an internal matter, not subject to UN "interference" and that South Africa must continue to have full authority over South-West Africa. Virtually all White South Africans seem clearly united on these points.

As an adjunct to any discussion of UN-South African relationships and controversy, it should be noted that the Republic has gradually been pushed out of membership in various UN specialized agencies, such as the International Labor Organization (ILO), the UN Educational, Scientific and Cultural Organization (UNESCO), and the UN Economic Commission for Africa. South Africa's last contribution to UNESCO was in 1956; its latest contribution to the ILO was made in 1963; its latest contribution to the Food and Agriculture Organization (FAO) was in 1964; and that to the World Health Organization (WHO) was made in 1965.[3] Her membership in other bodies such as the International Postal Union has also been threatened. It seems clear that South African political leaders must often have considered giving up their membership in the UN. They appear to have remained there, however, in the belief that they could, on occasion, better defend themselves by being present rather than by being absent. Statements of various recent prime ministers of the Republic tend to support an underlying hope that the UN, like its predecessor, the League of Nations, will eventually disintegrate.

It seems certain that South Africa's frictions with the UN are bound to continue. It seems likely, however, that the United States, the United Kingdom, and France, as permanent members of the Security Council and as leaders in the General Assembly, will continue to moderate debate in UN halls to avert having the South African situation judged a "Chapter 7" concern (one threatening world peace). Thereby, both the United States and the United Kingdom would avoid the necessity of supporting more forceful UN action in southern Africa and, at the same time, would avoid creating a precedent for UN "interference" into their own domestic problems of race or religion. There can never be set to rest, however, the thought that a major racial flare-up in southern Africa would require world attention, building up new pressure within the UN for sanctions and/or direct intervention.

SOUTH-WEST AFRICA

The international territory of South-West Africa (or Namibia) has a population of 630,000 and a land area of 318,000 square miles. Its capital is Windhoek, and its chief port is Walvis Bay. (The latter is administered as an integral part of the Cape Province within the Republic.)

South-West Africa is bordered on the north by Angola, on the west by the Atlantic Ocean, on the south and east by South Africa proper, and on the northeast by Botswana and Zambia. The greater part of the territory comprises an arid, high plateau, the continuation of the main South African highveld. The coastal strip is partially desert. The climate is hot and unusually dry, but periods of severe drought occasionally alternate with periods of excessive rainfall.

Blacks comprise about 85 percent of the total population of 630,000. Of the 95,000 Whites, some 60 percent are Afrikaners, 25 percent are Germans, and 15 percent of British extraction. Of the Blacks, differing ethnically and linguistically, the principal tribes are the Ovambo (numbering 300,000); the Dama (numbering 50,000); the Herero (numbering 40,000); the Nama, or Hottentot (numbering 40,000); and the Okavango (exceeding 30,000). Other tribes, smaller in number, include the Caprivian, Rehoboth Baster, Bushmen, and Tswana. There are also some 15,000 Cape Coloureds. The Ovambo are settled in the less-arid northern sector of the territory. They constitute the main farming and mining labor force. The majority of the Blacks remain animist, though many are adherents of the various Christian missions, these including Anglican, Lutheran, Roman Catholic, Methodist, and Dutch Reformed. Afrikaans and English are the official languages, but German is widely used, as are the tribal vernaculars. The literacy rate among Blacks is reported to be less than ten percent.

The territory is becoming increasingly important as a source of minerals, karakul wool, and fisheries. It is also considered highly strategic by South Africa as a buffer zone between the Republic and Angola. It is also increasingly important as a symbol of South African determination not to be overridden by militant UN and Black African opponents of Pretoria.

Although agriculture and stock raising occupy the largest working sector of the economy, mining contributes more than one-half the territorial GDP. Fishing is also a substantial income earner, while manufacturing is inconsequential. The territorial income has expanded tenfold since the end of World War II, with GDP in 1968 reaching $400 million. This represents some $600 per capita. However, it is estimated that some 20 percent of all profits and wages are repatriated from South-West Africa by nonresident firms and workers. Furthermore, there is no breakdown between White per capita income and that (obviously much smaller) received by Black labor. (See Chapter 7.) It is estimated that more than 50 percent of invested capital is from overseas sources, with most of the remainder controlled by South African ownership.

Although only 30 percent of all land is considered arable, there is a good deal of commercial agriculture, this concentrated in cattle raising and karakul wool. Production of some 5,000 commercial White-owned farms brought some $60 million in exports of these two commodities in 1969.

Mineral exports in 1967 were valued above $200 million. Diamonds were said to represent more than 60 percent of this total. The main diamond production is from alluvial soils and offshore diggings. This is controlled by Consolidated Diamond Mines, an offshoot of Anglo-American (and DeBeers) Corporation of South Africa. (This company is neither U.S.-owned nor U.S.-controlled.) Other mineral production, mainly from the American-owned mine at Tsumeb, includes production of copper, lead, zinc, vanadium, and manganese. (Majority stock in this mining enterprise is distributed between American Metals Climax and Newmount Mining.)

Fisheries processing is mainly controlled by South African interests. It accounts for only 4 percent of the territory's GDP but accounts for nearly 25 percent of the value of all exports.

South-West African trade figures are normally incorporated into South Africa's trade statistics, since these two and the independent nations of Botswana, Lesotho, and Swaziland form a customs-trade union and a rand currency zone. However, in 1966 South-West Africa's exports were estimated at $293 million. Imports in that year were estimated at $217 million. About 90 percent of territorial imports originate in South Africa, although 90 percent of South-West Africa's exports go overseas. As a result, the territory creates about 10 percent of all export income from the custom zone, earning some $250 million in foreign exchange for the customs group—principally South Africa.

Until now, both apartheid law and customary South African convention have been applied fully within South-West Africa. Contract labor terms have recently come under international scrutiny as a result of strong attack of the territory's Black labor leaders. Supported by the thesis that the oncoming Bantustans are soon to become autonomous, tribal leaders and their fellow workers have challenged the terms of their anachronistic labor contracts and have struck. The recent strike of Ovambo workmen, numbering 13,000, against the mining enterprise at Tsumeb was particularly effective. This new-found spirit of "independence" among the Black workers has given South African political leaders and foreign investors pause. (For details, see Chapter 7.)

Although non-White political organizations have been weak and ineffective, it now seems clear that creating the ten proposed Bantustans for South-West Africa will awaken or resuscitate Black nationalism and create new leaders. Ovambo and Herero leaders have long made their opposition to South African rule and apartheid well known to the world through exile petitions and mouthpieces at the UN.

These voices, too, are likely to be strengthened by the Bantustan concept and implementation.

At the same time it seems likely that the Whites (and possibly the few Coloureds) resident in South-West Africa will press to retain the status quo or will seek full integration with the Republic as a means of protecting themselves against any UN move to preempt the territory.

The present White population of the territory enjoys a limited amount of self-government, granted by South Africa in 1925. An administrator, appointed by the Republic's prime minister, is head of the territorial government. The National party holds control of the territorial Legislative Assembly. The opposition within that 18-member body is usually associated with the opposition United party of South Africa. The Legislative Assembly has authority over matters not reserved to South Africa and can make recommendations to the South African Parliament regarding the administration of the territory. However, full and final authority rests with the South African government.

As in South Africa, franchise is totally restricted to Whites. Political opposition parties formed in the territory by non-Whites have been considered "revolutionary." There have been three fairly active Black political groupings, however—the South-West Africa Peoples' Organization (SWAPO), the South-West Africa National Union (SWANU), and the South-West Africa National United Front (SWANUF). All these groups seek self-determination and independence for the territory.

While the territorial government has some legislative power, major power is retained by Pretoria/Capetown in areas ranging from railways to defense. The White South-West Africans are represented in the Republic's House of Assembly by six elected members and in the South African Senate by four nominated members (two of these chosen by the territorial Legislative Assembly and two chosen by the South African government).

Until development of the Bantustan concept, with its limited internal autonomy thesis, all power over Blacks, excepting local education, was retained in the hands of the Ministry of Bantu Affairs in Pretoria. As the Bantustans emerge, and as already apparent with the incipient Ovambo "nation," there is now a transitional phase in evidence. Some local governmental powers are moving into the hands of the Blacks through their Bantustan executives and Legislative assemblies. As with the Republic's Bantustans (such as the Transkei), the full extent and eventual goals of this transition are unclear. Here, as in South Africa, however, it would seem evident that dreams of self-determination awakened by the Bantustan ideas will be hard to stifle. Inauguration of the Bantustans in South-West Africa took place by unilateral action of the Republic government and without prior or subsequent approval of the UN. The first such Bantustan to be activated with its own Legislative Council and embryo internal autonomy was Ovamboland, established in 1968. Nine more are destined to follow.

During the hostilities of World War I, the territory of South-West Africa, then held as a colony by Germany, was occupied by South African troops. Germany lost South-West Africa and her other colonies following her defeat (under the terms of the Treaty of Versailles). At that time South-West Africa was placed under a League of Nations mandate to be administered by South Africa. With the demise of the League of Nations (1939), there followed the postwar (1945) creation of the UN (with its trusteeship system for mandates remaining dependent). Other such mandates from the defunct League were placed under this trusteeship. However, South Africa refused to relinquish to the UN its control over South-West Africa on grounds that it did (and does) not recognize the UN as legal successor to the League. South Africa does not deny that she has a kind of "international" obligation regarding her continuing administration of the territory of South-West Africa. Pretoria refuses, however, to accept the idea of a supervisory role for the UN over her conduct of that mandate. Even so, South Africa has, on occasion, submitted information to the UN regarding her administration of the territory and has admitted UN representatives into South Africa under South African escort. Pretoria also contends that it continues to administer South-West Africa "in the spirit of the mandate." In fact, however, she has increasingly applied apartheid legislation to the territory, including the Bantustan concept, and she administers the territory as a de facto annex of the Republic, without thought of its eventual independence as an entity.

The question of continuing administration over the territory, the unwillingness of the Republic to recognize UN supervisory authority, and its determination to apply the apartheid program to South-West Africa have frequently been the subjects of litigation before the World Court in the Hague. Several advisory opinions furnished by the World Court in the period 1950-60 tended to support the UN position with respect to South-West Africa. None of these was considered binding by the Republic. A subsequent formal case brought by Liberia and Ethiopia (acting as plaintiffs against South Africa) was long and drawn out. Rendering a judgment on this case by a one-vote margin on procedural grounds, the court contended that Liberia and Ethiopia were not proper plaintiffs. The court contended that those nations had nothing to do with the post-World War I handling of the mandate as signatories to the Treaty of Versailles. In the referenced case the court rendered no substantive judgment as to whether or not South Africa should continue its administration of the territory of South-West Africa. The General Assembly, despite the court's action, demanded expulsion of South Africa from the territory in 1966. These and previous UN demands were supported by a later (1971) World Court advisory opinion that South Africa's continuing presence in South-West Africa was illegal.

At the request of the UN Security Council, the new secretary-general of the UN, Kurt Waldheim, visited South Africa in March 1972. His task was to persuade Prime Minister Vorster that South Africa should give up control over South-West Africa. Even before his arrival, however, Prime Minister Vorster made it clear that his country was unwilling to give up its control over the territory. However, the secretary-general was able to visit South-West Africa and talk with opponents and proponents on the question of continuing South African control.

The Washington Post of March 6, 1972, characterized Waldheim's visit to southern Africa as a close-up look at one of the UN's "most prolonged and emotional issues. . . ." Commenting on the Waldheim tour, Newsweek of March 20, 1972, stated: "For the most part . . . Waldheim was held to the same old conveyor-belt tour to which all officials and journalistic visitors are treated by the South African Government—the irrigation projects, the schools, the hospitals and carefully chosen Africans. . . ."

In his talks with Vorster, Waldheim is reported to have proposed an independent federal status for South-West Africa. Although the prime minister is reported to have turned down the concept, the secretary-general is said to "see a ray of hope." Waldheim is reported by Newsweek as saying, "I believe it is the aim of the South African Government to grant self-determination to Namibia. . . ." That remark was received with skepticism by African diplomats at the UN and elsewhere.

An important sidelight on the Ovambo situation in international terms was the deportation, in March 1972, of an Anglican Bishop, Colin Winter, and two of his Anglican clergymen. These men had been assisting, financially and otherwise, in the legal defense of the striking Ovambos. It is especially noteworthy that these men were ordered expelled from an "international territory" by the Nationalist government of South Africa on grounds that they were "agitators." It is noteworthy, also, that their deportation came at the very moment that the UN secretary-general, Kurt Waldheim, was due to make his first visit to South and South-West Africa.

The United States has consistently maintained that South Africa is obliged, under the mandate (and the trust) to respect the rights of the inhabitants of South-West African and to accept UN supervision in administration of the territory. Various official U.S. representations, made in Washington and Pretoria and in the UN over recent years, have pointed out that South African apartheid (including Bantustans) legislation, made applicable to South-West Africa, is contrary to the Republic's mandatory obligations. The United States believes that, either as a UN trust or as a League mandate, the inhabitants of South-West Africa should have the right of self-determination and eventual independence. The United States maintains that, until the territory achieves that independence, the UN continues to have supervisory authority over South-West Africa and that South Africa, as de facto administrator, is accountable to the UN for its actions in the territory. The United States has repeatedly asked the South African government to cooperate with the UN and others in preparing the territory for independence.

As noted elsewhere, foreign investment (including U.S.) in South-West African mining properties is heavy. In May 1970 the United States declared its official discouragement of further U.S. investment in South-West Africa, then indicating that U.S. nationals and companies so investing there in the future will not receive U.S. investment protection and assistance against claims of future national (and lawful) governments for nationalization of those properties. Export-import guarantees and other U.S. government credit facilities, too, are no longer applicable in South-West Africa.

Pretoria recently offered to hold a plebiscite in South-West Africa, this to determine the real desires of the inhabitants on the question of independence. However, Pretoria later withdrew its offer, but continued to claim that the majority of the territory's indigenous inhabitants wish to remain associated with the Republic. Thus, the issue is stark—will South Africa ever give up control of South-West Africa, or, alternatively, will she lead that territory to real independence through the Bantustans or otherwise? If not, what are the UN and the international community to do about the case?

THE INDIAN OCEAN

The withdrawal of Britain from areas east of Suez and the power vacuum which that withdrawal has left in the Indian Ocean represents a new military-naval problem for the United States, the United Kingdom, and the Western allies. Though not formally a member of NATO, South Africa, by its peculiar geographic position, figures prominently in any Western plan to fill the Indian Ocean void as a counter to Russian naval influence there.

The closing of British bases and the departure or scale-down from Singapore to Aden during recent years represented the first step in creation of this vacuum. Emergence of the Persian Gulf states as independent authorities was recognized as the second. The India-Pakistan conflict, resulting in the enhancement of Russian influence on the Asian subcontinent at the expense of American influence, represented yet a third factor of diminishing Western power in the Indian Ocean area. Widespread Russian naval activity in the area represented a fourth important element for concern.

To counter all these the Americans have done the following: (a) reinforced slightly their existing Middle East naval command at Bahrein; (b) established, with British help, an austerity naval-air base at Diego Garcia in the Mauritian Archipelago (due for completion in 1973); (c) decided to send into the eastern Indian Ocean (January 1972) a flotilla from the U.S. seventh fleet, normally based in the far Pacific.

The American situation in the Indian Ocean has been compounded by the fact that, during the Johnson Administration, U.S. officials decreed a cessation of American naval visits to South African ports on grounds that non-White crew members were there exposed to the humiliations of apartheid. Thus, the proximity of the South African ports continue to be denied to the United States at a time when the value of those ports is undeniable in any effective Western surveillance of the Indian Ocean. America's self-denial of access to those South African ports is also important as regards fueling, provisioning, and shore leave. British naval units and those of other NATO powers are not so affected, as they continue to make use of those ports. As yet, no really useful alternative Afro-Asian ports of call for American naval units—such as those on Madagascar or Ceylon—have been formally established.

THE WHITE REDOUBT

There is yet one more concept of importance to describe in this section on the Republic's foreign relations. This is the concept that sees South African suzerainty extending over South-West Africa, Rhodesia, Angola, Mozambique, Malawi, Lesotho, Botswana, and Swaziland. As this suzerainty hardens it builds, with its buffer zone of satellite states, a White redoubt, or bastion, along the line of the Zambezi River. This bastion is stiffened through expansion of the military, political, economic, social, and cultural powers of South Africa, and, thereby, the Republic's hegemony throughout southern Africa is enhanced.

In various ways, in recent years, has this extension of suzerainty become more apparent. As to Rhodesia there have been the activities of the South African security forces on Rhodesian soil in allied actions against the "freedom fighters" from the north. There has also been the concerted effort by South African government and business to "protect" Rhodesia from the debilitating influences of the UN economic sanctions program directed against the Rhodesian regime. These efforts have included financial aid, free access to South African markets, and easy access through South Africa of goods transiting to and from the beleaguered country.

With the Portuguese, too, there have been concerted efforts by Pretoria and Lisbon to control infiltration of "freedom fighters." As well, there has been a certain concert of views on general defense matters and on UN agenda problems.

With Malawi, too, there has been a generous (by South African standards) extending of a helping hand. There have been South African loans for tourism and for the new Malawian capital. Pretoria is underwriting costs of a new rail link between Malawi and the port of Nacala in Mozambique. There has been South African technical assistance in support of agricultural production and tourism. There has been a considerable increase of Malawi's exports to South Africa, this export trade tripling within the past five years. There has been constant "dialogue" with Malawi in the form of state visits, official discussions, and formalized diplomatic relationships.

South Africa's relationships with Botswana, Lesotho, and Swaziland have extended far beyond ordinary trading spheres. (These have been described in previous pages.) In part they have developed from their peculiar geographical proximity to the Republic. That economic dominance—even intensified and extended to the political field—also is evident in the Republic's associations with South-West Africa. Cultural and financial intrusions by Pretoria into all these territories of southern Africa are deep. Even the dependence of the work forces of these territories on South Africa is clear-cut. Economically, all these territories are heavily dependent on the Republic. Politically and militarily, they also serve as important buffer zones against the Black nationalist drives from the north.

Long-range, it would appear that in all these subcontinental associations, with Black rulers and with White, South Africa is setting up her own sphere of influence, her own area of coexistence, her own role as suzerain over southern Africa. Thus is her hegemony over the White redoubt becoming solidified.

CHAPTER

11

CONCLUSIONS AND RECOMMENDATIONS

The Introduction to this book sets forth the dangers, internal and international, which South African racial and social tensions present. The Introduction also sets down a number of rhetorical questions, which the socioeconomic dissection of the country and people, made in pages following, seeks to clarify or to answer. The foregoing examination of South Africa's situation leaves little doubt that it is volatile, potentially explosive. In fact, that explosion might have come long before now had it not been for the effectiveness of the country's internal security network; the breadth of governmental regulation, which limits both freedom and opposition; and the exceptional forbearance of the non-Whites.

Despite these controls, however, there have been growing demands for change emanating from within the Republic. The inspiration for these demands has come from businessmen, clerics, and academics, as well as from some political opponents of the present regime. They ask for modification of social attitudes toward, and improved working conditions for, the non-Whites. Whether these demands are yet strong enough to excite real change and whether such change may come in time to avert widespread violence are questions yet to be answered.

The detailed analysis of the South African situation set forth in preceding pages reveals at least five specific areas in which constructive change could bring amelioration of the problem. Three of these are primarily internal in nature and application. Two areas are external and international, but require cooperation from South Africa. Improvements in these five areas of possible change might well provide catharsis and catalysis, thereby redirecting the country to a new and better destiny—splendid rather than sanguine.

The three internal areas or determinants are these: (a) as that program now seems irreversible, the Republic should give full public and private backing to the Bantustan program so as to insure its economic success and to clarify its political goals; (b) the Republic should encourage a program, public and private, to alleviate the country's social ills and to attain a modicum of harmony and social justice; and (c) the Republic should develop a program designed to move the South African economy onto higher ground for the benefit of all races.

The two external determinants requiring either tacit or active support from South Africa and other nations, are these: (a) a "meeting of minds" between the UN and South Africa as regards the future of the international territory of South-West Africa, and (b) improvement of South Africa's position within the family of nations, this to be accomplished by a multinational program of constructive diplomacy, redirecting the Republic into her natural role of economic leadership on the African continent.

A description of the nature and dimensions of these five areas of change, these determinants, follows.

The problems and prospects of the Bantustan program evident thus far are detailed in Chapter 5 of this book. To date, the accomplishments of that program appear to be both fragmentary and contradictory. Its aims appear murky. The program does not seem to meet the differing needs of urban and rural Blacks. The program does not yet seem to have been given the forethought, the financial backing, and the technical know-how essential to assure its viability, economic or political. Imperative questions remain. These include the nature of agricultural, industrial, and social development; settlement of land problems; clarification of citizenship and nationality; and the eventual political situation vis-à-vis the Republic. On the one hand, there is a centrifugal divisiveness to the Bantustan program—physically drawing the various tribes apart, further separating urban and rural Black African groupings, and further separating all races of the Republic. On the other hand, there is the centripetal influence of economic integration, of urbanization, and of a new political cohesion of reawakened non-White nationalism.

Perhaps, the most important result of the Bantustan program, as evolved thus far, has been the rebirth of Black African nationalism and the rejuvenation of Black African leadership. It would appear that these highly important results have not yet been assessed by White South African leaders. They can no longer ignore these political realities. The Bantustan program, as developed thus far, does not appear to have satisified the desires of the majority of either White South Africans or non-White South Africans. The program does not resolve present ambiguities and the future status of Coloured and Asian communities within the Republic. It does not clarify the future nature of the Republic—whether that be a federation, confederation, or a partitioned set of independent mini-nations. Is White hegemony over the Bantustans to be retained or abandoned?

To make the Bantustans succeed it will take foresighted partnership and mutual respect of both Blacks and Whites. It will take sagacity, courage, even longevity, on the part of responsible Black homeland and urban leaders. As a minimum, it seems essential that the government (a) give full financial and technical backing to the Bantustans; (b) give the Bantustans a full share of South Africa's natural resources, including land and infrastructure; (c) determine the future position of Coloured and Asian communities; (d) lay out in clearest terms the future shape and relationship of the Republic and homelands.

Can it be that the essence of the Bantustan program is simply to continue to divide and rule the Blacks—buying short-term political and economic expediency at the risk of long-term dangers to the Republic's nationhood? At this stage, it must be assumed that this program, now begun, is irreversible. It must also be presumed that South Africa's leaders mean to make the Bantustan program work. Here, as has been seen in other fields of activity in the Republic, there are basic inconsistencies and massive contradictions. It is this kind of dichotomy that weakens South Africa's reputation and veracity in the outside world and with her own people.

The history of the Black African in the Union and the Republic has demonstrated that, short of taking to the streets, he has had no way of initiating programs for his own social, economic, and political betterment. Thus, until the institution of the Bantustans (with their, as yet, unfulfilled promises for social betterment) the Black has had no means of instituting change legally within the system. He has had only two extralegal courses open to him. The one is that of nonviolence, such as passive resistance. The other is the desperate remedy of violence, of massive and forceful civil disobedience. With the exception of Gandhi's pre-Union efforts and the localized, mainly unsuccessful, nonviolent protests of Asians and Blacks in the two decades following the end of World War II, there were virtually no campaigns of nonviolence seen in the nation. All such efforts were regional and partial, not national nor majority supported. All the small-scale programs of sabotage and personalized violence of the early 1960's were illusory and abortive. The actions resulted only in heightened wrath of Whites toward Blacks and in ever more repressive apartheid legislation. The violence provided only a moral justification for the new ruthlessness of Whites toward Blacks.

It has been recognized by most responsible non-White leaders that any campaign based on violence would fail in South Africa to date. In the face of South Africa's efficient security-defense apparatus and a ruthless government, any such effort was bound to fail. However, a serious question now arises as to whether well planned, well-organized, and broad nonviolent campaigns—such as general (and still illegal) strikes, sit-ins, and so forth—would now succeed in shaking the national scene and the White polity. The question here is whether present and potential political leaders of South Africa are now willing to moderate the present apartheid system in the face of obvious social need and growing political danger.

In the face of prospects of bloody violence and/or nonviolent commotion, there is a case being made among thoughtful White South Africans demanding social change for all non-Whites, but especially for Blacks. This plea for social change is coming from academics and editors, from religious and civic leaders, and from businessmen of all political hues. Their voices are now joined by the powerful and persuasive voices of the Black Bantustan leaders and by responsible leaders of the Coloured and Asian communities. Their pleas are premised on the theory that such change must come in time to avoid violence, not alone in the Republic, but throughout southern Africa. While the majority of White South Africans continue to defend the status quo, those Whites appealing for change insist that such change must come in time, and not belatedly. They insist, too, that such change would be beneficial to all South Africans, not to non-Whites alone.

There are many ways in which such moderation can be accomplished. Of these possibilities the simplest would be to eliminate the petty apartheid harassments of Blacks—such as curfews, influx controls, inordinate legal procedures, pass-laws offenses, the denial of the right to own land, and inequity in education. The ruthless treatment of non-White prisoners (the extensive system of detentions and bannings) is an area in which, by curtailment alone, wholesale improvement of relations between the races could be expected. These changes would be simple, yet economically and socially beneficial.

Thus far, the Black Africans, Coloureds, and Asians have pled for change within the system for the following: (a) adequate lands, (b) improved living standards, (c) better labor conditions, and (d) basic civil rights with Whites. Thus far, they are insisting on a more just society for non-Whites in the Republic and homelands, this to be attained peacefully. They are fully aware that, until the creation of the Bantustans, their efforts to achieve that justice were scattered, desultory, and weak. The Bantustans have changed all that. The Black political platform is now available, and it is broad and strong. Coloured and Asian platforms are being built more slowly, via the communal councils, but they are rising into view. Leaders and platforms can now beget either violent change or nonviolent change, depending on the wisdom and immediacy of South African White response to non-White demands.

Today, in South Africa, the contention is being made by some that the much-needed social change can come by modifications in custom and convention. Others believe that essential social change can only come through governmental action. There may be some truth in both contentions. The first group makes the telling point that South Africa's non-Whites suffer as many embarrassing, humiliating, and brutalizing experiences at the hands of White persons and White society as they do by government edict. The second group believes that fundamental and useful change in this arena can only come from changes in law and administration. The foregoing study supports the thesis of beneficial change in both areas.

It seems certain that within many realms of social activity in the Republic, yet still within the purview of South African law, many social evils of the country could be remedied—such as payment of adequate wages, the upgrading of jobs for all non-Whites, and the provision of adequate housing, medical care, education, and amenities. Such improvements could be effected largely by the concerted action of employers, of churches, of trade unions, and of individuals.

On the government side, yet a different situation exists. Within the past two decades the South African ruling clique, by means of its internal security apparatus and its legal and extralegal fiats, succeeded in exiling, banning, imprisoning—figuratively beheading—all responsible non-White leadership. By these actions the government has crushed or suffocated the intellectual, social, and economic potential of Black, Coloured, and Asian communities. Thus, the lifeblood of the country was diluted, and the proper role of the non-White communities left incoherent and inchoate.

As these non-White leaders were gagged or eliminated, the socioeconomic and intellectual bridges of understanding between the various racial components of the Republic were also destroyed. In fact, those losses of contact only served to deepen and widen the chasms of misunderstanding between the races. Today, those chasms exhibit the breadth and depth of misunderstanding, bitterness, even hatred, between White and non-White and between the various non-White groupings themselves. This destruction of the bridges of understanding has also created a deceptive calm—which Whites, most unfortunately, have interpreted as a "happy" acceptance by non-Whites of the status quo. This false and dangerous presumption that Black, Coloured, and Asian are content with the "South African way of life" is entirely erroneous. The calm, the patience, and the surface placidity denote only withdrawal, innate hostility, and a biding of time. This situation, too, has changed with the beginnings of Bantustan. There remains the bitterness and dissatisfaction toward Whites. Yet, beyond this, is a new exhilaration, a new determination of all non-White groupings to improve their economic and social situations—

their educational and political status. This new sense of nationalism and of racial pride is not likely to be denied short of violence, unless certain of its demands are met. All this is bringing the Republic to a new era of unrest. Even Prime Minister Vorster has characterized the current situation within the Republic as "potentially explosive."

South Africa's economic goals—for mining, for agriculture, for industry, for commerce, for transport, and so forth—all aim at steady expansion and self-sufficiency for the country. Based on its natural resources, its geography, its present and potential markets, and proper utilization of its richest resource—its manpower—that movement toward ever higher economic ground would seem assured. Yet even greater economic achievements would appear to be in view if only a few formal actions were to be taken in the field of manpower usage—by government, by business, and by labor leaders. First of these moves would involve a relaxation of the "job reservations" policies toward non-Whites. The second would involve a massive program of apprenticeship training for non-Whites, especially for Blacks. This latter move appears to be as important to the success of the Bantustan program as it would be beneficial to the nation overall. A third essential would be a program whereby corporate and governmental employers would undertake enlightened programs to improve working conditions for their non-White employees. This would include equal pay for equal work; extensive in-house training and upgrading; fringe benefits, such as adequate housing for workers and their families, hospitalization, and retirement provisos; and minimum wage standards for all races. Thereafter, White trade unions might well be persuaded of the advantages accruing to their organizations from opening the doors of those unions to full non-White membership. Many of these foregoing ideas could be promulgated simply by corporate action or administrative fiat. Others would require changes in governmental legislation. To assure South Africa of attainment of its desired economic goals, these changes are essential. This point of view is already being forcefully stated by South Africa's business leaders and knowledgeable economists. Otherwise, economic stagnation may well occur, and that may be followed by economic strangulation.

The mere existence of gold and diamonds and coal and iron is not insurance enough. Production and utilization of all South Africa's natural resources necessitate massive injections of non-White labor to maintain output. Temporary expedients will not be enough to alleviate labor shortages, even if they include new labor controls, costly programs of subsidized immigration, further nationalization of industry, and broader import and financial controls. Temporary delaying action may have been bought by recent increases in the price of gold and by the devaluation of the rand. New Common Market relationships and increasing international market competition will counteract such temporary benefits. In an increasingly competitive modern world the South African economy, including labor, must become increasingly productive and increasingly competitive. The country's economy is irrevocably tied to continued and effective use of its non-White labor. To believe and to act otherwise is to tear the nation apart.

Many informed observers, foreign and South African (including American and South African Blacks), agree that it would serve no real purpose for American and other foreign corporations to pull out of South Africa. These observers contend that it is far better for enlightened foreign investors to remain on the scene. If those enlightened foreign corporations withdrew they would only forsake 18 million non-White South Africans to an ever harsher social and economic condition. Instead, their continued presence would permit the foreign firms to find and utilize means for breeching South African social and labor conventions and, operating within the law, to provide real opportunity for their non-White workers. The contention can be made, as well, that these enlightened foreign (including American) concerns, being backed by Western capital and know-how, should have the opportunity to operate in accordance with Western business ethics and labor principles. The long-term interests of U.S. and U.K. foreign policy and of Western-oriented, multinational business would support these propositions.

It should be recognized that higher wages, improved skills, and better working conditions should provide major incentives for greater productivity among the country's non-White workers. Improvements in living and health standards alone are bound to increase energies and thus output. Such changes and improvements in non-White working conditions might well help to find the quiet that the South African socioeconomic scene so desperately needs. The prototype experience of Polaroid and of other enlightened capital undertakings appear to be demonstrating their value. How much more effective would be the values and the social impetus if 100 or more large American and British corporations in the Republic were to adopt these new labor incentives for their non-White workers?

These corporate actions, combined with the geometrically progressive influences of governmental changes in job reservations and influx control legislation, could have yet other salutary effects. There are the prospects of broad new non-White markets arising out of new non-White purchasing power. These markets could be developed in tandem with the opening of untapped Black African markets north of the Zambezi River. Those markets will only be fully available after South Africa has recognized the economic benefits of social change and, thereby, has improved her international reputation. Those

Black African market opportunities are enormous for a country of South Africa's geographic location and present industrial-agricultural capacity. Such prospects cannot be overlooked by any South African statesman of vision.

As attested in preceding pages, the issue of South-West Africa will continue to create international abrasions, not alone in the UN or in various interested world capitals, but even within South-West Africa itself. In view of the sure prospect that tensions over that territory are bound to increase, it seems reasonable to assume that constructive diplomacy, bilateral and multilateral, should be employed. If that early preventive diplomacy is not utilized, then later, costlier and less effective corrective action will undoubtedly be required. Furthermore, preventive diplomacy must be timely—taken before the fact of imminent turmoil, rather than after the fact of oncoming turmoil. There appear to be some very useful diplomatic approaches that might be taken even today.

In the immediate future no single circumstance or combination of circumstances may be expected to force the leaders of South Africa, of whatever political hue, to give up their hold over South-West Africa. Those officials, of whatever party is in power, would refuse to remove their hands from the administrative controls of that territory, as long as it is not yet independent. They would make their judgments on grounds that their continuing de facto control is required in the Republic's national interests—strategic, political, and economic. At present, the best that can be expected is that South Africa's leaders, recognizing their own interests, might be prevailed upon to do more, socially and economically, for the indigenous inhabitants of South-West Africa. (This recognition would take into consideration, but goes beyond, the Republic's backup of the Bantustan program now being implemented in certain areas of South-West Africa.)

As one means of prodding South African leaders into constructive action, the Republic might again be persuaded to make annual and full socieconomic reports to the UN secretary-general with respect to the conditions of the territory's inhabitants. In this connection, it might also be practicable for South Africa to accept a resident UN representative for South-West Africa on mutually agreeable terms. The secretary-general might also attempt to persuade South Africa to apply a fixed percentage of profits from the territory's mining, commercial, agricultural, and fishing activities toward economic and social betterment of the indigenous inhabitants. It might also be possible for the UN secretary-general to persuade South Africa to bring the territory forward with a carefully tailored program of internal autonomy moving toward confederal autonomy and eventual independence. All these requirements would be in line with articles 73 and 94 of the UN Charter. (South African officials could be reminded that their nation remains a charter member of that organization and their own Prime Minister Smuts was an author of its charter.)

The recent World Court actions with respect to South-West Africa, pro and con; the recent visit of the UN secretary-general to the territory; the ubiquitous UN debate on the issue; the recent labor troubles among the Ovambo workers of the territory; the recent church-state conflicts there; the recent Bantustan development in the area—all these have brought into the open new political pressures and new security problems, for the Republic, for South-West Africa, and for the UN. With all these abrasions, past, present, and future, South-West Africa cannot be overlooked as the real "Achilles heel" of the Republic. The question facing all concerned is not whether South Africa will fail to face up to—and control—these clearly international difficulties, Control them she will—if necessary by force. The question rather will be—how best can the international community react?

In view of these certain prospects of internal trouble and even more troublesome international reaction, it would seem imperative that South Africa be persuaded to moderate those difficulties by its own program of preventive diplomacy. By resolving some of the territory's socioeconomic and planning problems, as well as with moves toward internal autonomy and eventual independence for the territory, the Republic's leaders can insure against an explosion. The case was proved historically in other nearby Black territories, now independent. Given establishment of target dates and of ever increasing autonomy, these nations and their leaders obtained assurance of movement toward nonviolent independence. The same case is now being made for the Bantustans by the Republic's own leaders. Thereby, it can give encouragement and inspiration as well to indigenous leaders of South-West Africa. It would give them the necessary inspiration to move their followers along peaceful paths.

The analysis made by this book has revealed that, in microcosm, South Africa contains most of the world's major social ills. There is the great economic disparity between the "haves" and "have-nots." There are the social inequalities of race, of color, of caste, of class, of culture. There are the massive labor and legal injustices, White versus non-White. There are the varied injustices of apartheid, which have created the chasms between the various races. There is vilification by government of all political opposition and criticism, most of which it labels subversive. There is the collision between Calvinist authoritarianism and Judeo-Christian libertarianism. There is, overall, the domination by Whites over non-Whites.

There is also the failure of most of the Republic's political leaders to comprehend the basic reasons for the condemnation by outsiders of the Republic's social and racial policies. The Republic's leaders either fail to understand or deliberately refuse to recognize that this outcry comes as much or more from an external comprehension of the international dangers of South Africa's internal situation as from a Christian sense of moral indignation. Outsiders contend that if South African political leaders plead that they are upholding Western civilization and culture, they must also uphold Western justice and social values. Further, there is a failure of White South Africans to realize that from their repressive racist crops can well come the harvest of a continental African race war. Seeds of such conflict are already extant. It is for these reasons that South Africa is asked to improve its internal conditions and, thereby, its international image.

Even in South Africa it is widely recognized that, lacking any improvement in her internal situation, there will be gradually increasing tension between Pretoria and neighboring Black nations. This deterioration of neighborliness is bound to be speeded by continuing militant pressures from the Black African nations to the north. Any effort at "dialogue" with these nations is bound to fail unless South Africa's leaders give proof of the earnestness of their intentions by making internal social improvements. If change does not come the present situation can only be followed by broad suzerainty of an all-White hegemony throughout southern Africa. These moves will simply cement into place a locally impregnable and tyrannical White redoubt. To counter these pessimistic prospects, some constructive and timely international action seems essential.

Mention has earlier been made of various international efforts, UN and other, for sanctions and boycotts against South Africa. Most, if not all, of these external pressures appear, thus far, to have only hardened South African White determination to resist change. Those external pressures, instead, have impelled the nation farther and faster toward economic nationalism and self-sufficiency. As preceeding pages record, in the face of outside pressures, South Africa has expanded her defense capabilities. Indicative of her attitude has been her drive for increased domestic components for many of her essential manufactures and her drive to overcome (or to store up against) petroleum shortages. There is no doubt but that she will continue these drives toward impregnability.

Though these drives may not be central to the thinking of the ordinary man in the street in Johannesburg, they are kept constantly in view by the country's leaders in Pretoria and by South African opponents overseas. Thus, in the interests of future peace on the African continent, and even globally, it is of paramount importance that nations considering themselves leaders and spokesmen of Western civilization—and especially those nations with their own delicate internal race problems—find a way to come into more constructive association with the Republic. It is realized that this association, involving nations with many high-priority international or national difficulties, would necessarily require new and higher-priority placement of the problem of South Africa. The United States for example, faced with Vietnam, with major economic difficulties, with her own civil rights conflicts, does not today place South Africa high on her list of foreign policy problems demanding immediate attention. Nor does Britain place South Africa high on her list of foreign policy issues—faced with Ulster, with Rhodesia, with the Common Market, and with Commonwealth matters. Yet no nation having world responsibilities can afford to overlook the boiling cauldron of racial turmoil in southern Africa. That cauldron could boil over at any time.

No Western nation can shirk the task of attempting some form of preventive diplomacy in a situation where later, and far costlier, actions will be required. It would appear then that, together, those Western nations most intimately concerned with South Africa, particularly the United States and the United Kingdom, could more forcefully register their concern with South Africa. They could join these with unequivocal appeals that steps be taken by South Africa to improve the situation. The Western nations could do so on grounds that threatening dangers of outbreak of racial violence in southern Africa must only concern world powers today but could find those powers engaged militarily on the African continent tomorrow.

Today, any nation that maintains foreign policy relationships with South Africa has three main strategies. One of these is a course of <u>dissociation</u>, even of total disengagement. For those nations heavily involved with South Africa in financial, trade, and defense areas, such as the United Kingdom or the United States, this option is impractical. The second option is one of <u>unfettered association</u> with South Africa, this involving unequivocal and uncritical acceptance of the concept of apartheid and White supremacy. On domestic political grounds alone, this option is impossible for both the United States and the United Kingdom. A third option is that of <u>ad hoc association</u>—this being an ambivalent, sometimes schizophrenic jumble of day-to-day determinations (political, economic, or whatever) vis-à-vis South Africa. This policy course, recently utilized by both the United Kingdom and the United States, seems to have satisfied no one. It sets up an impossible dichotomy—a mixture of views, reactions, attacks, and counterattacks. It gives foreign critics of South Africa justifiable room for criticism of murky, often self-defeating actions by their own governments. Likewise, it gives South African leaders reason to delay needed reform. This ad hoc strategy is bound to be inconsistent, inconclusive, and ineffective. For those reasons, therefore, a fourth, more carefully devised and orchestrated strategy is essential

This fourth strategy might be termed a <u>program of balanced equations</u>—a combination of carrots and sticks, of pressures and counterpressures. This could involve a specific grouping of interested nations—possibly six or seven member states, including the United States, the United Kingdom, Canada, the Netherlands, West Germany, and one or more Scandinavian nations. This group of Western democracies could then establish a formula or program of action. These nations could at once register concern over the problems and prospects of apartheid, while, at the same time, recognizing South Africa's sovereignty and position in the Western world. Such an association of nations need not require diplomatic accords, but simply informal working arrangements, either within or without the context of the UN. This should be a program aimed at emphasizing the internationalism rather than the isolationism of the Republic. It should emphasize to South Africa's leaders their responsibilities under the rule of law if they, as they do, contend theirs is a Western culture and civilization. Properly administered, the program could well weaken rather than stiffen South African White resistance to change.

Among others, the proposed international courses of action could and should include the following.

•Agreement by member states that those states will continue to honor the UN arms embargo against South Africa, and, if necessary, would stiffen or expand that embargo if, in two years, no social improvement is seen within South Africa.

•Member states would agree that ordinary trade and investment will be continued with South Africa. It should be stressed, however, that investors, industrialists, and commercial agents from those nations will be instructed to carry on programs of enlightened capitalism and social justice in all their South African activities. If these standards are not met, member states should invoke penalties for those businesses that do not maintain fair employment and labor practices in their South African operations. These penalties could include withdrawal of tax incentives, imposition of fines, refusal of government export loan benefits, and so forth.

•Member states should agree that South Africa will be prohibited from participation in international professional and amateur sporting events (including test match cricket, rugby, soccer, golf, tennis, swimming, boxing, Olympic meets, and so forth) unless non-White athletes of proven talent are included as full-fledged members of South African teams.

•Member states will persuade British, continental European, and American authors, dramatists, playwrights, musicians, and artists to permit showings of their talents in South Africa in the interests of keeping South Africa in direct touch with the outside world, thus hastening constructive change. (Similar efforts might be made with respect to American and European films, scripts, and TV video tapes.) It will be insisted, however, that, wherever possible, such showings be made available to mixed audiences and not be subject to South African political censorship.

•Member states (including the United States and the United Kingdom) should agree to permit informal visits to South African ports by their various naval vessels. This would be construed as a further important means of association and would be in the same spirit of relaxed informality that now prevails with respect to merchant ship and aircraft visits. It would mean, as well, that member states are fully cognizant not only of South Africa's responsibilities toward the West but of Western defense interest in the Republic and her resources.

•Member states should agree to carry out increased (some joint) programs of educational and cultural exchanges with the Republic. These visits and tours should be planned in both directions but would not condone visa difficulties or barriers at any point by any nation. Special attention should be given to exchange of students, academics, and artists of all races.

•Member states should cooperate to have South Africa restored to full membership in all UN specialized agencies including ILO, WHO, FAO, and so forth.

•Member states should act in concert, officially and unofficially, to create a fruitful "dialogue" between South Africa and Black African nations. This effort would be directed especially at averting open conflict in southern Africa. These talks, utilizing chiefs-of-state and diplomatic channels, as well as private contacts, should insist on a useful agenda for the dialogues and for inclusion of non-Whites on the South African side.

•Member states should agree to support large-scale World Bank or UN development programs in the Bantustans and South-West Africa. This effort, involving both low-interest loans and technical assistance, should aim at helping to build basic capital resources and infrastructure in the "homelands" and in South-West Africa. The program would not replace South Africa's responsibilities in those areas but would be supplemental thereto.

•Member states should insist that the government of South Africa take a more tolerant, pragmatic, and modern view of foreign and domestic churchmen and church activities within South Africa and South-West Africa. If, within two years, South Africa does not cease its persecution of these churchmen and religious bodies, the member states should then consider a "tit for tat" exclusion of South African clergymen, diplomats, and information and media officials from their respective nations.

•Member states should consider means whereby they can enter into formal discussions with South Africa in the fields of modern justice and the rule of law. These discussions might usefully be held under the aegis of the International Court of Justice or the UN and would involve legal authorities, academics, and officials.

•Member states could play an important part in supporting the efforts of the UN secretary-general with respect to South-West Africa.*

The foregoing represent only a few of the possibilities that might be advanced. Member states would undoubtedly wish to institute more. Imperative in such a program is the necessity to maintain a balanced, and if necessary graduated, set of pressures and counter-pressures, gifts, and penalties. Essential also is the matter of timing and of concerted action. The result should keep South Africa constantly aware of the necessity that she bow to constructive social change in time to avoid catastrophe for herself and for other nations. This is in the interest of the Western world—and of all humanity.

This carefully orchestrated program would recognize at once both the non-White cause and the cause of all the peoples of South Africa. Its duality of approach would recognize both the duality and complexity of the South African situation as depicted in this book. It would recognize the duality of the "haves" and "have-nots." It would recognize the complexities of a nation fully blessed with natural resources—which fails to utilize its best resource, its people. It would recognize the existence of arrogance and of forbearance, of humanity and of inhumanity, of democratic legalism and of totalitarian injustice, of urbanized society and of traditional tribalism, of internationalism and of isolationism—all the contradictions that make up the Republic. It would aim to rebuild bridges of peace between the races in South Africa, as these races lacking such bridges would otherwise surely become antagonists in a disastrous conflict.

There is no single program of action, internal or international—no magic wand—which will instantaneously produce changes so sorely needed within South Africa. All such programs must be devised for the long haul in the hope of awakening timely evolutionary change, rather than belated untimely action to bind revolutionary wounds. What is needed on all sides is understanding, imagination, determination, goodwill, compassion, and patience.

In the face of all the crosscurrents and multifaceted pressures, internal and international, a tiny White oligarchy located at the tip of an immense Black-ruled continent cannot long survive without making adequate and timely adaptations to a modern, multiracial world. Thus far, in both the Union and the Republic, this White oligarchy has survived only through a maze of schizophrenic laws; through a massive and sometimes brutal system of security and defense; and through anachronistic legalisms and inordinate repression

---

*For recommendations re South-West Africa, see subsection in Conclusions just preceding.

of a majority of its people. To capitalize on its superb gifts of natural resources, geography, climate, energy, and humanity, South Africa must abandon its own self-defeating contrariness. It must both accept and utilize its non-Whites as full-fledged South Africans. Ignoring that proponderant majority will destroy South Africa itself. If South Africa does not adapt to change in time by evolutionary means, then change will undoubtedly be forced upon the nation by revolution.

The answer to the riddle that is South Africa today rests with her rulers and with her peoples—White, Coloured, Asian, and Black. If her true national necessities are not squarely and timely met, then South Africa, in future history, will only be known, as stated in the outset of this book, as a long-gone and baffling anachronism—an enigma.

NOTES

CHAPTER 3

1. South African Institute of Race Relations, A Survey of Race Relations in South Africa (Johannesburg: the Institute, 1971), p. 73.

2. Ibid., p. 142.

3. Statistics taken from ibid. (1968, 1969, and 1971).

4. Anthony Mathews, Law, Order and Liberty in South Africa (Juta Press), reviewed in Sunday Tribune (Durban), December 12, 1971).

5. Natal Daily News, September 26 and 27, 1966.

6. U.S. News and World Report, November 14, 1966.

7. As reported in Natal Mercury (Durban), February 24, 1971.

CHAPTER 4

1. South African Institute of Race Relations, A Survey of Race Relations in South Africa (Johannesburg: the Institute, 1968), p. 1.

2. Sunday Tribune (Durban), August 30, 1970.

3. Background material on the council comes in part from Norman Middleton's article in Reality (Pietermaritzburg) (January 1972), pp. 10 ff.

4. Sunday Tribune (Durban), September 5, 1971.

5. Fatima Meer, Portraits of Indian South Africans (Durban: Avon, 1969).

6. Ibid.

7. Monica Wilson and Leonard Thompson, eds., The Oxford History of South Africa, Vol. II, South Africa, 1870-1966 (London: Oxford University Press, 1971).

CHAPTER 5

1. "A State in the Making—Transkei" (South African Department of Information, 1970).

2. The Christian Science Monitor, November 5, 1971.

3. Financial Times, February 9, 1972.

CHAPTER 6

1. South African Information Service figures.

2. Financial Mail (Johannesburg), December 13, 1968, special survey on coal.

3. South African Information Service.

4. U.S. Department of Commerce statistics.

5. South Africa: Key to a Continent (Johannesburg: Da Gama Publishers, 1970), p. 83.

6. Financial Mail (Johannesburg), October 17, 1969, special survey on fisheries.
7. Daily Telegraph (London), October 22, 1971.
8. South Africa: Key to a Continent.
9. Figures cited are from ibid.
10. Rand Daily Mail (Johannesburg), February 17, 1972.
11. Foregoing statistics on U.S. and U.K. investments compiled by UN, U.S., and other public media.
12. The Wall Street Journal, September 22, 1971, and The Christian Science Monitor, May 2, 1972.
13. Figures from U.S. Department of Commerce bulletins.
14. Ibid.
15. The Washington Post, January 15, 1972.

CHAPTER 7

1. Financial Mail (Johannesburg), January 15, 1972.
2. The Guardian (London), September 25, 1971.
3. Financial Mail (Johannesburg), April 21, 1972.

CHAPTER 8

1. Educational statistics following are culled from A Survey of Race Relations in South Africa (Johannesburg: South African Institute of Race Relations, 1968-71).
2. Sunday Tribune (Durban), August 8, 1971.
3. Ibid.
4. Sunday Tribune (Durban), September 5, 1971.
5. South African Institute of Race Relations, A Survey of Race Relations in South Africa (Johannesburg: the Institute, 1971), p. 65.

CHAPTER 9

1. Daily News (Durban), April 1, 1971.
2. The New York Times, December 12, 1971.
3. The Economist, December 18, 1971.
4. Sunday Tribune (Durban), December 12, 1971.
5. Sunday Telegraph (London), February 13, 1972.
6. The Dome, (University of Natal, Durban), March 31, 1971.
7. Ibid.

CHAPTER 10

1. The Washington Post, January 27, 1972 (article by former Ambassador Charles Yost, entitled "Must Africa's Problems Be Resolved By Violence ?").
2. The Washington Post, March 15, 1972.
3. South African Institute of Race Relations, A Survey of Race Relations in South Africa (Johannesburg: the Institute, 1968), p. 78.

BIBLIOGRAPHY

To the authors, editors, and publishers of the following newspapers, magazines, and books, the author gratefully acknowledges valued help in the factual and analytical presentations of this book.

NEWSPAPERS

Daily News (Durban)

Dome (University of Natal, Durban)

Natal Mercury (Durban)

Natal Witness (Pietermaritzburg)

Rand Daily Mail (Johannesburg)

Sunday Times (Johannesburg)

Sunday Tribune (Durban)

The Christian Science Monitor

---

*Various unclassified pamphlets and reports were used from the U.S. Department of Commerce and the U.S. Department of State, as well as various official South African publications, including South African statistical bulletins and South African informational releases, including "South African Quiz," "Industrial Development Corporation," "Taking Factories to the People," "South Africa's Outward Policy," "Scope for Investment" (Johannesburg: Union Acceptance Corp.), and "A State in the Making—Transkei." Also used were various pamphlets and publications of the United party and the Progressive party of South Africa, as well as various issues of the monthly Standard Bank Review and South African sugar industry publications. Various pamphlets issued, including notes of annual general meetings, published by the South African Institute of Race Relations, Johannesburg, were also used.

The Sunday Telegraph (London)

The Guardian (London)

The New York Times

The Star (Johannesburg)

The Sun (Baltimore)

The Times (London)

The Wall Street Journal

The Washington Post

MAGAZINES

Africa Report (Washington, D.C.)

The Economist (London)

Financial Mail (Johannesburg)

Newsweek

Reality (Pietermaritizburg)

Time

U.S. News and World Report

BOOKS

De Kiewiet, C. W. The Anatomy of South African Misery. London: Oxford University Press, 1956.

Hill, Christopher. Bantustans. London: Oxford University Press, 1964.

Hutt, W. H. Economics of the Colour Bar. London: Institute of Economic Affairs, 1964.

Keppel-Jones, Arthur. South Africa. Hutchinson, 1961.

Legum, Colin. South Africa: Crisis for the West. New York: Frederick A. Praeger, 1965.

Marquard, Leo. The Peoples and Policies of South Africa. London: Oxford University Press, 1952.

Meer, Fatima. Portraits of Indian South Africans. Durban: Avon House, 1969.

Paton, Alan. The Long View. Edward Callan. New York: Frederick A. Praeger, 1968.

South Africa: Key to a Continent. Johannesburg: Da Gama Publishers, 1970.

South African Institute of Race Relations. A Survey of Race Relations in South Africa. Johannesburg: the Institute. Vols. for 1966-71.

Wilson, Monica, and Leonard Thompson, eds. Oxford History of South Africa. Vol. I: South Africa to 1870. London: Oxford University Press, 1969.

Wilson, Monica, and Leonard Thompson, eds. Oxford History of South Africa. Vol. II: South Africa, 1870-1966. London: Oxford University Press, 1971.

ABOUT THE AUTHOR

WILLIAM REDMAN ("Red") DUGGAN, retired diplomat, lecturer, and author, is a recognized authority on sub-Saharan Africa. He served 28 years in the American Foreign Service, of which 20 years were spent living and working in Africa or dealing with African problems in the U.S. Department of State and the UN.

Of his African service Mr. Duggan spent seven years in South Africa and four years in Tanzania. He has traveled extensively throughout that continent. He has also served in Canada, in Denmark, at the UN, and in Washington. From 1956 to 1958 he was officer-in-charge, West African Affairs, U.S. Department of State. From 1962 to 1967 he served as African affairs specialist on the Department of State's prestigious Policy Planning Council. He retired from the Foreign Service and from his last post as American consul general in Durban, South Africa, in mid-1971. Mr. Duggan has been the recipient of two of the Department of State's highest awards—The Distinguished Honor Award (1971) and the Meritorious Service Medal (1963).

Born in Colorado and a graduate of the University of Notre Dame, Mr. Duggan holds a bachelor's degree in political science and a master's degree in politics and economics. He has also taken advanced training at the African Studies Center of Boston University. Mr. Duggan, now in retirement from government service, is engaged as a lecturer in international affairs at Willamette University, Salem, Oregon. He also serves as a consultant on African Affairs with the Ford Foundation. He is a fellow of the African Studies Association and a member of the Explorers Club.